The Story Girl

CW01072405

L. M. Montgomery

Alpha Editions

This edition published in 2024

ISBN : 9789362926449

Design and Setting By
Alpha Editions
www.alphaedis.com
Email - info@alphaedis.com

Contents

CHAPTER I.
THE HOME OF OUR FATHERS

"I do like a road, because you can be always wondering what is at the end of it."

The Story Girl said that once upon a time. Felix and I, on the May morning when we left Toronto for Prince Edward Island, had not then heard her say it, and, indeed, were but barely aware of the existence of such a person as the Story Girl. We did not know her at all under that name. We knew only that a cousin, Sara Stanley, whose mother, our Aunt Felicity, was dead, was living down on the Island with Uncle Roger and Aunt Olivia King, on a farm adjoining the old King homestead in Carlisle. We supposed we should get acquainted with her when we reached there, and we had an idea, from Aunt Olivia's letters to father, that she would be quite a jolly creature. Further than that we did not think about her. We were more interested in Felicity and Cecily and Dan, who lived on the homestead and would therefore be our roofmates for a season.

But the spirit of the Story Girl's yet unuttered remark was thrilling in our hearts that morning, as the train pulled out of Toronto. We were faring forth on a long road; and, though we had some idea what would be at the end of it, there was enough glamour of the unknown about it to lend a wonderful charm to our speculations concerning it.

We were delighted at the thought of seeing father's old home, and living among the haunts of his boyhood. He had talked so much to us about it, and described its scenes so often and so minutely, that he had inspired us with some of his own deep-seated affection for it—an affection that had never waned in all his years of exile. We had a vague feeling that we, somehow, belonged there, in that cradle of our family, though we had never seen it. We had always looked forward eagerly to the promised day when father would take us "down home," to the old house with the spruces behind it and the famous "King orchard" before it—when we might ramble in "Uncle Stephen's Walk," drink from the deep well with the Chinese roof over it, stand on "the Pulpit Stone," and eat apples from our "birthday trees."

The time had come sooner than we had dared to hope; but father could not take us after all. His firm asked him to go to Rio de Janeiro that spring to take charge of their new branch there. It was too good a chance to lose, for father was a poor man and it meant promotion and increase of salary; but it also meant the temporary breaking up of our home. Our mother had died before either of us was old enough to remember her; father could not take us to Rio de Janeiro. In the end he decided to send us to Uncle Alec and Aunt Janet down on the homestead; and our housekeeper, who belonged to the Island and was now returning to it, took charge of us on the journey. I fear she had an anxious trip of it, poor woman! She was constantly in a quite justifiable terror lest we should be lost or killed; she must have felt great relief when she reached Charlottetown and handed us over to the keeping of Uncle Alec. Indeed, she said as much.

"The fat one isn't so bad. He isn't so quick to move and get out of your sight while you're winking as the thin one. But the only safe way to travel with those young ones would be to have 'em both tied to you with a short rope—a MIGHTY short rope."

"The fat one" was Felix, who was very sensitive about his plumpness. He was always taking exercises to make him thin, with the dismal result that he became fatter all the time. He vowed that he didn't care; but he DID care terribly, and he glowered at Mrs. MacLaren in a most undutiful fashion. He had never liked her since the day she had told him he would soon be as broad as he was long.

For my own part, I was rather sorry to see her going; and she cried over us and wished us well; but we had forgotten all about her by the time we reached the open country, driving along, one on either side of Uncle Alec, whom we loved from the moment we saw him. He was a small man, with thin, delicate features, close-clipped gray beard, and large, tired, blue eyes— father's eyes over again. We knew that Uncle Alec was fond of children and was heart-glad to welcome "Alan's boys." We felt at home with him, and were not afraid to ask him questions on any subject that came uppermost in our minds. We became very good friends with him on that twenty-four mile drive.

Much to our disappointment it was dark when we reached Carlisle—too dark to see anything very distinctly, as we drove up the lane of the old King homestead on the hill. Behind us a young moon was hanging over southwestern meadows of spring-time peace, but all about us were the soft, moist shadows of a May night. We peered eagerly through the gloom.

"There's the big willow, Bev," whispered Felix excitedly, as we turned in at the gate.

There it was, in truth—the tree Grandfather King had planted when he returned one evening from ploughing in the brook field and stuck the willow switch he had used all day in the soft soil by the gate.

It had taken root and grown; our father and our uncles and aunts had played in its shadow; and now it was a massive thing, with a huge girth of trunk and great spreading boughs, each of them as large as a tree in itself.

"I'm going to climb it to-morrow," I said joyfully.

Off to the right was a dim, branching place which we knew was the orchard; and on our left, among sibilant spruces and firs, was the old, whitewashed house—from which presently a light gleamed through an open door, and Aunt Janet, a big, bustling, sonsy woman, with full-blown peony cheeks, came to welcome us.

Soon after we were at supper in the kitchen, with its low, dark, raftered ceiling from which substantial hams and flitches of bacon were hanging. Everything was just as father had described it. We felt that we had come home, leaving exile behind us.

Felicity, Cecily, and Dan were sitting opposite us, staring at us when they thought we would be too busy eating to see them. We tried to stare at them when THEY were eating; and as a result we were always catching each other at it and feeling cheap and embarrassed.

Dan was the oldest; he was my age—thirteen. He was a lean, freckled fellow with rather long, lank, brown hair and the shapely King nose. We recognized it at once. His mouth was his own, however, for it was like to no mouth on either the King or the Ward side; and nobody would have been anxious to claim it, for it was an undeniably ugly one—long and narrow and twisted. But it could grin in friendly fashion, and both Felix and I felt that we were going to like Dan.

Felicity was twelve. She had been called after Aunt Felicity, who was the twin sister of Uncle Felix. Aunt Felicity and Uncle Felix, as father had often told us, had died on the same day, far apart, and were buried side by side in the old Carlisle graveyard.

We had known from Aunt Olivia's letters, that Felicity was the beauty of the connection, and we had been curious to see her on that account. She fully justified our expectations. She was plump and dimpled, with big, dark-blue, heavy-lidded eyes, soft, feathery, golden curls, and a pink and white skin—"the King complexion." The Kings were noted for their noses and complexion. Felicity had also delightful hands and wrists. At every turn of them a dimple showed itself. It was a pleasure to wonder what her elbows must be like.

She was very nicely dressed in a pink print and a frilled muslin apron; and we understood, from something Dan said, that she had "dressed up" in honour of our coming. This made us feel quite important. So far as we knew, no feminine creatures had ever gone to the pains of dressing up on our account before.

Cecily, who was eleven, was pretty also—or would have been had Felicity not been there. Felicity rather took the colour from other girls. Cecily looked pale and thin beside her; but she had dainty little features, smooth brown hair of satin sheen, and mild brown eyes, with just a hint of demureness in them now and again. We remembered that Aunt Olivia had written to father that Cecily was a true Ward—she had no sense of humour. We did not know what this meant, but we thought it was not exactly complimentary.

Still, we were both inclined to think we would like Cecily better than Felicity. To be sure, Felicity was a stunning beauty. But, with the swift and unerring intuition of childhood, which feels in a moment what it sometimes takes maturity much time to perceive, we realized that she was rather too well aware of her good looks. In brief, we saw that Felicity was vain.

"It's a wonder the Story Girl isn't over to see you," said Uncle Alec. "She's been quite wild with excitement about your coming."

"She hasn't been very well all day," explained Cecily, "and Aunt Olivia wouldn't let her come out in the night air. She made her go to bed instead. The Story Girl was awfully disappointed."

"Who is the Story Girl?" asked Felix.

"Oh, Sara—Sara Stanley. We call her the Story Girl partly because she's such a hand to tell stories—oh, I can't begin to describe it—and partly because Sara Ray, who lives at the foot of the hill, often comes up to play with us, and it is awkward to have two girls of the same name in the same crowd. Besides, Sara Stanley doesn't like her name and she'd rather be called the Story Girl."

Dan speaking for the first time, rather sheepishly volunteered the information that Peter had also been intending to come over but had to go home to take some flour to his mother instead.

"Peter?" I questioned. I had never heard of any Peter.

"He is your Uncle Roger's handy boy," said Uncle Alec. "His name is Peter Craig, and he is a real smart little chap. But he's got his share of mischief, that same lad."

"He wants to be Felicity's beau," said Dan slyly.

"Don't talk silly nonsense, Dan," said Aunt Janet severely.

Felicity tossed her golden head and shot an unsisterly glance at Dan.

"I wouldn't be very likely to have a hired boy for a beau," she observed.

We saw that her anger was real, not affected. Evidently Peter was not an admirer of whom Felicity was proud.

We were very hungry boys; and when we had eaten all we could—and oh, what suppers Aunt Janet always spread!—we discovered that we were very tired also—too tired to go out and explore our ancestral domains, as we would have liked to do, despite the dark.

We were quite willing to go to bed; and presently we found ourselves tucked away upstairs in the very room, looking out eastward into the spruce grove, which father had once occupied. Dan shared it with us, sleeping in a bed of his own in the opposite corner. The sheets and pillow-slips were fragrant with lavender, and one of Grandmother King's noted patchwork quilts was over us. The window was open and we heard the frogs singing down in the swamp of the brook meadow. We had heard frogs sing in Ontario, of course; but certainly Prince Edward Island frogs were more tuneful and mellow. Or was it simply the glamour of old family traditions and tales which was over us, lending its magic to all sights and sounds around us? This was home—father's home—OUR home! We had never lived long enough in any one house to develop a feeling of affection for it; but here, under the roof-tree built by Great-Grandfather King ninety years ago, that feeling swept into our boyish hearts and souls like a flood of living sweetness and tenderness.

"Just think, those are the very frogs father listened to when he was a little boy," whispered Felix.

"They can hardly be the SAME frogs," I objected doubtfully, not feeling very certain about the possible longevity of frogs. "It's twenty years since father left home."

"Well, they're the descendants of the frogs he heard," said Felix, "and they're singing in the same swamp. That's near enough."

Our door was open and in their room across the narrow hall the girls were preparing for bed, and talking rather more loudly than they might have done had they realized how far their sweet, shrill voices carried.

"What do you think of the boys?" asked Cecily.

"Beverley is handsome, but Felix is too fat," answered Felicity promptly.

Felix twitched the quilt rather viciously and grunted. But I began to think I would like Felicity. It might not be altogether her fault that she was vain. How could she help it when she looked in the mirror?

"I think they're both nice and nice looking," said Cecily.

Dear little soul!

"I wonder what the Story Girl will think of them," said Felicity, as if, after all, that was the main thing.

Somehow, we, too, felt that it was. We felt that if the Story Girl did not approve of us it made little difference who else did or did not.

"I wonder if the Story Girl is pretty," said Felix aloud.

"No, she isn't," said Dan instantly, from across the room. "But you'll think she is while she's talking to you. Everybody does. It's only when you go away from her that you find out she isn't a bit pretty after all."

The girls' door shut with a bang. Silence fell over the house. We drifted into the land of sleep, wondering if the Story Girl would like us.

CHAPTER II.
A QUEEN OF HEARTS

I wakened shortly after sunrise. The pale May sunshine was showering through the spruces, and a chill, inspiring wind was tossing the boughs about.

"Felix, wake up," I whispered, shaking him.

"What's the matter?" he murmured reluctantly.

"It's morning. Let's get up and go down and out. I can't wait another minute to see the places father has told us of."

We slipped out of bed and dressed, without arousing Dan, who was still slumbering soundly, his mouth wide open, and his bed-clothes kicked off on the floor. I had hard work to keep Felix from trying to see if he could "shy" a marble into that tempting open mouth. I told him it would waken Dan, who would then likely insist on getting up and accompanying us, and it would be so much nicer to go by ourselves for the first time.

Everything was very still as we crept downstairs. Out in the kitchen we heard some one, presumably Uncle Alec, lighting the fire; but the heart of house had not yet begun to beat for the day.

We paused a moment in the hall to look at the big "Grandfather" clock. It was not going, but it seemed like an old, familiar acquaintance to us, with the gilt balls on its three peaks; the little dial and pointer which would indicate the changes of the moon, and the very dent in its wooden door which father had made when he was a boy, by kicking it in a fit of naughtiness.

Then we opened the front door and stepped out, rapture swelling in our bosoms. There was a rare breeze from the south blowing to meet us; the shadows of the spruces were long and clear-cut; the exquisite skies of early morning, blue and wind-winnowed, were over us; away to the west, beyond the brook field, was a long valley and a hill purple with firs and laced with still leafless beeches and maples.

Behind the house was a grove of fir and spruce, a dim, cool place where the winds were fond of purring and where there was always a resinous, woodsy odour. On the further side of it was a thick plantation of slender silver birches and whispering poplars; and beyond it was Uncle Roger's house.

Right before us, girt about with its trim spruce hedge, was the famous King orchard, the history of which was woven into our earliest recollections. We knew all about it, from father's descriptions, and in fancy we had roamed in it many a time and oft.

It was now nearly sixty years since it had had its beginning, when Grandfather King brought his bride home. Before the wedding he had fenced off the big south meadow that sloped to the sun; it was the finest, most fertile field on the farm, and the neighbours told young Abraham King that he would raise many a fine crop of wheat in that meadow. Abraham King smiled and, being a man of few words, said nothing; but in his mind he had a vision of the years to be, and in that vision he saw, not rippling acres of harvest gold, but great, leafy avenues of wide-spreading trees laden with fruit to gladden the eyes of children and grandchildren yet unborn.

It was a vision to develop slowly into fulfilment. Grandfather King was in no hurry. He did not set his whole orchard out at once, for he wished it to grow with his life and history, and be bound up with all of good and joy that should come to his household. So the morning after he had brought his young wife home they went together to the south meadow and planted their bridal trees. These trees were no longer living; but they had been when father was a boy, and every spring bedecked themselves in blossom as delicately tinted as Elizabeth King's face when she walked through the old south meadow in the morn of her life and love.

When a son was born to Abraham and Elizabeth a tree was planted in the orchard for him. They had fourteen children in all, and each child had its "birth tree." Every family festival was commemorated in like fashion, and every beloved visitor who spent a night under their roof was expected to plant a tree in the orchard. So it came to pass that every tree in it was a fair green monument to some love or delight of the vanished years. And each grandchild had its tree, there, also, set out by grandfather when the tidings of its birth reached him; not always an apple tree—perhaps it was a plum, or cherry or pear. But it was always known by the name of the person for whom, or by whom, it was planted; and Felix and I knew as much about "Aunt Felicity's pears," and "Aunt Julia's cherries," and "Uncle Alec's apples," and the "Rev. Mr. Scott's plums," as if we had been born and bred among them.

And now we had come to the orchard; it was before us; we had only to open that little whitewashed gate in the hedge and we might find ourselves in its storied domain. But before we reached the gate we glanced to our left, along the grassy, spruce-bordered lane which led over to Uncle Roger's; and at the entrance of that lane we saw a girl standing, with a gray cat at her feet. She lifted her hand and beckoned blithely to us; and, the orchard forgotten, we followed her summons. For we knew that this must be the Story Girl; and in that gay and graceful gesture was an allurement not to be gainsaid or denied.

We looked at her as we drew near with such interest that we forgot to feel shy. No, she was not pretty. She was tall for her fourteen years, slim and straight; around her long, white face—rather too long and too white—fell sleek, dark-brown curls, tied above either ear with rosettes of scarlet ribbon. Her large, curving mouth was as red as a poppy, and she had brilliant, almond-shaped, hazel eyes; but we did not think her pretty.

Then she spoke; she said,

"Good morning."

Never had we heard a voice like hers. Never, in all my life since, have I heard such a voice. I cannot describe it. I might say it was clear; I might say it was sweet; I might say it was vibrant and far-reaching and bell-like; all this would be true, but it would give you no real idea of the peculiar quality which made the Story Girl's voice what it was.

If voices had colour, hers would have been like a rainbow. It made words LIVE. Whatever she said became a breathing entity, not a mere verbal statement or utterance. Felix and I were too young to understand or analyze the impression it made upon us; but we instantly felt at her greeting that it WAS a good morning—a surpassingly good morning—the very best morning that had ever happened in this most excellent of worlds.

"You are Felix and Beverley," she went on, shaking our hands with an air of frank comradeship, which was very different from the shy, feminine advances of Felicity and Cecily. From that moment we were as good friends as if we had known each other for a hundred years. "I am glad to see you. I was so disappointed I couldn't go over last night. I got up early this morning, though, for I felt sure you would be up early, too, and that you'd like to have me tell you about things. I can tell things so much better than Felicity or Cecily. Do you think Felicity is VERY pretty?"

"She's the prettiest girl I ever saw," I said enthusiastically, remembering that Felicity had called me handsome.

"The boys all think so," said the Story Girl, not, I fancied, quite well pleased. "And I suppose she is. She is a splendid cook, too, though she is only twelve. I can't cook. I am trying to learn, but I don't make much progress. Aunt Olivia says I haven't enough natural gumption ever to be a cook; but I'd love to be able to make as good cakes and pies as Felicity can make. But then, Felicity is stupid. It's not ill-natured of me to say that. It's just the truth, and you'd soon find it out for yourselves. I like Felicity very well, but she IS stupid. Cecily is ever so much cleverer. Cecily's a dear. So is Uncle Alec; and Aunt Janet is pretty nice, too."

"What is Aunt Olivia like?" asked Felix.

"Aunt Olivia is very pretty. She is just like a pansy—all velvety and purply and goldy."

Felix and I SAW, somewhere inside of our heads, a velvet and purple and gold pansy-woman, just as the Story Girl spoke.

"But is she NICE?" I asked. That was the main question about grown-ups. Their looks mattered little to us.

"She is lovely. But she is twenty-nine, you know. That's pretty old. She doesn't bother me much. Aunt Janet says that I'd have no bringing up at all, if it wasn't for her. Aunt Olivia says children should just be let COME up—that everything else is settled for them long before they are born. I don't understand that. Do you?"

No, we did not. But it was our experience that grown-ups had a habit of saying things hard to understand.

"What is Uncle Roger like?" was our next question.

"Well, I like Uncle Roger," said the Story Girl meditatively. "He is big and jolly. But he teases people too much. You ask him a serious question and you get a ridiculous answer. He hardly ever scolds or gets cross, though, and THAT is something. He is an old bachelor."

"Doesn't he ever mean to get married?" asked Felix.

"I don't know. Aunt Olivia wishes he would, because she's tired keeping house for him, and she wants to go to Aunt Julia in California. But she says he'll never get married, because he is looking for perfection, and when he finds her she won't have HIM."

By this time we were all sitting down on the gnarled roots of the spruces, and the big gray cat came over and made friends with us. He was a lordly animal, with a silver-gray coat beautifully marked with darker stripes. With such colouring most cats would have had white or silver feet; but he had four black paws and a black nose. Such points gave him an air of distinction, and marked him out as quite different from the common or garden variety of cats. He seemed to be a cat with a tolerably good opinion of himself, and his response to our advances was slightly tinged with condescension.

"This isn't Topsy, is it?" I asked. I knew at once that the question was a foolish one. Topsy, the cat of which father had talked, had flourished thirty years before, and all her nine lives could scarcely have lasted so long.

"No, but it is Topsy's great-great-great-great-grandson," said the Story Girl gravely. "His name is Paddy and he is my own particular cat. We have barn cats, but Paddy never associates with them. I am very good friends with all cats. They are so sleek and comfortable and dignified. And it is so easy to make them happy. Oh, I'm so glad you boys have come to live here. Nothing ever happens here, except days, so we have to make our own good times. We were short of boys before—only Dan and Peter to four girls."

"FOUR girls? Oh, yes, Sara Ray. Felicity mentioned her. What is she like? Where does she live?"

"Just down the hill. You can't see the house for the spruce bush. Sara is a nice girl. She's only eleven, and her mother is dreadfully strict. She never allows Sara to read a single story. JUST you fancy! Sara's conscience is always troubling her for doing things she's sure her mother won't approve, but it never prevents her from doing them. It only spoils her fun. Uncle Roger says that a mother who won't let you do anything, and a conscience that won't let you enjoy anything is an awful combination, and he doesn't wonder Sara is pale and thin and nervous. But, between you and me, I believe the real reason is that her mother doesn't give her half enough to eat. Not that she's mean, you know—but she thinks it isn't healthy for children to eat much, or anything but certain things. Isn't it fortunate we weren't born into that sort of a family?"

"I think it's awfully lucky we were all born into the same family," Felix remarked.

"Isn't it? I've often thought so. And I've often thought what a dreadful thing it would have been if Grandfather and Grandmother King had never got married to each other. I don't suppose there would have been a single one of us children here at all; or if we were, we would be part somebody else and that would be almost as bad. When I think it all over I can't feel too thankful that Grandfather and Grandmother King happened to marry each other, when there were so many other people they might have married."

Felix and I shivered. We felt suddenly that we had escaped a dreadful danger—the danger of having been born somebody else. But it took the Story Girl to make us realize just how dreadful it was and what a terrible risk we had run years before we, or our parents either, had existed.

"Who lives over there?" I asked, pointing to a house across the fields.

"Oh, that belongs to the Awkward Man. His name is Jasper Dale, but everybody calls him the Awkward Man. And they do say he writes poetry. He calls his place Golden Milestone. I know why, because I've read Longfellow's poems. He never goes into society because he is so awkward. The girls laugh at him and he doesn't like it. I know a story about him and I'll tell it to you sometime."

"And who lives in that other house?" asked Felix, looking over the westering valley where a little gray roof was visible among the trees.

"Old Peg Bowen. She's very queer. She lives there with a lot of pet animals in winter, and in summer she roams over the country and begs her meals. They say she is crazy. People have always tried to frighten us children into good behaviour by telling us that Peg Bowen would catch us if we didn't behave. I'm not so frightened of her as I once was, but I don't think I would like to be caught by her. Sara Ray is dreadfully scared of her. Peter Craig says she is a witch and that he bets she's at the bottom of it when the butter won't come. But I don't believe THAT. Witches are so scarce nowadays. There may be some somewhere in the world, but it's not likely there are any here right in Prince Edward Island. They used to be very plenty long ago. I know some splendid witch stories I'll tell you some day. They'll just make your blood freeze in your veins."

We hadn't a doubt of it. If anybody could freeze the blood in our veins this girl with the wonderful voice could. But it was a May morning, and our young blood was running blithely in our veins. We suggested a visit to the orchard would be more agreeable.

"All right. I know stories about it, too," she said, as we walked across the yard, followed by Paddy of the waving tail. "Oh, aren't you glad it is spring? The beauty of winter is that it makes you appreciate spring."

The latch of the gate clicked under the Story Girl's hand, and the next moment we were in the King orchard.

CHAPTER III.
LEGENDS OF THE OLD ORCHARD

Outside of the orchard the grass was only beginning to grow green; but here, sheltered by the spruce hedges from uncertain winds and sloping to southern suns, it was already like a wonderful velvet carpet; the leaves on the trees were beginning to come out in woolly, grayish clusters; and there were purple-pencilled white violets at the base of the Pulpit Stone.

"It's all just as father described it," said Felix with a blissful sigh, "and there's the well with the Chinese roof."

We hurried over to it, treading on the spears of mint that were beginning to shoot up about it. It was a very deep well, and the curb was of rough, undressed stones. Over it, the queer, pagoda-like roof, built by Uncle Stephen on his return from a voyage to China, was covered with yet leafless vines.

"It's so pretty, when the vines leaf out and hang down in long festoons," said the Story Girl. "The birds build their nests in it. A pair of wild canaries come here every summer. And ferns grow out between the stones of the well as far down as you can see. The water is lovely. Uncle Edward preached his finest sermon about the Bethlehem well where David's soldiers went to get him water, and he illustrated it by describing his old well at the homestead—this very well—and how in foreign lands he had longed for its sparkling water. So you see it is quite famous."

"There's a cup just like the one that used to be here in father's time," exclaimed Felix, pointing to an old-fashioned shallow cup of clouded blue ware on a little shelf inside the curb.

"It is the very same cup," said the Story Girl impressively. "Isn't it an amazing thing? That cup has been here for forty years, and hundreds of people have drunk from it, and it has never been broken. Aunt Julia dropped it down the well once, but they fished it up, not hurt a bit except for that little nick in the rim. I think it is bound up with the fortunes of the King family, like the Luck of Edenhall in Longfellow's poem. It is the last cup of Grandmother King's second best set. Her best set is still complete. Aunt Olivia has it. You must get her to show it to you. It's so pretty, with red berries all over it, and the funniest little pot-bellied cream jug. Aunt Olivia never uses it except on a family anniversary."

We took a drink from the blue cup and then went to find our birthday trees. We were rather disappointed to find them quite large, sturdy ones. It seemed to us that they should still be in the sapling stage corresponding to our boyhood.

"Your apples are lovely to eat," the Story Girl said to me, "but Felix's are only good for pies. Those two big trees behind them are the twins' trees— my mother and Uncle Felix, you know. The apples are so dead sweet that nobody but us children and the French boys can eat them. And that tall, slender tree over there, with the branches all growing straight up, is a seedling that came up of itself, and NOBODY can eat its apples, they are so sour and bitter. Even the pigs won't eat them. Aunt Janet tried to make pies of them once, because she said she hated to see them going to waste. But she never tried again. She said it was better to waste apples alone than apples and sugar too. And then she tried giving them away to the French hired men, but they wouldn't even carry them home."

The Story Girl's words fell on the morning air like pearls and diamonds. Even her prepositions and conjunctions had untold charm, hinting at mystery and laughter and magic bound up in everything she mentioned. Apple pies and sour seedlings and pigs became straightway invested with a glamour of romance.

"I like to hear you talk," said Felix in his grave, stodgy way.

"Everybody does," said the Story Girl coolly. "I'm glad you like the way I talk. But I want you to like ME, too—AS WELL as you like Felicity and Cecily. Not BETTER. I wanted that once but I've got over it. I found out in Sunday School, the day the minister taught our class, that it was selfish. But I want you to like me AS WELL."

"Well, I will, for one," said Felix emphatically. I think he was remembering that Felicity had called him fat.

Cecily now joined us. It appeared that it was Felicity's morning to help prepare breakfast, therefore she could not come. We all went to Uncle Stephen's Walk.

This was a double row of apple trees, running down the western side of the orchard. Uncle Stephen was the first born of Abraham and Elizabeth King. He had none of grandfather's abiding love for woods and meadows and the kindly ways of the warm red earth. Grandmother King had been a Ward, and in Uncle Stephen the blood of the seafaring race claimed its own. To sea he must go, despite the pleadings and tears of a reluctant mother; and it was from the sea he came to set out his avenue in the orchard with trees brought from a foreign land.

Then he sailed away again—and the ship was never heard of more. The gray first came in grandmother's brown hair in those months of waiting.

The, for the first time, the orchard heard the sound of weeping and was consecrated by a sorrow.

"When the blossoms come out it's wonderful to walk here," said the Story Girl. "It's like a dream of fairyland—as if you were walking in a king's palace. The apples are delicious, and in winter it's a splendid place for coasting."

From the Walk we went to the Pulpit Stone—a huge gray boulder, as high as a man's head, in the southeastern corner. It was straight and smooth in front, but sloped down in natural steps behind, with a ledge midway on which one could stand. It had played an important part in the games of our uncles and aunts, being fortified castle, Indian ambush, throne, pulpit, or concert platform, as occasion required. Uncle Edward had preached his first sermon at the age of eight from that old gray boulder; and Aunt Julia, whose voice was to delight thousands, sang her earliest madrigals there.

The Story Girl mounted to the ledge, sat on the rim, and looked at us. Pat sat gravely at its base and daintily washed his face with his black paws.

"Now for your stories about the orchard," said I.

"There are two important ones," said the Story Girl. "The story of the Poet Who Was Kissed, and the Tale of the Family Ghost. Which one shall I tell?"

"Tell them both," said Felix greedily, "but tell the ghost one first."

"I don't know." The Story Girl looked dubious. "That sort of story ought to be told in the twilight among the shadows. Then it would frighten the souls out of your bodies."

We thought it might be more agreeable not to have the souls frightened out of our bodies, and we voted for the Family Ghost.

"Ghost stories are more comfortable in daytime," said Felix.

The Story Girl began it and we listened avidly. Cecily, who had heard it many times before, listened just as eagerly as we did. She declared to me afterwards that no matter how often the Story Girl told a story it always seemed as new and exciting as if you had just heard it for the first time.

"Long, long ago," began the Story Girl, her voice giving us an impression of remote antiquity, "even before Grandfather King was born, an orphan cousin of his lived here with his parents. Her name was Emily King. She was very small and very sweet. She had soft brown eyes that were too timid to look straight at anybody—like Cecily's there—and long, sleek, brown curls—like mine; and she had a tiny birthmark like a pink butterfly on one cheek—right here.

"Of course, there was no orchard here then. It was just a field; but there was a clump of white birches in it, right where that big, spreading tree of Uncle Alec's is now, and Emily liked to sit among the ferns under the birches and read or sew. She had a lover. His name was Malcolm Ward and he was as handsome as a prince. She loved him with all her heart and he loved her the same; but they had never spoken about it. They used to meet under the birches and talk about everything except love. One day he told her he was coming the next day to ask A VERY IMPORTANT QUESTION, and he wanted to find her under the birches when he came. Emily promised to meet him there. I am sure she stayed awake that night, thinking about it, and wondering what the important question would be, although she knew perfectly well. I would have. And the next day she dressed herself beautifully in her best pale blue muslin and sleeked her curls and went smiling to the birches. And while she was waiting there, thinking such lovely thoughts, a neighbour's boy came running up—a boy who didn't know about her romance—and cried out that Malcolm Ward had been killed by his gun going off accidentally. Emily just put her hands to her heart—so—and fell, all white and broken among the ferns. And when she came back to life she never cried or lamented. She was CHANGED. She was never, never like herself again; and she was never contented unless she was dressed in her blue muslin and waiting under the birches. She got paler and paler every day, but the pink butterfly grew redder, until it looked just like a stain of blood on her white cheek. When the winter came she died. But next spring"—the Story Girl dropped her voice to a whisper that was as audible and thrilling as her louder tones—"people began to tell that Emily was sometimes seen waiting under the birches still. Nobody knew just who told it first. But more than one person saw her. Grandfather saw her when he was a little boy. And my mother saw her once."

"Did YOU ever see her?" asked Felix skeptically.

"No, but I shall some day, if I keep on believing in her," said the Story Girl confidently.

"I wouldn't like to see her. I'd be afraid," said Cecily with a shiver.

"There wouldn't be anything to be afraid of," said the Story Girl reassuringly. "It's not as if it were a strange ghost. It's our own family ghost, so of course it wouldn't hurt us."

We were not so sure of this. Ghosts were unchancy folk, even if they were our family ghosts. The Story Girl had made the tale very real to us. We were glad we had not heard it in the evening. How could we ever have got back to the house through the shadows and swaying branches of a darkening orchard? As it was, we were almost afraid to look up it, lest we should see the waiting, blue-clad Emily under Uncle Alec's tree. But all we saw was

Felicity, tearing over the green sward, her curls streaming behind her in a golden cloud.

"Felicity's afraid she's missed something," remarked the Story Girl in a tone of quiet amusement. "Is your breakfast ready, Felicity, or have I time to tell the boys the Story of the Poet Who Was Kissed?"

"Breakfast is ready, but we can't have it till father is through attending to the sick cow, so you will likely have time," answered Felicity.

Felix and I couldn't keep our eyes off her. Crimson-cheeked, shining-eyed from her haste, her face was like a rose of youth. But when the Story Girl spoke, we forgot to look at Felicity.

"About ten years after Grandfather and Grandmother King were married, a young man came to visit them. He was a distant relative of grandmother's and he was a Poet. He was just beginning to be famous. He was VERY famous afterward. He came into the orchard to write a poem, and he fell asleep with his head on a bench that used to be under grandfather's tree. Then Great-Aunt Edith came into the orchard. She was not a Great-Aunt then, of course. She was only eighteen, with red lips and black, black hair and eyes. They say she was always full of mischief. She had been away and had just come home, and she didn't know about the Poet. But when she saw him, sleeping there, she thought he was a cousin they had been expecting from Scotland. And she tiptoed up—so—and bent over—so—and kissed his cheek. Then he opened his big blue eyes and looked up into Edith's face. She blushed as red as a rose, for she knew she had done a dreadful thing. This could not be her cousin from Scotland. She knew, for he had written so to her, that he had eyes as black as her own. Edith ran away and hid; and of course she felt still worse when she found out that he was a famous poet. But he wrote one of his most beautiful poems on it afterwards and sent it to her—and it was published in one of his books."

We had SEEN it all—the sleeping genius—the roguish, red-lipped girl— the kiss dropped as lightly as a rose-petal on the sunburned cheek.

"They should have got married," said Felix.

"Well, in a book they would have, but you see this was in real life," said the Story Girl. "We sometimes act the story out. I like it when Peter plays the poet. I don't like it when Dan is the poet because he is so freckled and screws his eyes up so tight. But you can hardly ever coax Peter to be the poet—except when Felicity is Edith—and Dan is so obliging that way."

"What is Peter like?" I asked.

"Peter is splendid. His mother lives on the Markdale road and washes for a living. Peter's father ran away and left them when Peter was only three years old. He has never come back, and they don't know whether he is alive or dead. Isn't that a nice way to behave to your family? Peter has worked for his board ever since he was six. Uncle Roger sends him to school, and pays him wages in summer. We all like Peter, except Felicity."

"I like Peter well enough in his place," said Felicity primly, "but you make far too much of him, mother says. He is only a hired boy, and he hasn't been well brought up, and hasn't much education. I don't think you should make such an equal of him as you do."

Laughter rippled over the Story Girl's face as shadow waves go over ripe wheat before a wind.

"Peter is a real gentleman, and he is more interesting than YOU could ever be, if you were brought up and educated for a hundred years," she said.

"He can hardly write," said Felicity.

"William the Conqueror couldn't write at all," said the Story Girl crushingly.

"He never goes to church, and he never says his prayers," retorted Felicity, uncrushed.

"I do, too," said Peter himself, suddenly appearing through a little gap in the hedge. "I say my prayers sometimes."

This Peter was a slim, shapely fellow, with laughing black eyes and thick black curls. Early in the season as it was, he was barefooted. His attire consisted of a faded, gingham shirt and a scanty pair of corduroy knickerbockers; but he wore it with such an unconscious air of purple and fine linen that he seemed to be much better dressed than he really was.

"You don't pray very often," insisted Felicity.

"Well, God will be all the more likely to listen to me if I don't pester Him all the time," argued Peter.

This was rank heresy to Felicity, but the Story Girl looked as if she thought there might be something in it.

"You NEVER go to church, anyhow," continued Felicity, determined not to be argued down.

"Well, I ain't going to church till I've made up my mind whether I'm going to be a Methodist or a Presbyterian. Aunt Jane was a Methodist. My mother ain't much of anything but I mean to be something. It's more respectable to be a Methodist or a Presbyterian, or SOMETHING, than not to be anything. When I've settled what I'm to be I'm going to church same as you."

"That's not the same as being BORN something," said Felicity loftily.

"I think it's a good deal better to pick your own religion than have to take it just because it was what your folks had," retorted Peter.

"Now, never mind quarrelling," said Cecily. "You leave Peter alone, Felicity. Peter, this is Beverley King, and this is Felix. And we're all going to be good friends and have a lovely summer together. Think of the games we can have! But if you go squabbling you'll spoil it all. Peter, what are you going to do to-day?"

"Harrow the wood field and dig your Aunt Olivia's flower beds."

"Aunt Olivia and I planted sweet peas yesterday," said the Story Girl, "and I planted a little bed of my own. I am NOT going to dig them up this year to see if they have sprouted. It is bad for them. I shall try to cultivate patience, no matter how long they are coming up."

"I am going to help mother plant the vegetable garden to-day," said Felicity.

"Oh, I never like the vegetable garden," said the Story Girl. "Except when I am hungry. Then I DO like to go and look at the nice little rows of onions and beets. But I love a flower garden. I think I could be always good if I lived in a garden all the time."

"Adam and Eve lived in a garden all the time," said Felicity, "and THEY were far from being always good."

"They mightn't have kept good as long as they did if they hadn't lived in a garden," said the Story Girl.

We were now summoned to breakfast. Peter and the Story Girl slipped away through the gap, followed by Paddy, and the rest of us walked up the orchard to the house.

"Well, what do you think of the Story Girl?" asked Felicity.

"She's just fine," said Felix, enthusiastically. "I never heard anything like her to tell stories."

"She can't cook," said Felicity, "and she hasn't a good complexion. Mind you, she says she's going to be an actress when she grows up. Isn't that dreadful?"

We didn't exactly see why.

"Oh, because actresses are always wicked people," said Felicity in a shocked tone. "But I daresay the Story Girl will go and be one just as soon as she can. Her father will back her up in it. He is an artist, you know."

Evidently Felicity thought artists and actresses and all such poor trash were members one of another.

"Aunt Olivia says the Story Girl is fascinating," said Cecily.

The very adjective! Felix and I recognized its beautiful fitness at once. Yes, the Story Girl WAS fascinating and that was the final word to be said on the subject.

Dan did not come down until breakfast was half over, and Aunt Janet talked to him after a fashion which made us realize that it would be well to keep, as the piquant country phrase went, from the rough side of her tongue. But all things considered, we liked the prospect of our summer very much. Felicity to look at—the Story Girl to tell us tales of wonder—Cecily to admire us—Dan and Peter to play with—what more could reasonable fellows want?

CHAPTER IV.
THE WEDDING VEIL OF THE PROUD PRINCESS

When we had lived for a fortnight in Carlisle we belonged there, and the freedom of all its small fry was conferred on us. With Peter and Dan, with Felicity and Cecily and the Story Girl, with pale, gray-eyed little Sara Ray, we were boon companions. We went to school, of course; and certain home chores were assigned to each of us for the faithful performance of which we were held responsible. But we had long hours for play. Even Peter had plenty of spare time when the planting was over.

We got along very well with each other in the main, in spite of some minor differences of opinion. As for the grown-up denizens of our small world, they suited us also.

We adored Aunt Olivia; she was pretty and merry and kind; and, above all, she had mastered to perfection the rare art of letting children alone. If we kept ourselves tolerably clean, and refrained from quarrelling or talking slang, Aunt Olivia did not worry us. Aunt Janet, on the contrary, gave us so much good advice and was so constantly telling us to do this or not to do the other thing, that we could not remember half her instructions, and did not try.

Uncle Roger was, as we had been informed, quite jolly and fond of teasing. We liked him; but we had an uncomfortable feeling that the meaning of his remarks was not always that which met the ear. Sometimes we believed Uncle Roger was making fun of us, and the deadly seriousness of youth in us resented that.

To Uncle Alec we gave our warmest love. We felt that we always had a friend at court in Uncle Alec, no matter what we did or left undone. And we never had to turn HIS speeches inside out to discover their meaning.

The social life of juvenile Carlisle centred in the day and Sunday Schools. We were especially interested in our Sunday School, for we were fortunate enough to be assigned to a teacher who made our lessons so interesting that we no longer regarded Sunday School attendance as a disagreeable weekly duty; but instead looked forward to it with pleasure, and tried to carry out our teacher's gentle precepts—at least on Mondays and Tuesdays. I am afraid the remembrance grew a little dim the rest of the week.

She was also deeply interested in missions; and one talk on this subject inspired the Story Girl to do a little home missionary work on her own account. The only thing she could think of, along this line, was to persuade Peter to go to church.

Felicity did not approve of the design, and said so plainly.

"He won't know how to behave, for he's never been inside a church door in his life," she warned the Story Girl. "He'll likely do something awful, and then you'll feel ashamed and wish you'd never asked him to go, and we'll all be disgraced. It's all right to have our mite boxes for the heathen, and send missionaries to them. They're far away and we don't have to associate with them. But I don't want to have to sit in a pew with a hired boy."

But the Story Girl undauntedly continued to coax the reluctant Peter. It was not an easy matter. Peter did not come of a churchgoing stock; and besides, he alleged, he had not yet made up his mind whether to be a Presbyterian or a Methodist.

"It isn't a bit of difference which you are," pleaded the Story Girl. "They both go to heaven."

"But one way must be easier or better than the other, or else they'd all be one kind," argued Peter. "I want to find the easiest way. And I've got a hankering after the Methodists. My Aunt Jane was a Methodist."

"Isn't she one still?" asked Felicity pertly.

"Well, I don't know exactly. She's dead," said Peter rebukingly. "Do people go on being just the same after they're dead?"

"No, of course not. They're angels then—not Methodists or anything, but just angels. That is, if they go to heaven."

"S'posen they went to the other place?"

But Felicity's theology broke down at this point. She turned her back on Peter and walked disdainfully away.

The Story Girl returned to the main point with a new argument.

"We have such a lovely minister, Peter. He looks just like the picture of St. John my father sent me, only he is old and his hair is white. I know you'd like him. And even if you are going to be a Methodist it won't hurt you to go to the Presbyterian church. The nearest Methodist church is six miles away, at Markdale, and you can't attend there just now. Go to the Presbyterian church until you're old enough to have a horse."

"But s'posen I got too fond of being Presbyterian and couldn't change if I wanted to?" objected Peter.

Altogether, the Story Girl had a hard time of it; but she persevered; and one day she came to us with the announcement that Peter had yielded.

"He's going to church with us to-morrow," she said triumphantly.

We were out in Uncle Roger's hill pasture, sitting on some smooth, round stones under a clump of birches. Behind us was an old gray fence, with violets and dandelions thick in its corners. Below us was the Carlisle valley, with its orchard-embowered homesteads, and fertile meadows. Its upper end was dim with a delicate spring mist. Winds blew up the field like wave upon wave of sweet savour—spice of bracken and balsam.

We were eating little jam "turnovers," which Felicity had made for us. Felicity's turnovers were perfection. I looked at her and wondered why it was not enough that she should be so pretty and capable of making such turnovers. If she were only more interesting! Felicity had not a particle of the nameless charm and allurement which hung about every motion of the Story Girl, and made itself manifest in her lightest word and most careless glance. Ah well, one cannot have every good gift! The Story Girl had no dimples at her slim, brown wrists.

We all enjoyed our turnovers except Sara Ray. She ate hers but she knew she should not have done so. Her mother did not approve of snacks between meals, or of jam turnovers at any time. Once, when Sara was in a brown study, I asked her what she was thinking of.

"I'm trying to think of something ma hasn't forbid," she answered with a sigh.

We were all glad to hear that Peter was going to church, except Felicity. She was full of gloomy forebodings and warnings.

"I'm surprised at you, Felicity King," said Cecily severely. "You ought to be glad that poor boy is going to get started in the right way."

"There's a great big patch on his best pair of trousers," protested Felicity.

"Well, that's better than a hole," said the Story Girl, addressing herself daintily to her turnover. "God won't notice the patch."

"No, but the Carlisle people will," retorted Felicity, in a tone which implied that what the Carlisle people thought was far more important. "And I don't believe that Peter has got a decent stocking to his name. What will you feel like if he goes to church with the skin of his legs showing through the holes, Miss Story Girl?"

"I'm not a bit afraid," said the Story Girl staunchly. "Peter knows better than that."

"Well, all I hope is that he'll wash behind his ears," said Felicity resignedly.

"How is Pat to-day?" asked Cecily, by way of changing the conversation.

"Pat isn't a bit better. He just mopes about the kitchen," said the Story Girl anxiously. "I went out to the barn and I saw a mouse. I had a stick in my hand and I fetched a swipe at it—so. I killed it stone dead. Then I took it in to Paddy. Will you believe it? He wouldn't even look at it. I'm so worried. Uncle Roger says he needs a dose of physic. But how is he to be made take it, that's the question. I mixed a powder in some milk and tried to pour it down his throat while Peter held him. Just look at the scratches I got! And the milk went everywhere except down Pat's throat."

"Wouldn't it be awful if—if anything happened to Pat?" whispered Cecily.

"Well, we could have a jolly funeral, you know," said Dan.

We looked at him in such horror that Dan hastened to apologize.

"I'd be awful sorry myself if Pat died. But if he DID, we'd have to give him the right kind of a funeral," he protested. "Why, Paddy just seems like one of the family."

The Story Girl finished her turnover, and stretched herself out on the grasses, pillowing her chin in her hands and looking at the sky. She was bare headed, as usual, and her scarlet ribbon was bound filletwise about her head. She had twined freshly plucked dandelions around it and the effect was that of a crown of brilliant golden stars on her sleek, brown curls.

"Look at that long, thin, lacy cloud up there," she said. "What does it make you think of, girls?"

"A wedding veil," said Cecily.

"That is just what it is—the Wedding Veil of the Proud Princess. I know a story about it. I read it in a book. Once upon a time"—the Story Girl's eyes grew dreamy, and her accents floated away on the summer air like wind-blown rose petals—"there was a princess who was the most beautiful princess in the world, and kings from all lands came to woo her for a bride. But she was as proud as she was beautiful. She laughed all her suitors to scorn. And when her father urged her to choose one of them as her husband she drew herself up haughtily—so—"

The Story Girl sprang to her feet and for a moment we saw the proud princess of the old tale in all her scornful loveliness—

"and she said,

"'I will not wed until a king comes who can conquer all kings. Then I shall be the wife of the king of the world and no one can hold herself higher than I.'

"So every king went to war to prove that he could conquer every one else, and there was a great deal of bloodshed and misery. But the proud princess laughed and sang, and she and her maidens worked at a wonderful lace veil which she meant to wear when the king of all kings came. It was a very beautiful veil; but her maidens whispered that a man had died and a woman's heart had broken for every stitch set in it.

"Just when a king thought he had conquered everybody some other king would come and conquer HIM; and so it went on until it did not seem likely the proud princess would ever get a husband at all. But still her pride was so great that she would not yield, even though everybody except the kings who wanted to marry her, hated her for the suffering she had caused. One day a horn was blown at the palace gate; and there was one tall man in complete armor with his visor down, riding on a white horse. When he said he had come to marry the princess every one laughed, for he had no retinue and no beautiful apparel, and no golden crown.

"'But I am the king who conquers all kings,' he said.

"'You must prove it before I shall marry you,' said the proud princess. But she trembled and turned pale, for there was something in his voice that frightened her. And when he laughed, his laughter was still more dreadful.

"'I can easily prove it, beautiful princess,' he said, 'but you must go with me to my kingdom for the proof. Marry me now, and you and I and your father and all your court will ride straightway to my kingdom; and if you are not satisfied then that I am the king who conquers all kings you may give me back my ring and return home free of me forever more.'

"It was a strange wooing and the friends of the princess begged her to refuse. But her pride whispered that it would be such a wonderful thing to be the queen of the king of the world; so she consented; and her maidens dressed her, and put on the long lace veil that had been so many years a-making. Then they were married at once, but the bridegroom never lifted his visor and no one saw his face. The proud princess held herself more proudly than ever, but she was as white as her veil. And there was no laughter or merry-making, such as should be at a wedding, and every one looked at every one else with fear in his eyes.

"After the wedding the bridegroom lifted his bride before him on his white horse, and her father and all the members of his court mounted, too, and rode after them. On and on they rode, and the skies grew darker and the wind blew and wailed, and the shades of evening came down. And just in the twilight they rode into a dark valley, filled with tombs and graves.

"'Why have you brought me here?' cried the proud princess angrily.

"'This is my kingdom,' he answered. 'These are the tombs of the kings I have conquered. Behold me, beautiful princess. I am Death!'

"He lifted his visor. All saw his awful face. The proud princess shrieked.

"'Come to my arms, my bride,' he cried. 'I have won you fairly. I am the king who conquers all kings!'

"He clasped her fainting form to his breast and spurred his white horse to the tombs. A tempest of rain broke over the valley and blotted them from sight. Very sadly the old king and courtiers rode home, and never, never again did human eye behold the proud princess. But when those long, white clouds sweep across the sky, the country people in the land where she lived say, 'Look you, there is the Wedding Veil of the Proud Princess.'"

The weird spell of the tale rested on us for some moments after the Story Girl had finished. We had walked with her in the place of death and grown cold with the horror that chilled the heart of the poor princess. Dan presently broke the spell.

"You see it doesn't do to be too proud, Felicity," he remarked, giving her a poke. "You'd better not say too much about Peter's patches."

CHAPTER V.
PETER GOES TO CHURCH

There was no Sunday School the next afternoon, as superintendent and teachers wished to attend a communion service at Markdale. The Carlisle service was in the evening, and at sunset we were waiting at Uncle Alec's front door for Peter and the Story Girl.

None of the grown-ups were going to church. Aunt Olivia had a sick headache and Uncle Roger stayed home with her. Aunt Janet and Uncle Alec had gone to the Markdale service and had not yet returned.

Felicity and Cecily were wearing their new summer muslins for the first time—and were acutely conscious of the fact. Felicity, her pink and white face shadowed by her drooping, forget-me-not-wreathed, leghorn hat, was as beautiful as usual; but Cecily, having tortured her hair with curl papers all night, had a rampant bush of curls all about her head which quite destroyed the sweet, nun-like expression of her little features. Cecily cherished a grudge against fate because she had not been given naturally curly hair as had the other two girls. But she attained the desire of her heart on Sundays at least, and was quite well satisfied. It was impossible to convince her that the satin smooth lustre of her week-day tresses was much more becoming to her.

Presently Peter and the Story Girl appeared, and we were all more or less relieved to see that Peter looked quite respectable, despite the indisputable patch on his trousers. His face was rosy, his thick black curls were smoothly combed, and his tie was neatly bowed; but it was his legs which we scrutinized most anxiously. At first glance they seemed well enough; but closer inspection revealed something not altogether customary.

"What is the matter with your stockings, Peter?" asked Dan bluntly.

"Oh, I hadn't a pair without holes in the legs," answered Peter easily, "because ma hadn't time to darn them this week. So I put on two pairs. The holes don't come in the same places, and you'd never notice them unless you looked right close."

"Have you got a cent for collection?" demanded Felicity.

"I've got a Yankee cent. I s'pose it will do, won't it?"

Felicity shook her head vehemently.

"Oh, no, no. It may be all right to pass a Yankee cent on a store keeper or an egg peddler, but it would never do for church."

"I'll have to go without any, then," said Peter. "I haven't another cent. I only get fifty cents a week and I give it all to ma last night."

But Peter must have a cent. Felicity would have given him one herself— and she was none too lavish of her coppers—rather than have him go without one. Dan, however, lent him one, on the distinct understanding that it was to be repaid the next week.

Uncle Roger wandered by at this moment and, beholding Peter, said,

"'Is Saul also among the prophets?' What can have induced you to turn church-goer, Peter, when all Olivia's gentle persuasions were of no avail? The old, old argument I suppose—'beauty draws us with a single hair.'"

Uncle Roger looked quizzically at Felicity. We did not know what his quotations meant, but we understood he thought Peter was going to church because of Felicity. Felicity tossed her head.

"It isn't my fault that he's going to church," she said snappishly. "It's the Story Girl's doings."

Uncle Roger sat down on the doorstep, and gave himself over to one of the silent, inward paroxysms of laughter we all found so very aggravating. He shook his big, blond head, shut his eyes, and murmured,

"Not her fault! Oh, Felicity, Felicity, you'll be the death of your dear Uncle yet if you don't watch out."

Felicity started off indignantly, and we followed, picking up Sara Ray at the foot of the hill.

The Carlisle church was a very old-fashioned one, with a square, ivy-hung tower. It was shaded by tall elms, and the graveyard surrounded it completely, many of the graves being directly under its windows. We always took the corner path through it, passing the King plot where our kindred of four generations slept in a green solitude of wavering light and shadow.

There was Great-grandfather King's flat tombstone of rough Island sandstone, so overgrown with ivy that we could hardly read its lengthy inscription, recording his whole history in brief, and finishing with eight lines of original verse composed by his widow. I do not think that poetry was Great-grandmother King's strong point. When Felix read it, on our first Sunday in Carlisle, he remarked dubiously that it LOOKED like poetry but didn't SOUND like it.

There, too, slept the Emily whose faithful spirit was supposed to haunt the orchard; but Edith who had kissed the poet lay not with her kindred. She had died in a far, foreign land, and the murmur of an alien sea sounded about her grave.

White marble tablets, ornamented with weeping willow trees, marked where Grandfather and Grandmother King were buried, and a single shaft of red Scotch granite stood between the graves of Aunt Felicity and Uncle Felix. The Story Girl lingered to lay a bunch of wild violets, misty blue and faintly sweet, on her mother's grave; and then she read aloud the verse on the stone.

"'They were lovely and pleasant in their lives and in their death they were not divided.'"

The tones of her voice brought out the poignant and immortal beauty and pathos of that wonderful old lament. The girls wiped their eyes; and we boys felt as if we might have done so, too, had nobody been looking. What better epitaph could any one wish than to have it said that he was lovely and pleasant in his life? When I heard the Story Girl read it I made a secret compact with myself that I would try to deserve such an epitaph.

"I wish I had a family plot," said Peter, rather wistfully. "I haven't ANYTHING you fellows have. The Craigs are just buried anywhere they happen to die."

"I'd like to be buried here when I die," said Felix. "But I hope it won't be for a good while yet," he added in a livelier tone, as we moved onward to the church.

The interior of the church was as old-fashioned as its exterior. It was furnished with square box pews; the pulpit was a "wine-glass" one, and was reached by a steep, narrow flight of steps. Uncle Alec's pew was at the top of the church, quite near the pulpit.

Peter's appearance did not attract as much attention as we had fondly expected. Indeed, nobody seemed to notice him at all. The lamps were not yet lighted and the church was filled with a soft twilight and hush. Outside, the sky was purple and gold and silvery green, with a delicate tangle of rosy cloud above the elms.

"Isn't it awful nice and holy in here?" whispered Peter reverently. "I didn't know church was like this. It's nice."

Felicity frowned at him, and the Story Girl touched her with her slippered foot to remind him that he must not talk in church. Peter stiffened up and sat at attention during the service. Nobody could have behaved better. But when the sermon was over and the collection was being taken up, he made the sensation which his entrance had not produced.

Elder Frewen, a tall, pale man, with long, sandy side-whiskers, appeared at the door of our pew with the collection plate. We knew Elder Frewen quite well and liked him; he was Aunt Janet's cousin and often visited her. The contrast between his week-day jollity and the unearthly solemnity of his countenance on Sundays always struck us as very funny. It seemed so to strike Peter; for as Peter dropped his cent into the plate he laughed aloud!

Everybody looked at our pew. I have always wondered why Felicity did not die of mortification on the spot. The Story Girl turned white, and Cecily turned red. As for that poor, unlucky Peter, the shame of his countenance was pitiful to behold. He never lifted his head for the remainder of the service; and he followed us down the aisle and across the graveyard like a beaten dog. None of us uttered a word until we reached the road, lying in the white moonshine of the May night. Then Felicity broke the tense silence by remarking to the Story Girl,

"I told you so!"

The Story Girl made no response. Peter sidled up to her.

"I'm awful sorry," he said contritely. "I never meant to laugh. It just happened before I could stop myself. It was this way—"

"Don't you ever speak to me again," said the Story Girl, in a tone of cold concentrated fury. "Go and be a Methodist, or a Mohammedan, or ANYTHING! I don't care what you are! You have HUMILIATED me!"

She marched off with Sara Ray, and Peter dropped back to us with a frightened face.

"What is it I've done to her?" he whispered. "What does that big word mean?"

"Oh, never mind," I said crossly—for I felt that Peter HAD disgraced us—"She's just mad—and no wonder. Whatever made you act so crazy, Peter?"

"Well, I didn't mean to. And I wanted to laugh twice before that and DIDN'T. It was the Story Girl's stories made me want to laugh, so I don't think it's fair for her to be mad at me. She hadn't ought to tell me stories about people if she don't want me to laugh when I see them. When I looked at Samuel Ward I thought of him getting up in meeting one night, and praying that he might be guided in his upsetting and downrising. I remembered the way she took him off, and I wanted to laugh. And then I looked at the pulpit and thought of the story she told about the old Scotch minister who was too fat to get in at the door of it, and had to h'ist himself by his two hands over it, and then whispered to the other minister so that everybody heard him.

"'This pulpit door was made for speerits'—and I wanted to laugh. And then Mr. Frewen come—and I thought of her story about his sidewhiskers—how when his first wife died of information of the lungs he went courting Celia Ward, and Celia told him she wouldn't marry him unless he shaved them whiskers off. And he wouldn't, just to be stubborn. And one day one of them caught fire, when he was burning brush, and burned off, and every one thought he'd HAVE to shave the other off then. But he didn't and just went round with one whisker till the burned one grew out. And then Celia gave in and took him, because she saw there wasn't no hope of HIM ever giving in. I just remembered that story, and I thought I could see him, taking up the cents so solemn, with one long whisker; and the laugh just laughed itself before I could help it."

We all exploded with laughter on the spot, much to the horror of Mrs. Abraham Ward, who was just driving past, and who came up the next day and told Aunt Janet we had "acted scandalous" on the road home from church. We felt ashamed ourselves, because we knew people should conduct themselves decently and in order on Sunday farings-forth. But, as with Peter, it "had laughed itself."

Even Felicity laughed. Felicity was not nearly so angry with Peter as might have been expected. She even walked beside him and let him carry her Bible. They talked quite confidentially. Perhaps she forgave him the more easily, because he had justified her in her predictions, and thus afforded her a decided triumph over the Story Girl.

"I'm going to keep on going to church," Peter told her. "I like it. Sermons are more int'resting than I thought, and I like the singing. I wish I could make up my mind whether to be a Presbyterian or a Methodist. I s'pose I might ask the ministers about it."

"Oh, no, no, don't do that," said Felicity in alarm. "Ministers wouldn't want to be bothered with such questions."

"Why not? What are ministers for if they ain't to tell people how to get to heaven?"

"Oh, well, it's all right for grown-ups to ask them things, of course. But it isn't respectful for little boys—especially hired boys."

"I don't see why. But anyhow, I s'pose it wouldn't be much use, because if he was a Presbyterian minister he'd say I ought to be a Presbyterian, and if he was a Methodist he'd tell me to be one, too. Look here, Felicity, what IS the difference between them?"

"I—I don't know," said Felicity reluctantly. "I s'pose children can't understand such things. There must be a great deal of difference, of course, if we only knew what it was. Anyhow, I am a Presbyterian, and I'm glad of it."

We walked on in silence for a time, thinking our own young thoughts. Presently they were scattered by an abrupt and startling question from Peter.

"What does God look like?" he said.

It appeared that none of us had any idea.

"The Story Girl would prob'ly know," said Cecily.

"I wish I knew," said Peter gravely. "I wish I could see a picture of God. It would make Him seem lots more real."

"I've often wondered myself what he looks like," said Felicity in a burst of confidence. Even in Felicity, so it would seem, there were depths of thought unplumbed.

"I've seen pictures of Jesus," said Felix meditatively. "He looks just like a man, only better and kinder. But now that I come to think of it, I've never seen a picture of God."

"Well, if there isn't one in Toronto it isn't likely there's one anywhere," said Peter disappointedly. "I saw a picture of the devil once," he added. "It was in a book my Aunt Jane had. She got it for a prize in school. My Aunt Jane was clever."

"It couldn't have been a very good book if there was such a picture in it," said Felicity.

"It was a real good book. My Aunt Jane wouldn't have a book that wasn't good," retorted Peter sulkily.

He refused to discuss the subject further, somewhat to our disappointment. For we had never seen a picture of the person referred to, and we were rather curious regarding it.

"We'll ask Peter to describe it sometime when he's in a better humour," whispered Felix.

Sara Ray having turned in at her own gate, I ran ahead to join the Story Girl, and we walked up the hill together. She had recovered her calmness of mind, but she made no reference to Peter. When we reached our lane and passed under Grandfather King's big willow the fragrance of the orchard struck us in the face like a wave. We could see the long rows of trees, a white gladness in the moonshine. It seemed to us that there was in the orchard something different from other orchards that we had known. We were too young to analyze the vague sensation. In later years we were to understand that it was because the orchard blossomed not only apple blossoms but all the love, faith, joy, pure happiness and pure sorrow of those who had made it and walked there.

"The orchard doesn't seem the same place by moonlight at all," said the Story Girl dreamily. "It's lovely, but it's different. When I was very small I used to believe the fairies danced in it on moonlight nights. I would like to believe it now but I can't."

"Why not?"

"Oh, it's so hard to believe things you know are not true. It was Uncle Edward who told me there were no such things as fairies. I was just seven. He is a minister, so of course I knew he spoke the truth. It was his duty to tell me, and I do not blame him, but I have never felt quite the same to Uncle Edward since."

Ah, do we ever "feel quite the same" towards people who destroy our illusions? Shall I ever be able to forgive the brutal creature who first told me there was no such person as Santa Claus? He was a boy, three years older than myself; and he may now, for aught I know, be a most useful and respectable member of society, beloved by his kind. But I know what he must ever seem to me!

We waited at Uncle Alec's door for the others to come up. Peter was by way of skulking shamefacedly past into the shadows; but the Story Girl's brief, bitter anger had vanished.

"Wait for me, Peter," she called.

She went over to him and held out her hand.

"I forgive you," she said graciously.

Felix and I felt that it would really be worth while to offend her, just to be forgiven in such an adorable voice. Peter eagerly grasped her hand.

"I tell you what, Story Girl, I'm awfully sorry I laughed in church, but you needn't be afraid I ever will again. No, sir! And I'm going to church and Sunday School regular, and I'll say my prayers every night. I want to be like the rest of you. And look here! I've thought of the way my Aunt Jane used to give medicine to a cat. You mix the powder in lard, and spread it on his paws and his sides and he'll lick it off, 'cause a cat can't stand being messy. If Paddy isn't any better to-morrow, we'll do that."

They went away together hand in hand, children-wise, up the lane of spruces crossed with bars of moonlight. And there was peace over all that fresh and flowery land, and peace in our little hearts.

CHAPTER VI.
THE MYSTERY OF GOLDEN MILESTONE

Paddy was smeared with medicated lard the next day, all of us assisting at the rite, although the Story Girl was high priestess. Then, out of regard for mats and cushions, he was kept in durance vile in the granary until he had licked his fur clean. This treatment being repeated every day for a week, Pat recovered his usual health and spirits, and our minds were set at rest to enjoy the next excitement—collecting for a school library fund.

Our teacher thought it would be an excellent thing to have a library in connection with the school; and he suggested that each of the pupils should try to see how much money he or she could raise for the project during the month of June. We might earn it by honest toil, or gather it in by contributions levied on our friends.

The result was a determined rivalry as to which pupil should collect the largest sum; and this rivalry was especially intense in our home coterie.

Our relatives started us with a quarter apiece. For the rest, we knew we must depend on our own exertions. Peter was handicapped at the beginning by the fact that he had no family friend to finance him.

"If my Aunt Jane'd been living she'd have given me something," he remarked. "And if my father hadn't run away he might have given me something too. But I'm going to do the best I can anyhow. Your Aunt Olivia says I can have the job of gathering the eggs, and I'm to have one egg out of every dozen to sell for myself."

Felicity made a similar bargain with her mother. The Story Girl and Cecily were each to be paid ten cents a week for washing dishes in their respective homes. Felix and Dan contracted to keep the gardens free from weeds. I caught brook trout in the westering valley of spruces and sold them for a cent apiece.

Sara Ray was the only unhappy one among us. She could do nothing. She had no relatives in Carlisle except her mother, and her mother did not approve of the school library project, and would not give Sara a cent, or put her in any way of earning one. To Sara, this was humiliation indescribable. She felt herself an outcast and an alien to our busy little circle, where each member counted every day, with miserly delight, his slowly increasing hoard of small cash.

"I'm just going to pray to God to send me some money," she announced desperately at last.

"I don't believe that will do any good," said Dan. "He gives lots of things, but he doesn't give money, because people can earn that for themselves."

"I can't," said Sara, with passionate defiance. "I think He ought to take that into account."

"Don't worry, dear," said Cecily, who always poured balm. "If you can't collect any money everybody will know it isn't your fault."

"I won't ever feel like reading a single book in the library if I can't give something to it," mourned Sara.

Dan and the girls and I were sitting in a row on Aunt Olivia's garden fence, watching Felix weed. Felix worked well, although he did not like weeding—"fat boys never do," Felicity informed him. Felix pretended not to hear her, but I knew he did, because his ears grew red. Felix's face never blushed, but his ears always gave him away. As for Felicity, she did not say things like that out of malice prepense. It never occurred to her that Felix did not like to be called fat.

"I always feel so sorry for the poor weeds," said the Story Girl dreamily. "It must be very hard to be rooted up."

"They shouldn't grow in the wrong place," said Felicity mercilessly.

"When weeds go to heaven I suppose they will be flowers," continued the Story Girl.

"You do think such queer things," said Felicity.

"A rich man in Toronto has a floral clock in his garden," I said. "It looks just like the face of a clock, and there are flowers in it that open at every hour, so that you can always tell the time."

"Oh, I wish we had one here," exclaimed Cecily.

"What would be the use of it?" asked the Story Girl a little disdainfully. "Nobody ever wants to know the time in a garden."

I slipped away at this point, suddenly remembering that it was time to take a dose of magic seed. I had bought it from Billy Robinson three days before in school. Billy had assured me that it would make me grow fast.

I was beginning to feel secretly worried because I did not grow. I had overheard Aunt Janet say I was going to be short, like Uncle Alec. Now, I loved Uncle Alec, but I wanted to be taller than he was. So when Billy confided to me, under solemn promise of secrecy, that he had some "magic seed," which would make boys grow, and would sell me a box of it for ten cents, I jumped at the offer. Billy was taller than any boy of his age in Carlisle, and he assured me it all came from taking magic seed.

"I was a regular runt before I begun," he said, "and look at me now. I got it from Peg Bowen. She's a witch, you know. I wouldn't go near her again for a bushel of magic seed. It was an awful experience. I haven't much left, but I guess I've enough to do me till I'm as tall as I want to be. You must take a pinch of the seed every three hours, walking backward, and you must never tell a soul you're taking it, or it won't work. I wouldn't spare any of it to any one but you."

I felt deeply grateful to Billy, and sorry that I had not liked him better. Somehow, nobody did like Billy Robinson over and above. But I vowed I WOULD like him in future. I paid him the ten cents cheerfully and took the magic seed as directed, measuring myself carefully every day by a mark on the hall door. I could not see any advance in growth yet, but then I had been taking it only three days.

One day the Story Girl had an inspiration.

"Let us go and ask the Awkward Man and Mr. Campbell for a contribution to the library fund," she said. "I am sure no one else has asked them, because nobody in Carlisle is related to them. Let us all go, and if they give us anything we'll divide it equally among us."

It was a daring proposition, for both Mr. Campbell and the Awkward Man were regarded as eccentric personages; and Mr. Campbell was supposed to detest children. But where the Story Girl led we would follow to the death. The next day being Saturday, we started out in the afternoon.

We took a short cut to Golden Milestone, over a long, green, dewy land full of placid meadows, where sunshine had fallen asleep. At first all was not harmonious. Felicity was in an ill humour; she had wanted to wear her second best dress, but Aunt Janet had decreed that her school clothes were good enough to go "traipsing about in the dust." Then the Story Girl arrived, arrayed not in any second best but in her very best dress and hat, which her father had sent her from Paris—a dress of soft, crimson silk, and a white leghorn hat encircled by flame-red poppies. Neither Felicity nor Cecily could have worn it; but it became the Story Girl perfectly. In it she was a thing of fire and laughter and glow, as if the singular charm of her temperament were visible and tangible in its vivid colouring and silken texture.

"I shouldn't think you'd put on your best clothes to go begging for the library in," said Felicity cuttingly.

"Aunt Olivia says that when you are going to have an important interview with a man you ought to look your very best," said the Story Girl, giving her skirt a lustrous swirl and enjoying the effect.

"Aunt Olivia spoils you," said Felicity.

"She doesn't either, Felicity King! Aunt Olivia is just sweet. She kisses me good-night every night, and your mother NEVER kisses you."

"My mother doesn't make kisses so common," retorted Felicity. "But she gives us pie for dinner every day."

"So does Aunt Olivia."

"Yes, but look at the difference in the size of the pieces! And Aunt Olivia only gives you skim milk. My mother gives us cream."

"Aunt Olivia's skim milk is as good as your mother's cream," cried the Story Girl hotly.

"Oh, girls, don't fight," said Cecily, the peacemaker. "It's such a nice day, and we'll have a nice time if you don't spoil it by fighting."

"We're NOT fighting," said Felicity. "And I like Aunt Olivia. But my mother is just as good as Aunt Olivia, there now!"

"Of course she is. Aunt Janet is splendid," agreed the Story Girl.

They smiled at each other amicably. Felicity and the Story Girl were really quite fond of each other, under the queer surface friction that commonly resulted from their intercourse.

"You said once you knew a story about the Awkward Man," said Felix. "You might tell it to us."

"All right," agreed the Story Girl. "The only trouble is, I don't know the whole story. But I'll tell you all I do know. I call it 'The Mystery of the Golden Milestone.'"

"Oh, I don't believe that story is true," said Felicity. "I believe Mrs. Griggs was just romancing. She DOES romance, mother says."

"Yes; but I don't believe she could ever have thought of such a thing as this herself, so I believe it must be true," said the Story Girl. "Anyway, this is the story, boys. You know the Awkward Man has lived alone ever since his mother died, ten years ago. Abel Griggs is his hired man, and he and his wife live in a little house down the Awkward Man's lane. Mrs. Griggs makes his bread for him, and she cleans up his house now and then. She says he keeps it very neat. But till last fall there was one room she never saw. It was always locked—the west one, looking out over his garden. One day last fall the Awkward Man went to Summerside, and Mrs. Griggs scrubbed his kitchen. Then she went over the whole house and she tried the door of the west room. Mrs. Griggs is a VERY curious woman. Uncle Roger says all women have as much curiosity as is good for them, but Mrs. Griggs has more. She expected to find the door locked as usual. It was NOT locked. She opened it and went in. What do you suppose she found?"

"Something like—like Bluebeard's chamber?" suggested Felix in a scared tone.

"Oh, no, NO! Nothing like THAT could happen in Prince Edward Island. But if there HAD been beautiful wives hanging up by their hair all round the walls I don't believe Mrs. Griggs could have been much more astonished. The room had never been furnished in his mother's time, but now it was ELEGANTLY furnished, though Mrs. Griggs says SHE doesn't know when or how that furniture was brought there. She says she never saw a room like it in a country farmhouse. It was like a bed-room and sitting-room combined. The floor was covered with a carpet like green velvet. There were fine lace curtains at the windows and beautiful pictures on the walls. There was a little white bed, and a dressing-table, a bookcase full of books, a stand with a work basket on it, and a rocking-chair. There was a woman's picture above the bookcase. Mrs. Griggs says she thinks it was a coloured photograph, but she didn't know who it was. Anyway, it was a very pretty girl. But the most amazing thing of all was that A WOMAN'S DRESS was hanging over a chair by the table. Mrs. Griggs says it NEVER belonged to Jasper Dale's mother, for she thought it a sin to wear anything but print and drugget; and this dress was of PALE BLUE silk. Besides that, there was a pair of blue satin slippers on the floor beside it—HIGH-HEELED slippers. And on the fly-leaves of the books the name 'Alice' was written. Now, there never was an Alice in the Dale connection and nobody ever heard of the Awkward Man having a sweetheart. There, isn't that a lovely mystery?"

"It's a pretty queer yarn," said Felix. "I wonder if it is true—and what it means."

"I intend to find out what it means," said the Story Girl. "I am going to get acquainted with the Awkward Man sometime, and then I'll find out his Alice-secret."

"I don't see how you'll ever get acquainted with him," said Felicity. "He never goes anywhere except to church. He just stays home and reads books when he isn't working. Mother says he is a perfect hermit."

"I'll manage it somehow," said the Story Girl—and we had no doubt that she would. "But I must wait until I'm a little older, for he wouldn't tell the secret of the west room to a little girl. And I mustn't wait till I'm TOO old, for he is frightened of grown-up girls, because he thinks they laugh at his awkwardness. I know I will like him. He has such a nice face, even if he is awkward. He looks like a man you could tell things to."

"Well, I'd like a man who could move around without falling over his own feet," said Felicity. "And then the look of him! Uncle Roger says he is long, lank, lean, narrow, and contracted."

"Things always sound worse than they are when Uncle Roger says them," said the Story Girl. "Uncle Edward says Jasper Dale is a very clever man and it's a great pity he wasn't able to finish his college course. He went to college two years, you know. Then his father died, and he stayed home with his mother because she was very delicate. I call him a hero. I wonder if it is true that he writes poetry. Mrs. Griggs says it is. She says she has seen him writing it in a brown book. She said she couldn't get near enough to read it, but she knew it was poetry by the shape of it."

"Very likely. If that blue silk dress story is true, I'd believe ANYTHING of him," said Felicity.

We were near Golden Milestone now. The house was a big, weather-gray structure, overgrown with vines and climbing roses. Something about the three square windows in the second story gave it an appearance of winking at us in a friendly fashion through its vines—at least, so the Story Girl said; and, indeed, we could see it for ourselves after she had once pointed it out to us.

We did not get into the house, however. We met the Awkward man in his yard, and he gave us a quarter apiece for our library. He did not seem awkward or shy; but then we were only children, and his foot was on his native heath.

He was a tall, slender man, who did not look his forty years, so unwrinkled was his high, white forehead, so clear and lustrous his large, dark-blue eyes, so free from silver threads his rather long black hair. He had large hands and feet, and walked with a slight stoop. I am afraid we stared at him rather rudely while the Story Girl talked to him. But was not an Awkward Man, who was also a hermit and kept blue silk dresses in a locked room, and possibly wrote poetry, a legitimate object of curiosity? I leave it to you.

When we got away we compared notes, and found that we all liked him—and this, although he had said little and had appeared somewhat glad to get rid of us.

"He gave us the money like a gentleman," said the Story Girl. "I felt he didn't grudge it. And now for Mr. Campbell. It was on HIS account I put on my red silk. I don't suppose the Awkward Man noticed it at all, but Mr. Campbell will, or I'm much mistaken."

CHAPTER VII.
HOW BETTY SHERMAN WON A HUSBAND

The rest of us did not share the Story Girl's enthusiasm regarding our call on Mr. Campbell. We secretly dreaded it. If, as was said, he detested children, who knew what sort of a reception we might meet?

Mr. Campbell was a rich, retired farmer, who took life easily. He had visited New York and Boston, Toronto and Montreal; he had even been as far as the Pacific coast. Therefore he was regarded in Carlisle as a much travelled man; and he was known to be "well read" and intelligent. But it was also known that Mr. Campbell was not always in a good humour. If he liked you there was nothing he would not do for you; if he disliked you—well, you were not left in ignorance of it. In short, we had the impression that Mr. Campbell resembled the famous little girl with the curl in the middle of her forehead. "When he was good, he was very, very good, and when he was bad he was horrid." What if this were one of his horrid days?

"He can't DO anything to us, you know," said the Story Girl. "He may be rude, but that won't hurt any one but himself."

"Hard words break no bones," observed Felicity philosophically.

"But they hurt your feelings. I am afraid of Mr. Campbell," said Cecily candidly.

"Perhaps we'd better give up and go home," suggested Dan.

"You can go home if you like," said the Story Girl scornfully. "But I am going to see Mr. Campbell. I know I can manage him. But if I have to go alone, and he gives me anything, I'll keep it all for my own collection, mind you."

That settled it. We were not going to let the Story Girl get ahead of us in the manner of collecting.

Mr. Campbell's housekeeper ushered us into his parlour and left us. Presently Mr. Campbell himself was standing in the doorway, looking us over. We took heart of grace. It seemed to be one of his good days, for there was a quizzical smile on his broad, clean-shaven, strongly-featured face. Mr. Campbell was a tall man, with a massive head, well thatched with thick, black hair, gray-streaked. He had big, black eyes, with many wrinkles around them, and a thin, firm, long-lipped mouth. We thought him handsome, for an old man.

His gaze wandered over us with uncomplimentary indifference until it fell on the Story Girl, leaning back in an arm-chair. She looked like a slender red lily in the unstudied grace of her attitude. A spark flashed into Mr. Campbell's black eyes.

"Is this a Sunday School deputation?" he inquired rather ironically.

"No. We have come to ask a favour of you," said the Story Girl.

The magic of her voice worked its will on Mr. Campbell, as on all others. He came in, sat down, hooked his thumb into his vest pocket, and smiled at her.

"What is it?" he asked.

"We are collecting for our school library, and we have called to ask you for a contribution," she replied.

"Why should I contribute to your school library?" demanded Mr. Campbell.

This was a poser for us. Why should he, indeed? But the Story Girl was quite equal to it. Leaning forward, and throwing an indescribable witchery into tone and eyes and smile, she said,

"Because a lady asks you."

Mr. Campbell chuckled.

"The best of all reasons," he said. "But see here, my dear young lady, I'm an old miser and curmudgeon, as you may have heard. I HATE to part with my money, even for a good reason. And I NEVER part with any of it, unless I am to receive some benefit from the expenditure. Now, what earthly good could I get from your three by six school library? None whatever. But I shall make you a fair offer. I have heard from my housekeeper's urchin of a son that you are a 'master hand' to tell stories. Tell me one, here and now. I shall pay you in proportion to the entertainment you afford me. Come now, and do your prettiest."

There was a fine mockery in his tone that put the Story Girl on her mettle instantly. She sprang to her feet, an amazing change coming over her. Her eyes flashed and burned; crimson spots glowed in her cheeks.

"I shall tell you the story of the Sherman girls, and how Betty Sherman won a husband," she said.

We gasped. Was the Story Girl crazy? Or had she forgotten that Betty Sherman was Mr. Campbell's own great-grandmother, and that her method of winning a husband was not exactly in accordance with maidenly traditions.

But Mr. Campbell chuckled again.

"An excellent test," he said. "If you can amuse ME with that story you must be a wonder. I've heard it so often that it has no more interest for me than the alphabet."

"One cold winter day, eighty years ago," began the Story Girl without further parley, "Donald Fraser was sitting by the window of his new house, playing his fiddle for company, and looking out over the white, frozen bay before his door. It was bitter, bitter cold, and a storm was brewing. But, storm, or no storm, Donald meant to go over the bay that evening to see Nancy Sherman. He was thinking of her as he played 'Annie Laurie,' for Nancy was more beautiful than the lady of the song. 'Her face, it is the fairest that e'er the sun shone on,' hummed Donald—and oh, he thought so, too! He did not know whether Nancy cared for him or not. He had many rivals. But he knew that if she would not come to be the mistress of his new house no one else ever should. So he sat there that afternoon and dreamed of her, as he played sweet old songs and rollicking jigs on his fiddle.

"While he was playing a sleigh drove up to the door, and Neil Campbell came in. Donald was not overly glad to see him, for he suspected where he was going. Neil Campbell, who was Highland Scotch and lived down at Berwick, was courting Nancy Sherman, too; and, what was far worse, Nancy's father favoured him, because he was a richer man than Donald Fraser. But Donald was not going to show all he thought—Scotch people never do—and he pretended to be very glad to see Neil and made him heartily welcome.

"Neil sat down by the roaring fire, looking quite well satisfied with himself. It was ten miles from Berwick to the bay shore, and a call at a half way house was just the thing. Then Donald brought out the whisky. They always did that eighty years ago, you know. If you were a woman, you could give your visitors a dish of tea; but if you were a man and did not offer them a 'taste' of whisky, you were thought either very mean or very ignorant.

"'You look cold,' said Donald, in his great, hearty voice. 'Sit nearer the fire, man, and put a bit of warmth in your veins. It's bitter cold the day. And now tell me the Berwick news. Has Jean McLean made up with her man yet? And is it true that Sandy McQuarrie is to marry Kate Ferguson? 'Twill be a match now! Sure, with her red hair, Sandy will not be like to lose his bride past finding.'

"Neil had plenty of news to tell. And the more whisky he drank the more he told. He didn't notice that Donald was not taking much. Neil talked on and on, and of course he soon began to tell things it would have been much wiser not to tell. Finally he told Donald that he was going over the bay to ask Nancy Sherman that very night to marry him. And if she would have him, then Donald and all the folks should see a wedding that WAS a wedding.

"Oh, wasn't Donald taken aback! This was more than he had expected. Neil hadn't been courting Nancy very long, and Donald never dreamed he would propose to her QUITE so soon.

"At first Donald didn't know what to do. He felt sure deep down in his heart, that Nancy liked HIM. She was very shy and modest, but you know a girl can let a man see she likes him without going out of her way. But Donald knew that if Neil proposed first he would have the best chance. Neil was rich and the Shermans were poor, and old Elias Sherman would have the most to say in the matter. If he told Nancy she must take Neil Campbell she would never dream of disobeying him. Old Elias Sherman was a man who had to be obeyed. But if Nancy had only promised some one else first her father would not make her break her word.

"Wasn't it a hard plight for poor Donald? But he was a Scotchman, you know, and it's pretty hard to stick a Scotchman long. Presently a twinkle came into his eyes, for he remembered that all was fair in love and war. So he said to Neil, oh, so persuasively,

"'Have some more, man, have some more. 'Twill keep the heart in you in the teeth of that wind. Help yourself. There's plenty more where that came from.'

"Neil didn't want MUCH persuasion. He took some more, and said slyly,

"'Is it going over the bay the night that yourself will be doing?'

"Donald shook his head.

"'I had thought of it,' he owned, 'but it looks a wee like a storm, and my sleigh is at the blacksmith's to be shod. If I went it must be on Black Dan's back, and he likes a canter over the ice in a snow-storm as little as I. His own fireside is the best place for a man to-night, Campbell. Have another taste, man, have another taste.'

"Neil went on 'tasting,' and that sly Donald sat there with a sober face, but laughing eyes, and coaxed him on. At last Neil's head fell forward on his breast, and he was sound asleep. Donald got up, put on his overcoat and cap, and went to the door.

"'May your sleep be long and sweet, man,' he said, laughing softly, 'and as for the waking, 'twill be betwixt you and me.'

"With that he untied Neil's horse, climbed into Neil's sleigh, and tucked Neil's buffalo robe about him.

"'Now, Bess, old girl, do your bonniest,' he said. 'There's more than you know hangs on your speed. If the Campbell wakes too soon Black Dan could show you a pair of clean heels for all your good start. On, my girl.'

"Brown Bess went over the ice like a deer, and Donald kept thinking of what he should say to Nancy—and more still of what she would say to him. SUPPOSE he was mistaken. SUPPOSE she said 'no!'

"'Neil would have the laugh on me then. Sure he's sleeping well. And the snow is coming soon. There'll be a bonny swirl on the bay ere long. I hope no harm will come to the lad if he starts to cross. When he wakes he'll be in such a fine Highland temper that he'll never stop to think of danger. Well, Bess, old girl, here we are. Now, Donald Fraser, pluck up heart and play the man. Never flinch because a slip of a lass looks scornful at you out of the bonniest dark-blue eyes on earth.'

"But in spite of his bold words Donald's heart was thumping as he drove into the Sherman yard. Nancy was there milking a cow by the stable door, but she stood up when she saw Donald coming. Oh, she was very beautiful! Her hair was like a skein of golden silk, and her eyes were as blue as the gulf water when the sun breaks out after a storm. Donald felt more nervous than ever. But he knew he must make the most of his chance. He might not see Nancy alone again before Neil came. He caught her hand and stammered out,

"'Nan, lass, I love you. You may think 'tis a hasty wooing, but that's a story I can tell you later maybe. I know well I'm not worthy of you, but if true love could make a man worthy there'd be none before me. Will you have me, Nan?'

"Nancy didn't SAY she would have him. She just LOOKED it, and Donald kissed her right there in the snow.

"The next morning the storm was over. Donald knew Neil must be soon on his track. He did not want to make the Sherman house the scene of a quarrel, so he resolved to get away before the Campbell came. He persuaded Nancy to go with him to visit some friends in another settlement. As he brought Neil's sleigh up to the door he saw a black speck far out on the bay and laughed.

"'Black Dan goes well, but he'll not be quick enough,' he said.

"Half an hour later Neil Campbell rushed into the Sherman kitchen and oh, how angry he was! There was nobody there but Betty Sherman, and Betty was not afraid of him. She was never afraid of anybody. She was very handsome, with hair as brown as October nuts and black eyes and crimson cheeks; and she had always been in love with Neil Campbell herself.

"'Good morning, Mr. Campbell,' she said, with a toss of her head. 'It's early abroad you are. And on Black Dan, no less! Was I mistaken in thinking that Donald Fraser said once that his favourite horse should never be backed by any man but him? But doubtless a fair exchange is no robbery, and Brown Bess is a good mare in her way.'

"'Where is Donald Fraser?' said Neil, shaking his fist. 'It's him I'm seeking, and it's him I will be finding. Where is he, Betty Sherman?'

"'Donald Fraser is far enough away by this time,' mocked Betty. 'He is a prudent fellow, and has some quickness of wit under that sandy thatch of his. He came here last night at sunset, with a horse and sleigh not his own, or lately gotten, and he asked Nan in the stable yard to marry him. Did a man ask ME to marry him at the cow's side with a milking pail in my hand, it's a cold answer he'd get for his pains. But Nan thought differently, and they sat late together last night, and 'twas a bonny story Nan wakened me to hear when she came to bed—the story of a braw lover who let his secret out when the whisky was above the wit, and then fell asleep while his rival was away to woo and win his lass. Did you ever hear a like story, Mr. Campbell?'

"'Oh, yes,' said Neil fiercely. 'It is laughing at me over the country side and telling that story that Donald Fraser will be doing, is it? But when I meet him it is not laughing he will be doing. Oh, no. There will be another story to tell!'

"'Now, don't meddle with the man,' cried Betty. 'What a state to be in because one good-looking lass likes sandy hair and gray eyes better than Highland black and blue! You have not the spirit of a wren, Neil Campbell. Were I you, I would show Donald Fraser that I could woo and win a lass as speedily as any Lowlander of them all; that I would! There's many a girl would gladly say 'yes' for your asking. And here stands one! Why not marry ME, Neil Campbell? Folks say I'm as bonny as Nan—and I could love you as well as Nan loves her Donald—ay, and ten times better!'

"What do you suppose the Campbell did? Why, just the thing he ought to have done. He took Betty at her word on the spot; and there was a double wedding soon after. And it is said that Neil and Betty were the happiest couple in the world—happier even than Donald and Nancy. So all was well because it ended well!"

The Story Girl curtsied until her silken skirts swept the floor. Then she flung herself in her chair and looked at Mr. Campbell, flushed, triumphant, daring.

The story was old to us. It had once been published in a Charlottetown paper, and we had read in Aunt Olivia's scrapbook, where the Story Girl had learned it. But we had listened entranced. I have written down the bare words of the story, as she told it; but I can never reproduce the charm and colour and spirit she infused into it. It LIVED for us. Donald and Neil, Nancy and Betty, were there in that room with us. We saw the flashes of expression on their faces, we heard their voices, angry or tender, mocking or merry, in Lowland and Highland accent. We realized all the mingled coquetry and feeling and defiance and archness in Betty Sherman's daring speech. We had even forgotten all about Mr. Campbell.

That gentleman, in silence, took out his wallet, extracted a note therefrom, and handed it gravely to the Story Girl.

"There are five dollars for you," he said, "and your story was well worth it. You ARE a wonder. Some day you will make the world realize it. I've been about a bit, and heard some good things, but I've never enjoyed anything more than that threadbare old story I heard in my cradle. And now, will you do me a favour?"

"Of course," said the delighted Story Girl.

"Recite the multiplication table for me," said Mr. Campbell.

We stared. Well might Mr. Campbell be called eccentric. What on earth did he want the multiplication table recited for? Even the Story Girl was surprised. But she began promptly, with twice one and went through it to twelve times twelve. She repeated it simply, but her voice changed from one tone to another as each in succession grew tired. We had never dreamed that there was so much in the multiplication table. As she announced it, the fact that three times three was nine was exquisitely ridiculous, five times six almost brought tears to our eyes, eight times seven was the most tragic and frightful thing ever heard of, and twelve times twelve rang like a trumpet call to victory.

Mr. Campbell nodded his satisfaction.

"I thought you could do it," he said. "The other day I found this statement in a book. 'Her voice would have made the multiplication table charming!' I thought of it when I heard yours. I didn't believe it before, but I do now."

Then he let us go.

"You see," said the Story Girl as we went home, "you need never be afraid of people."

"But we are not all Story Girls," said Cecily.

That night we heard Felicity talking to Cecily in their room.

"Mr. Campbell never noticed one of us except the Story Girl," she said, "but if I had put on MY best dress as she did maybe she wouldn't have taken all the attention."

"Could you ever do what Betty Sherman did, do you suppose?" asked Cecily absently.

"No; but I believe the Story Girl could," answered Felicity rather snappishly.

CHAPTER VIII.
A TRAGEDY OF CHILDHOOD

The Story Girl went to Charlottetown for a week in June to visit Aunt Louisa. Life seemed very colourless without her, and even Felicity admitted that it was lonesome. But three days after her departure Felix told us something on the way home from school which lent some spice to existence immediately.

"What do you think?" he said in a very solemn, yet excited, tone. "Jerry Cowan told me at recess this afternoon that he HAD SEEN A PICTURE OF GOD—that he has it at home in an old, red-covered history of the world, and has looked at it OFTEN."

To think that Jerry Cowan should have seen such a picture often! We were as deeply impressed as Felix had meant us to be.

"Did he say what it was like?" asked Peter.

"No—only that it was a picture of God, walking in the garden of Eden."

"Oh," whispered Felicity—we all spoke in low tones on the subject, for, by instinct and training, we thought and uttered the Great Name with reverence, in spite of our devouring curiosity—"oh, WOULD Jerry Cowan bring it to school and let us see it?"

"I asked him that, soon as ever he told me," said Felix. "He said he might, but he couldn't promise, for he'd have to ask his mother if he could bring the book to school. If she'll let him he'll bring it to-morrow."

"Oh, I'll be almost afraid to look at it," said Sara Ray tremulously.

I think we all shared her fear to some extent. Nevertheless, we went to school the next day burning with curiosity. And we were disappointed. Possibly night had brought counsel to Jerry Cowan; or perhaps his mother had put him up to it. At all events, he announced to us that he couldn't bring the red-covered history to school, but if we wanted to buy the picture outright he would tear it out of the book and sell it to us for fifty cents.

We talked the matter over in serious conclave in the orchard that evening. We were all rather short of hard cash, having devoted most of our spare means to the school library fund. But the general consensus of opinion was that we must have the picture, no matter what pecuniary sacrifices were involved. If we could each give about seven cents we would have the amount. Peter could only give four, but Dan gave eleven, which squared matters.

"Fifty cents would be pretty dear for any other picture, but of course this is different," said Dan.

"And there's a picture of Eden thrown in, too, you know," added Felicity.

"Fancy selling God's picture," said Cecily in a shocked, awed tone.

"Nobody but a Cowan would do it, and that's a fact," said Dan.

"When we get it we'll keep it in the family Bible," said Felicity. "That's the only proper place."

"Oh, I wonder what it will be like," breathed Cecily.

We all wondered. Next day in school we agreed to Jerry Cowan's terms, and Jerry promised to bring the picture up to Uncle Alec's the following afternoon.

We were all intensely excited Saturday morning. To our dismay, it began to rain just before dinner.

"What if Jerry doesn't bring the picture to-day because of the rain?" I suggested.

"Never you fear," answered Felicity decidedly. "A Cowan would come through ANYTHING for fifty cents."

After dinner we all, without any verbal decision about it, washed our faces and combed our hair. The girls put on their second best dresses, and we boys donned white collars. We all had the unuttered feeling that we must do such honour to that Picture as we could. Felicity and Dan began a small spat over something, but stopped at once when Cecily said severely,

"How DARE you quarrel when you are going to look at a picture of God to-day?"

Owing to the rain we could not foregather in the orchard, where we had meant to transact the business with Jerry. We did not wish our grown-ups around at our great moment, so we betook ourselves to the loft of the granary in the spruce wood, from whose window we could see the main road and hail Jerry. Sara Ray had joined us, very pale and nervous, having had, so it appeared, a difference of opinion with her mother about coming up the hill in the rain.

"I'm afraid I did very wrong to come against ma's will," she said miserably, "but I COULDN'T wait. I wanted to see the picture as soon as you did."

We waited and watched at the window. The valley was full of mist, and the rain was coming down in slanting lines over the tops of the spruces. But as we waited the clouds broke away and the sun came out flashingly; the drops on the spruce boughs glittered like diamonds.

"I don't believe Jerry can be coming," said Cecily in despair. "I suppose his mother must have thought it was dreadful, after all, to sell such a picture."

"There he is now!" cried Dan, waving excitedly from the window.

"He's carrying a fish-basket," said Felicity. "You surely don't suppose he would bring THAT picture in a fish-basket!"

Jerry HAD brought it in a fish-basket, as appeared when he mounted the granary stairs shortly afterwards. It was folded up in a newspaper packet on top of the dried herring with which the basket was filled. We paid him his money, but we would not open the packet until he had gone.

"Cecily," said Felicity in a hushed tone. "You are the best of us all. YOU open the parcel."

"Oh, I'm no gooder than the rest of you," breathed Cecily, "but I'll open it if you like."

With trembling fingers Cecily opened the parcel. We stood around, hardly breathing. She unfolded it and held it up. We saw it.

Suddenly Sara began to cry.

"Oh, oh, oh, does God look like THAT?" she wailed.

Felix and I spoke not. Disappointment, and something worse, sealed our speech. DID God look like that—like that stern, angrily frowning old man with the tossing hair and beard of the wood-cut Cecily held.

"I suppose He must, since that is His picture," said Dan miserably.

"He looks awful cross," said Peter simply.

"Oh, I wish we'd never, never seen it," cried Cecily.

We all wished that—too late. Our curiosity had led us into some Holy of Holies, not to be profaned by human eyes, and this was our punishment.

"I've always had a feeling right along," wept Sara, "that it wasn't RIGHT to buy—or LOOK AT—God's picture."

As we stood there wretchedly we heard flying feet below and a blithe voice calling,

"Where are you, children?"

The Story Girl had returned! At any other moment we would have rushed to meet her in wild joy. But now we were too crushed and miserable to move.

"Whatever is the matter with you all?" demanded the Story Girl, appearing at the top of the stairs. "What is Sara crying about? What have you got there?"

"A picture of God," said Cecily with a sob in her voice, "and oh, it is so dreadful and ugly. Look!"

The Story Girl looked. An expression of scorn came over her face.

"Surely you don't believe God looks like that," she said impatiently, while her fine eyes flashed. "He doesn't—He couldn't. He is wonderful and beautiful. I'm surprised at you. THAT is nothing but the picture of a cross old man."

Hope sprang up in our hearts, although we were not wholly convinced.

"I don't know," said Dan dubiously. "It says under the picture 'God in the Garden of Eden.' It's PRINTED."

"Well, I suppose that's what the man who drew it thought God was like," answered the Story Girl carelessly. "But HE couldn't have known any more than you do. HE had never seen Him."

"It's all very well for you to say so," said Felicity, "but YOU don't know either. I wish I could believe that isn't like God—but I don't know what to believe."

"Well, if you won't believe me, I suppose you'll believe the minister," said the Story Girl. "Go and ask him. He's in the house this very minute. He came up with us in the buggy."

At any other time we would never have dared catechize the minister about anything. But desperate cases call for desperate measures. We drew straws to see who should go and do the asking, and the lot fell to Felix.

"Better wait until Mr. Marwood leaves, and catch him in the lane," advised the Story Girl. "You'll have a lot of grown-ups around you in the house."

Felix took her advice. Mr. Marwood, presently walking benignantly along the lane, was confronted by a fat, small boy with a pale face but resolute eyes.

The rest of us remained in the background but within hearing.

"Well, Felix, what is it?" asked Mr. Marwood kindly.

"Please, sir, does God really look like this?" asked Felix, holding out the picture. "We hope He doesn't—but we want to know the truth, and that is why I'm bothering you. Please excuse us and tell me."

The minister looked at the picture. A stern expression came into his gentle blue eyes and he got as near to frowning as it was possible for him to get.

"Where did you get that thing?" he asked.

THING! We began to breathe easier.

"We bought it from Jerry Cowan. He found it in a red-covered history of the world. It SAYS it's God's picture," said Felix.

"It is nothing of the sort," said Mr. Marwood indignantly. "There is no such thing as a picture of God, Felix. No human being knows what he looks like—no human being CAN know. We should not even try to think what He looks like. But, Felix, you may be sure that God is infinitely more beautiful and loving and tender and kind than anything we can imagine of Him. Never believe anything else, my boy. As for this—this SACRILEGE—take it and burn it."

We did not know what a sacrilege meant, but we knew that Mr. Marwood had declared that the picture was not like God. That was enough for us. We felt as if a terrible weight had been lifted from our minds.

"I could hardly believe the Story Girl, but of course the minister KNOWS," said Dan happily.

"We've lost fifty cents because of it," said Felicity gloomily.

We had lost something of infinitely more value than fifty cents, although we did not realize it just then. The minister's words had removed from our minds the bitter belief that God was like that picture; but on something deeper and more enduring than mind an impression had been made that was never to be removed. The mischief was done. From that day to this the thought or the mention of God brings up before us involuntarily the vision of a stern, angry, old man. Such was the price we were to pay for the indulgence of a curiosity which each of us, deep in our hearts, had, like Sara Ray, felt ought not to be gratified.

"Mr. Marwood told me to burn it," said Felix.

"It doesn't seem reverent to do that," said Cecily. "Even if it isn't God's picture, it has His name on it."

"Bury it," said the Story Girl.

We did bury it after tea, in the depths of the spruce grove; and then we went into the orchard. It was so nice to have the Story Girl back again. She had wreathed her hair with Canterbury Bells, and looked like the incarnation of rhyme and story and dream.

"Canterbury Bells is a lovely name for a flower, isn't it?" she said. "It makes you think of cathedrals and chimes, doesn't it? Let's go over to Uncle Stephen's Walk, and sit on the branches of the big tree. It's too wet on the grass, and I know a story—a TRUE story, about an old lady I saw in town at Aunt Louisa's. Such a dear old lady, with lovely silvery curls."

After the rain the air seemed dripping with odours in the warm west wind—the tang of fir balsam, the spice of mint, the wild woodsiness of ferns, the aroma of grasses steeping in the sunshine,—and with it all a breath of wild sweetness from far hill pastures.

Scattered through the grass in Uncle Stephen's Walk, were blossoming pale, aerial flowers which had no name that we could ever discover. Nobody seemed to know anything about them. They had been there when Great-grandfather King bought the place. I have never seen them elsewhere, or found them described in any floral catalogue. We called them the White Ladies. The Story Girl gave them the name. She said they looked like the souls of good women who had had to suffer much and had been very patient. They were wonderfully dainty, with a strange, faint, aromatic perfume which was only to be detected at a little distance and vanished if you bent over them. They faded soon after they were plucked; and, although strangers, greatly admiring them, often carried away roots and seeds, they could never be coaxed to grow elsewhere.

"My story is about Mrs. Dunbar and the Captain of the FANNY," said the Story Girl, settling herself comfortably on a bough, with her brown head against a gnarled trunk. "It's sad and beautiful—and true. I do love to tell stories that I know really happened. Mrs. Dunbar lives next door to Aunt Louisa in town. She is so sweet. You wouldn't think to look at her that she had a tragedy in her life, but she has. Aunt Louisa told me the tale. It all happened long, long ago. Interesting things like this all did happen long ago, it seems to me. They never seem to happen now. This was in '49, when people were rushing to the gold fields in California. It was just like a fever, Aunt Louisa says. People took it, right here on the Island; and a number of young men determined they would go to California.

"It is easy to go to California now; but it was a very different matter then. There were no railroads across the land, as there are now, and if you wanted to go to California you had to go in a sailing vessel, all the way around Cape Horn. It was a long and dangerous journey; and sometimes it took over six months. When you got there you had no way of sending word home again except by the same plan. It might be over a year before your people at home heard a word about you—and fancy what their feelings would be!

"But these young men didn't think of these things; they were led on by a golden vision. They made all their arrangements, and they chartered the brig Fanny to take them to California.

"The captain of the Fanny is the hero of my story. His name was Alan Dunbar, and he was young and handsome. Heroes always are, you know, but Aunt Louisa says he really was. And he was in love—wildly in love,— with Margaret Grant. Margaret was as beautiful as a dream, with soft blue eyes and clouds of golden hair; and she loved Alan Dunbar just as much as he loved her. But her parents were bitterly opposed to him, and they had forbidden Margaret to see him or speak to him. They hadn't anything against him as a MAN, but they didn't want her to throw herself away on a sailor.

"Well, when Alan Dunbar knew that he must go to California in the Fanny he was in despair. He felt that he could NEVER go so far away for so long and leave his Margaret behind. And Margaret felt that she could never let him go. I know EXACTLY how she felt."

"How can you know?" interrupted Peter suddenly. "You ain't old enough to have a beau. How can you know?"

The Story Girl looked at Peter with a frown. She did not like to be interrupted when telling a story.

"Those are not things one KNOWS about," she said with dignity. "One FEELS about them."

Peter, crushed but not convinced, subsided, and the Story Girl went on.

"Finally, Margaret ran away with Alan, and they were married in Charlottetown. Alan intended to take his wife with him to California in the Fanny. If it was a hard journey for a man it was harder still for a woman, but Margaret would have dared anything for Alan's sake. They had three days—ONLY three days—of happiness, and then the blow fell. The crew and the passengers of the Fanny refused to let Captain Dunbar take his wife with him. They told him he must leave her behind. And all his prayers were of no avail. They say he stood on the deck of the Fanny and pleaded with the men while the tears ran down his face; but they would not yield, and he had to leave Margaret behind. Oh, what a parting it was!"

There was heartbreak in the Story Girl's voice and tears came into our eyes. There, in the green bower of Uncle Stephen's Walk, we cried over the pathos of a parting whose anguish had been stilled for many years.

"When it was all over, Margaret's father and mother forgave her, and she went back home to wait—to WAIT. Oh, it is so dreadful just to WAIT, and do nothing else. Margaret waited for nearly a year. How long it must have seemed to her! And at last there came a letter—but not from Alan. Alan was DEAD. He had died in California and had been buried there. While Margaret had been thinking of him and longing for him and praying for him he had been lying in his lonely, faraway grave."

Cecily sprang up, shaking with sobs.

"Oh, don't—don't go on," she implored. "I CAN'T bear any more."

"There is no more," said the Story Girl. "That was the end of it—the end of everything for Margaret. It didn't kill HER, but her heart died."

"I just wish I'd hold of those fellows who wouldn't let the Captain take his wife," said Peter savagely.

"Well, it was awful said," said Felicity, wiping her eyes. "But it was long ago and we can't do any good by crying over it now. Let us go and get something to eat. I made some nice little rhubarb tarts this morning."

We went. In spite of new disappointments and old heartbreaks we had appetites. And Felicity did make scrumptious rhubarb tarts!

CHAPTER IX.
MAGIC SEED

When the time came to hand in our collections for the library fund Peter had the largest—three dollars. Felicity was a good second with two and a half. This was simply because the hens had laid so well.

"If you'd had to pay father for all the extra handfuls of wheat you've fed to those hens, Miss Felicity, you wouldn't have so much," said Dan spitefully.

"I didn't," said Felicity indignantly. "Look how Aunt Olivia's hens laid, too, and she fed them herself just the same as usual."

"Never mind," said Cecily, "we have all got something to give. If you were like poor Sara Ray, and hadn't been able to collect anything, you might feel bad."

But Sara Ray HAD something to give. She came up the hill after tea, all radiant. When Sara Ray smiled—and she did not waste her smiles—she was rather pretty in a plaintive, apologetic way. A dimple or two came into sight, and she had very nice teeth—small and white, like the traditional row of pearls.

"Oh, just look," she said. "Here are three dollars—and I'm going to give it all to the library fund. I had a letter to-day from Uncle Arthur in Winnipeg, and he sent me three dollars. He said I was to use it ANY way I liked, so ma couldn't refuse to let me give it to the fund. She thinks it's an awful waste, but she always goes by what Uncle Arthur says. Oh, I've prayed so hard that some money might come some way, and now it has. See what praying does!"

I was very much afraid that we did not rejoice quite as unselfishly in Sara's good fortune as we should have done. WE had earned our contributions by the sweat of our brow, or by the scarcely less disagreeable method of "begging." And Sara's had as good as descended upon her out of the skies, as much like a miracle as anything you could imagine.

"She prayed for it, you know," said Felix, after Sara had gone home.

"That's too easy a way of earning money," grumbled Peter resentfully. "If the rest of us had just set down and done nothing, only prayed, how much do you s'pose we'd have? It don't seem fair to me."

"Oh, well, it's different with Sara," said Dan. "We COULD earn money and she COULDN'T. You see? But come on down to the orchard. The

Story Girl had a letter from her father to-day and she's going to read it to us."

We went promptly. A letter from the Story Girl's father was always an event; and to hear her read it was almost as good as hearing her tell a story.

Before coming to Carlisle, Uncle Blair Stanley had been a mere name to us. Now he was a personality. His letters to the Story Girl, the pictures and sketches he sent her, her adoring and frequent mention of him, all combined to make him very real to us.

We FELT then, what we did not understand till later years, that our grown-up relatives did not altogether admire or approve of Uncle Blair. He belonged to a different world from theirs. They had never known him very intimately or understood him. I realize now that Uncle Blair was a bit of a Bohemian—a respectable sort of tramp. Had he been a poor man he might have been a more successful artist. But he had a small fortune of his own and, lacking the spur of necessity, or of disquieting ambition, he remained little more than a clever amateur. Once in a while he painted a picture which showed what he could do; but for the rest, he was satisfied to wander over the world, light-hearted and content. We knew that the Story Girl was thought to resemble him strongly in appearance and temperament, but she had far more fire and intensity and strength of will—her inheritance from King and Ward. She would never be satisfied as a dabbler; whatever her future career should be, into it she would throw all her powers of mind and heart and soul.

But Uncle Blair could do at least one thing surpassingly well. He could write letters. Such letters! By contrast, Felix and I were secretly ashamed of father's epistles. Father could talk well but, as Felix said, he couldn't write worth a cent. The letters we had received from him since his arrival in Rio de Janeiro were mere scrawls, telling us to be good boys and not trouble Aunt Janet, incidentally adding that he was well and lonesome. Felix and I were always glad to get his letters, but we never read them aloud to an admiring circle in the orchard.

Uncle Blair was spending the summer in Switzerland; and the letter the Story Girl read to us, among the fair, frail White Ladies of the Walk, where the west wind came now with a sigh, and again with a rush, and then brushed our faces as softly as the down of a thistle, was full of the glamour of mountain-rimmed lakes, and purple chalets, and "snowy summits old in story." We climbed Mount Blanc, saw the Jungfrau soaring into cloudland, and walked among the gloomy pillars of Bonnivard's prison. Finally, the Story Girl told us the tale of the Prisoner of Chillon, in words that were Byron's, but in a voice that was all her own.

"It must be splendid to go to Europe," sighed Cecily longingly.

"I am going some day," said the Story Girl airily.

We looked at her with a slightly incredulous awe. To us, in those years, Europe seemed almost as remote and unreachable as the moon. It was hard to believe that one of US should ever go there. But Aunt Julia had gone— and SHE had been brought up in Carlisle on this very farm. So it was possible that the Story Girl might go too.

"What will you do there?" asked Peter practically.

"I shall learn how to tell stories to all the world," said the Story Girl dreamily.

It was a lovely, golden-brown evening; the orchard, and the farm-lands beyond, were full of ruby lights and kissing shadows. Over in the east, above the Awkward Man's house, the Wedding Veil of the Proud Princess floated across the sky, presently turning as rosy as if bedewed with her heart's blood. We sat there and talked until the first star lighted a white taper over the beech hill.

Then I remembered that I had forgotten to take my dose of magic seed, and I hastened to do it, although I was beginning to lose faith in it. I had not grown a single bit, by the merciless testimony of the hall door.

I took the box of seed out of my trunk in the twilit room and swallowed the decreed pinch. As I did so, Dan's voice rang out behind me.

"Beverley King, what have you got there?"

I thrust the box hastily into my trunk and confronted Dan.

"None of your business," I said defiantly.

"Yes, 'tis." Dan was too much in earnest to resent my blunt speech. "Look here, Bev, is that magic seed? And did you get it from Billy Robinson?"

Dan and I looked at each other, suspicion dawning in our eyes.

"What do you know about Billy Robinson and his magic seed?" I demanded.

"Just this. I bought a box from him for—for—something. He said he wasn't going to sell any of it to anybody else. Did he sell any to you?"

"Yes, he did," I said in disgust—for I was beginning to understand that Billy and his magic seed were arrant frauds.

"What for? YOUR mouth is a decent size," said Dan.

"Mouth? It had nothing to do with my mouth! He said it would make me grow tall. And it hasn't—not an inch! I don't see what you wanted it for! You are tall enough."

"I got it for my mouth," said Dan with a shame-faced grin. "The girls in school laugh at it so. Kate Marr says it's like a gash in a pie. Billy said that seed would shrink it for sure."

Well, there it was! Billy had deceived us both. Nor were we the only victims. We did not find the whole story out at once. Indeed, the summer was almost over before, in one way or another, the full measure of that shameless Billy Robinson's iniquity was revealed to us. But I shall anticipate the successive relations in this chapter. Every pupil of Carlisle school, so it eventually appeared, had bought magic seed, under solemn promise of secrecy. Felix had believed blissfully that it would make him thin. Cecily's hair was to become naturally curly, and Sara Ray was not to be afraid of Peg Bowen any more. It was to make Felicity as clever as the Story Girl and it was to make the Story Girl as good a cook as Felicity. What Peter had bought magic seed for remained a secret longer than any of the others. Finally—it was the night before what we expected would be the Judgment Day—he confessed to me that he had taken it to make Felicity fond of him. Skilfully indeed had that astute Billy played on our respective weaknesses.

The keenest edge to our humiliation was given by the discovery that the magic seed was nothing more or less than caraway, which grew in abundance at Billy Robinson's uncle's in Markdale. Peg Bowen had had nothing to do with it.

Well, we had all been badly hoaxed. But we did not trumpet our wrongs abroad. We did not even call Billy to account. We thought that least said was soonest mended in such a matter. We went very softly indeed, lest the grown-ups, especially that terrible Uncle Roger, should hear of it.

"We should have known better than to trust Billy Robinson," said Felicity, summing up the case one evening when all had been made known. "After all, what could you expect from a pig but a grunt?"

We were not surprised to find that Billy Robinson's contribution to the library fund was the largest handed in by any of the scholars. Cecily said she didn't envy him his conscience. But I am afraid she measured his conscience by her own. I doubt very much if Billy's troubled him at all.

CHAPTER X.
A DAUGHTER OF EVE

"I hate the thought of growing up," said the Story Girl reflectively, "because I can never go barefooted then, and nobody will ever see what beautiful feet I have."

She was sitting, the July sunlight, on the ledge of the open hayloft window in Uncle Roger's big barn; and the bare feet below her print skirt WERE beautiful. They were slender and shapely and satin smooth with arched insteps, the daintiest of toes, and nails like pink shells.

We were all in the hayloft. The Story Girl had been telling us a tale

"Of old, unhappy, far-off things,

And battles long ago."

Felicity and Cecily were curled up in a corner, and we boys sprawled idly on the fragrant, sun-warm heaps. We had "stowed" the hay in the loft that morning for Uncle Roger, so we felt that we had earned the right to loll on our sweet-smelling couch. Haylofts are delicious places, with just enough of shadow and soft, uncertain noises to give an agreeable tang of mystery. The swallows flew in and out of their nest above our heads, and whenever a sunbeam fell through a chink the air swarmed with golden dust. Outside of the loft was a vast, sunshiny gulf of blue sky and mellow air, wherein floated argosies of fluffy cloud, and airy tops of maple and spruce.

Pat was with us, of course, prowling about stealthily, or making frantic, bootless leaps at the swallows. A cat in a hayloft is a beautiful example of the eternal fitness of things. We had not heard of this fitness then, but we all felt that Paddy was in his own place in a hayloft.

"I think it is very vain to talk about anything you have yourself being beautiful," said Felicity.

"I am not a bit vain," said the Story Girl, with entire truthfulness. "It is not vanity to know your own good points. It would just be stupidity if you didn't. It's only vanity when you get puffed up about them. I am not a bit pretty. My only good points are my hair and eyes and feet. So I think it's real mean that one of them has to be covered up the most of the time. I'm always glad when it gets warm enough to go barefooted. But, when I grow up they'll have to covered all the time. It IS mean."

"You'll have to put your shoes and stockings on when you go to the magic lantern show to-night," said Felicity in a tone of satisfaction.

"I don't know that. I'm thinking of going barefooted."

"Oh, you wouldn't! Sara Stanley, you're not in earnest!" exclaimed Felicity, her blue eyes filling with horror.

The Story Girl winked with the side of her face next to Felix and me, but the side next the girls changed not a muscle. She dearly loved to "take a rise" out of Felicity now and then.

"Indeed, I would if I just made up my mind to. Why not? Why not bare feet—if they're clean—as well as bare hands and face?"

"Oh, you wouldn't! It would be such a disgrace!" said poor Felicity in real distress.

"We went to school barefooted all June," argued that wicked Story Girl. "What is the difference between going to the schoolhouse barefooted in the daytime and going in the evening?"

"Oh, there's EVERY difference. I can't just explain it—but every one KNOWS there is a difference. You know it yourself. Oh, PLEASE, don't do such a thing, Sara."

"Well, I won't, just to oblige you," said the Story Girl, who would have died the death before she would have gone to a "public meeting" barefooted.

We were all rather excited over the magic lantern show which an itinerant lecturer was to give in the schoolhouse that evening. Even Felix and I, who had seen such shows galore, were interested, and the rest were quite wild. There had never been such a thing in Carlisle before. We were all going, Peter included. Peter went everywhere with us now. He was a regular attendant at church and Sunday School, where his behaviour was as irreproachable as if he had been "raised" in the caste of Vere de Vere. It was a feather in the Story Girl's cap, for she took all the credit of having started Peter on the right road. Felicity was resigned, although the fatal patch on Peter's best trousers was still an eyesore to her. She declared she never got any good of the singing, because Peter stood up then and every one could see the patch. Mrs. James Clark, whose pew was behind ours, never took her eye off it—or so Felicity averred.

But Peter's stockings were always darned. Aunt Olivia had seen to that, ever since she heard of Peter's singular device regarding them on his first Sunday. She had also given Peter a Bible, of which he was so proud that he hated to use it lest he should soil it.

"I think I'll wrap it up and keep it in my box," he said. "I've an old Bible of Aunt Jane's at home that I can use. I s'pose it's just the same, even if it is old, isn't it?"

"Oh, yes," Cecily had assured him. "The Bible is always the same."

"I thought maybe they'd got some new improvements on it since Aunt Jane's day," said Peter, relieved.

"Sara Ray is coming along the lane, and she's crying," announced Dan, who was peering out of a knot-hole on the opposite side of the loft.

"Sara Ray is crying half her time," said Cecily impatiently. "I'm sure she cries a quartful of tears a month. There are times when you can't help crying. But I hide then. Sara just goes and cries in public."

The lachrymose Sara presently joined us and we discovered the cause of her tears to be the doleful fact that her mother had forbidden her to go to the magic lantern show that night. We all showed the sympathy we felt.

"She SAID yesterday you could go," said the Story Girl indignantly. "Why has she changed her mind?"

"Because of the measles in Markdale," sobbed Sara. "She says Markdale is full of them, and there'll be sure to be some of the Markdale people at the show. So I'm not to go. And I've never seen a magic lantern—I've never seen ANYTHING."

"I don't believe there's any danger of catching measles," said Felicity. "If there was we wouldn't be allowed to go."

"I wish I COULD get the measles," said Sara defiantly. "Maybe I'd be of some importance to ma then."

"Suppose Cecily goes down with you and coaxes your mother," suggested the Story Girl. "Perhaps she'd let you go then. She likes Cecily. She doesn't like either Felicity or me, so it would only make matters worse for us to try."

"Ma's gone to town—pa and her went this afternoon—and they're not coming back till to-morrow. There's nobody home but Judy Pineau and me."

"Then," said the Story Girl, "why don't you just go to the show anyhow? Your mother won't ever know, if you coax Judy to hold her tongue."

"Oh, but that's wrong," said Felicity. "You shouldn't put Sara up to disobeying her mother."

Now, Felicity for once was undoubtedly right. The Story Girl's suggestion WAS wrong; and if it had been Cecily who protested, the Story Girl would probably have listened to her, and proceeded no further in the matter. But Felicity was one of those unfortunate people whose protests against wrong-doing serve only to drive the wrong-doer further on her sinful way.

The Story Girl resented Felicity's superior tone, and proceeded to tempt Sara in right good earnest. The rest of us held our tongues. It was, we told ourselves, Sara's own lookout.

"I have a good mind to do it," said Sara, "but I can't get my good clothes; they're in the spare room, and ma locked the door, for fear somebody would get at the fruit cake. I haven't a single thing to wear, except my school gingham."

"Well, that's new and pretty," said the Story Girl. "We'll lend you some things. You can have my lace collar. That'll make the gingham quite elegant. And Cecily will lend you her second best hat."

"But I've no shoes or stockings. They're locked up too."

"You can have a pair of mine," said Felicity, who probably thought that since Sara was certain to yield to temptation, she might as well be garbed decently for her transgression.

Sara did yield. When the Story Girl's voice entreated it was not easy to resist its temptation, even if you wanted to. That evening, when we started for the schoolhouse, Sara Ray was among us, decked out in borrowed plumes.

"Suppose she DOES catch the measles?" Felicity said aside.

"I don't believe there'll be anybody there from Markdale. The lecturer is going to Markdale next week. They'll wait for that," said the Story Girl airily.

It was a cool, dewy evening, and we walked down the long, red hill in the highest of spirits. Over a valley filled with beech and spruce was a sunset afterglow—creamy yellow and a hue that was not so much red as the dream of red, with a young moon swung low in it. The air was sweet with the breath of mown hayfields where swaths of clover had been steeping in the sun. Wild roses grew pinkly along the fences, and the roadsides were star-dusted with buttercups.

Those of us who had nothing the matter with our consciences enjoyed our walk to the little whitewashed schoolhouse in the valley. Felicity and Cecily were void of offence towards all men. The Story Girl walked uprightly like an incarnate flame in her crimson silk. Her pretty feet were hidden in the tan-coloured, buttoned Paris boots which were the secret envy of every school girl in Carlisle.

But Sara Ray was not happy. Her face was so melancholy that the Story Girl lost patience with her. The Story Girl herself was not altogether at ease. Probably her own conscience was troubling her. But admit it she would not.

"Now, Sara," she said, "you just take my advice and go into this with all your heart if you go at all. Never mind if it is bad. There's no use being naughty if you spoil your fun by wishing all the time you were good. You can repent afterwards, but there is no use in mixing the two things together."

"I'm not repenting," protested Sara. "I'm only scared of ma finding it out."

"Oh!" The Story Girl's voice expressed her scorn. For remorse she had understanding and sympathy; but fear of her fellow creatures was something unknown to her. "Didn't Judy Pineau promise you solemnly she wouldn't tell?"

"Yes; but maybe some one who sees me there will mention it to ma."

"Well, if you're so scared you'd better not go. It isn't too late. Here's your own gate," said Cecily.

But Sara could not give up the delights of the show. So she walked on, a small, miserable testimony that the way of the transgressor is never easy, even when said transgressor is only a damsel of eleven.

The magic lantern show was a splendid one. The views were good and the lecturer witty. We repeated his jokes to each other all the way home. Sara, who had not enjoyed the exhibition at all, seemed to feel more cheerful when it was over and she was going home. The Story Girl on the contrary was gloomy.

"There WERE Markdale people there," she confided to me, "and the Williamsons live next door to the Cowans, who have measles. I wish I'd never egged Sara on to going—but don't tell Felicity I said so. If Sara Ray had really enjoyed the show I wouldn't mind. But she didn't. I could see that. So I've done wrong and made her do wrong—and there's nothing to show for it."

The night was scented and mysterious. The wind was playing an eerie fleshless melody in the reeds of the brook hollow. The sky was dark and starry, and across it the Milky Way flung its shimmering misty ribbons.

"There's four hundred million stars in the Milky Way," quoth Peter, who frequently astonished us by knowing more than any hired boy could be expected to. He had a retentive memory, and never forgot anything he heard or read. The few books left to him by his oft-referred-to Aunt Jane had stocked his mind with a miscellaneous information which sometimes made Felix and me doubt if we knew as much as Peter after all. Felicity was so impressed by his knowledge of astronomy that she dropped back from the other girls and walked beside him. She had not done so before because he was barefooted. It was permissible for hired boys to go to public meetings—when not held in the church—with bare feet, and no particular disgrace attached to it. But Felicity would not walk with a barefooted companion. It was dark now, so nobody would notice his feet.

"I know a story about the Milky Way," said the Story Girl, brightening up. "I read it in a book of Aunt Louisa's in town, and I learned it off by heart. Once there were two archangels in heaven, named Zerah and Zulamith—"

"Have angels names—same as people?" interrupted Peter.

"Yes, of course. They MUST have. They'd be all mixed up if they hadn't."

"And when I'm an angel—if I ever get to be one—will my name still be Peter?"

"No. You'll have a new name up there," said Cecily gently. "It says so in the Bible."

"Well, I'm glad of that. Peter would be such a funny name for an angel. And what is the difference between angels and archangels?"

"Oh, archangels are angels that have been angels so long that they've had time to grow better and brighter and more beautiful than newer angels," said the Story Girl, who probably made that explanation up on the spur of the moment, just to pacify Peter.

"How long does it take for an angel to grow into an archangel?" pursued Peter.

"Oh, I don't know. Millions of years likely. And even then I don't suppose ALL the angels do. A good many of them must just stay plain angels, I expect."

"I shall be satisfied just to be a plain angel," said Felicity modestly.

"Oh, see here, if you're going to interrupt and argue over everything, we'll never get the story told," said Felix. "Dry up, all of you, and let the Story Girl go on."

We dried up, and the Story Girl went on.

"Zerah and Zulamith loved each other, just as mortals love, and this is forbidden by the laws of the Almighty. And because Zerah and Zulamith had so broken God's law they were banished from His presence to the uttermost bounds of the universe. If they had been banished TOGETHER it would have been no punishment; so Zerah was exiled to a star on one side of the universe, and Zulamith was sent to a star on the other side of the universe; and between them was a fathomless abyss which thought itself could not cross. Only one thing could cross it—and that was love. Zulamith yearned for Zerah with such fidelity and longing that he began to build up a bridge of light from his star; and Zerah, not knowing this, but loving and longing for him, began to build a similar bridge of light from her star. For a thousand thousand years they both built the bridge of light, and at last they met and sprang into each other's arms. Their toil and loneliness and suffering were all over and forgotten, and the bridge they had built spanned the gulf between their stars of exile.

"Now, when the other archangels saw what had been done they flew in fear and anger to God's white throne, and cried to Him,

"'See what these rebellious ones have done! They have built them a bridge of light across the universe, and set Thy decree of separation at naught. Do Thou, then, stretch forth Thine arm and destroy their impious work.'

"They ceased—and all heaven was hushed. Through the silence sounded the voice of the Almighty.

"'Nay,' He said, 'whatsoever in my universe true love hath builded not even the Almighty can destroy. The bridge must stand forever.'

"And," concluded the Story Girl, her face upturned to the sky and her big eyes filled with starlight, "it stands still. That bridge is the Milky Way."

"What a lovely story," sighed Sara Ray, who had been wooed to a temporary forgetfulness of her woes by its charm.

The rest of us came back to earth, feeling that we had been wandering among the hosts of heaven. We were not old enough to appreciate fully the wonderful meaning of the legend; but we felt its beauty and its appeal. To us forevermore the Milky Way would be, not Peter's overwhelming garland of suns, but the lucent bridge, love-created, on which the banished archangels crossed from star to star.

We had to go up Sara Ray's lane with her to her very door, for she was afraid Peg Bowen would catch her if she went alone. Then the Story Girl and I walked up the hill together. Peter and Felicity lagged behind. Cecily and Dan and Felix were walking before us, hand in hand, singing a hymn. Cecily had a very sweet voice, and I listened in delight. But the Story Girl sighed.

"What if Sara does take the measles?" she asked miserably.

"Everyone has to have the measles sometime," I said comfortingly, "and the younger you are the better."

CHAPTER XI.
THE STORY GIRL DOES PENANCE

Ten days later, Aunt Olivia and Uncle Roger went to town one evening, to remain over night, and the next day. Peter and the Story Girl were to stay at Uncle Alec's during their absence.

We were in the orchard at sunset, listening to the story of King Cophetua and the beggar maid—all of us, except Peter, who was hoeing turnips, and Felicity, who had gone down the hill on an errand to Mrs. Ray.

The Story Girl impersonated the beggar maid so vividly, and with such an illusion of beauty, that we did not wonder in the least at the king's love for her. I had read the story before, and it had been my opinion that it was "rot." No king, I felt certain, would ever marry a beggar maid when he had princesses galore from whom to choose. But now I understood it all.

When Felicity returned we concluded from her expression that she had news. And she had.

"Sara is real sick," she said, with regret, and something that was not regret mingled in her voice. "She has a cold and sore throat, and she is feverish. Mrs. Ray says if she isn't better by the morning she's going to send for the doctor. AND SHE IS AFRAID IT'S THE MEASLES."

Felicity flung the last sentence at the Story Girl, who turned very pale.

"Oh, do you suppose she caught them at the magic lantern show?" she said miserably.

"Where else could she have caught them?" said Felicity mercilessly. "I didn't see her, of course—Mrs. Ray met me at the door and told me not to come in. But Mrs. Ray says the measles always go awful hard with the Rays—if they don't die completely of them it leaves them deaf or half blind, or something like that. Of course," added Felicity, her heart melting at sight of the misery in the Story Girl's piteous eyes, "Mrs. Ray always looks on the dark side, and it may not be the measles Sara has after all."

But Felicity had done her work too thoroughly. The Story Girl was not to be comforted.

"I'd give anything if I'd never put Sara up to going to that show," she said. "It's all my fault—but the punishment falls on Sara, and that isn't fair. I'd go this minute and confess the whole thing to Mrs. Ray; but if I did it might get Sara into more trouble, and I mustn't do that. I sha'n't sleep a wink to-night."

I don't think she did. She looked very pale and woebegone when she came down to breakfast. But, for all that, there was a certain exhilaration about her.

"I'm going to do penance all day for coaxing Sara to disobey her mother," she announced with chastened triumph.

"Penance?" we murmured in bewilderment.

"Yes. I'm going to deny myself everything I like, and do everything I can think of that I don't like, just to punish myself for being so wicked. And if any of you think of anything I don't, just mention it to me. I thought it out last night. Maybe Sara won't be so very sick if God sees I'm truly sorry."

"He can see it anyhow, without your doing anything," said Cecily.

"Well, my conscience will feel better."

"I don't believe Presbyterians ever do penance," said Felicity dubiously. "I never heard of one doing it."

But the rest of us rather looked with favour on the Story Girl's idea. We felt sure that she would do penance as picturesquely and thoroughly as she did everything else.

"You might put peas in your shoes, you know," suggested Peter.

"The very thing! I never thought of that. I'll get some after breakfast. I'm not going to eat a single thing all day, except bread and water—and not much of that!"

This, we felt, was a heroic measure indeed. To sit down to one of Aunt Janet's meals, in ordinary health and appetite, and eat nothing but bread and water—that would be penance with a vengeance! We felt WE could never do it. But the Story Girl did it. We admired and pitied her. But now I do not think that she either needed our pity or deserved our admiration. Her ascetic fare was really sweeter to her than honey of Hymettus. She was, though quite unconsciously, acting a part, and tasting all the subtle joy of the artist, which is so much more exquisite than any material pleasure.

Aunt Janet, of course, noticed the Story Girl's abstinence and asked if she was sick.

"No. I am just doing penance, Aunt Janet, for a sin I committed. I can't confess it, because that would bring trouble on another person. So I'm going to do penance all day. You don't mind, do you?"

Aunt Janet was in a very good humour that morning, so she merely laughed.

"Not if you don't go too far with your nonsense," she said tolerantly.

"Thank you. And will you give me a handful of hard peas after breakfast, Aunt Janet? I want to put them in my shoes."

"There isn't any; I used the last in the soup yesterday."

"Oh!" The Story Girl was much disappointed. "Then I suppose I'll have to do without. The new peas wouldn't hurt enough. They're so soft they'd just squash flat."

"I'll tell you," said Peter, "I'll pick up a lot of those little round pebbles on Mr. King's front walk. They'll be just as good as peas."

"You'll do nothing of the sort," said Aunt Janet. "Sara must not do penance in that way. She would wear holes in her stockings, and might seriously bruise her feet."

"What would you say if I took a whip and whipped my bare shoulders till the blood came?" demanded the Story Girl aggrieved.

"I wouldn't SAY anything," retorted Aunt Janet. "I'd simply turn you over my knee and give you a sound, solid spanking, Miss Sara. You'd find that penance enough."

The Story Girl was crimson with indignation. To have such a remark made to you—when you were fourteen and a half—and before the boys, too! Really, Aunt Janet could be very dreadful.

It was vacation, and there was not much to do that day; we were soon free to seek the orchard. But the Story Girl would not come. She had seated herself in the darkest, hottest corner of the kitchen, with a piece of old cotton in her hand.

"I am not going to play to-day," she said, "and I'm not going to tell a single story. Aunt Janet won't let me put pebbles in my shoes, but I've put a thistle next my skin on my back and it sticks into me if I lean back the least bit. And I'm going to work buttonholes all over this cotton. I hate working buttonholes worse than anything in the world, so I'm going to work them all day."

"What's the good of working buttonholes on an old rag?" asked Felicity.

"It isn't any good. The beauty of penance is that it makes you feel uncomfortable. So it doesn't matter what you do, whether it's useful or not, so long as it's nasty. Oh, I wonder how Sara is this morning."

"Mother's going down this afternoon," said Felicity. "She says none of us must go near the place till we know whether it is the measles or not."

"I've thought of a great penance," said Cecily eagerly. "Don't go to the missionary meeting to-night."

The Story Girl looked piteous.

"I thought of that myself—but I CAN'T stay home, Cecily. It would be more than flesh and blood could endure. I MUST hear that missionary speak. They say he was all but eaten by cannibals once. Just think how many new stories I'd have to tell after I'd heard him! No, I must go, but I'll tell you what I'll do. I'll wear my school dress and hat. THAT will be penance. Felicity, when you set the table for dinner, put the broken-handled knife for me. I hate it so. And I'm going to take a dose of Mexican Tea every two hours. It's such dreadful tasting stuff—but it's a good blood purifier, so Aunt Janet can't object to it."

The Story Girl carried out her self-imposed penance fully. All day she sat in the kitchen and worked buttonholes, subsisting on bread and water and Mexican Tea.

Felicity did a mean thing. She went to work and made little raisin pies, right there in the kitchen before the Story Girl. The smell of raisin pies is something to tempt an anchorite; and the Story Girl was exceedingly fond of them. Felicity ate two in her very presence, and then brought the rest out to us in the orchard. The Story Girl could see us through the window, carousing without stint on raisin pies and Uncle Edward's cherries. But she worked on at her buttonholes. She would not look at the exciting serial in the new magazine Dan brought home from the post-office, neither would she open a letter from her father. Pat came over, but his most seductive purrs won no notice from his mistress, who refused herself the pleasure of even patting him.

Aunt Janet could not go down the hill in the afternoon to find out how Sara was because company came to tea—the Millwards from Markdale. Mr. Millward was a doctor, and Mrs. Millward was a B.A. Aunt Janet was very desirous that everything should be as nice as possible, and we were all sent to our rooms before tea to wash and dress up. The Story Girl slipped over home, and when she came back we gasped. She had combed her hair out straight, and braided it in a tight, kinky, pudgy braid; and she wore an old dress of faded print, with holes in the elbows and ragged flounces, which was much too short for her.

"Sara Stanley, have you taken leave of your senses?" demanded Aunt Janet. "What do you mean by putting on such a rig! Don't you know I have company to tea?"

"Yes, and that is just why I put it on, Aunt Janet. I want to mortify the flesh—"

"I'll 'mortify' you, if I catch you showing yourself to the Millwards like that, my girl! Go right home and dress yourself decently—or eat your supper in the kitchen."

The Story Girl chose the latter alternative. She was highly indignant. I verily believe that to sit at the dining-room table, in that shabby, outgrown dress, conscious of looking her ugliest, and eating only bread and water before the critical Millwards would have been positive bliss to her.

When we went to the missionary meeting that evening, the Story Girl wore her school dress and hat, while Felicity and Cecily were in their pretty muslins. And she had tied her hair with a snuff-brown ribbon which was very unbecoming to her.

The first person we saw in the church porch was Mrs. Ray. She told us that Sara had nothing worse than a feverish cold.

The missionary had at least seven happy listeners that night. We were all glad that Sara did not have measles, and the Story Girl was radiant.

"Now you see all your penance was wasted," said Felicity, as we walked home, keeping close together because of the rumour that Peg Bowen was abroad.

"Oh, I don't know. I feel better since I punished myself. But I'm going to make up for it to-morrow," said the Story Girl energetically. "In fact, I'll begin to-night. I'm going to the pantry as soon as I get home, and I'll read father's letter before I go to bed. Wasn't the missionary splendid? That cannibal story was simply grand. I tried to remember every word, so that I can tell it just as he told it. Missionaries are such noble people."

"I'd like to be a missionary and have adventures like that," said Felix.

"It would be all right if you could be sure the cannibals would be interrupted in the nick of time as his were," said Dan. "But sposen they weren't?"

"Nothing would prevent cannibals from eating Felix if they once caught him," giggled Felicity. "He's so nice and fat."

I am sure Felix felt very unlike a missionary at that precise moment.

"I'm going to put two cents more a week in my missionary box than I've been doing," said Cecily determinedly.

Two cents more a week out of Cecily's egg money, meant something of a sacrifice. It inspired the rest of us. We all decided to increase our weekly contribution by a cent or so. And Peter, who had had no missionary box at all, up to this time, determined to start one.

"I don't seem to be able to feel as int'rested in missionaries as you folks do," he said, "but maybe if I begin to give something I'll get int'rested. I'll want to know how my money's being spent. I won't be able to give much. When your father's run away, and your mother goes out washing, and you're only old enough to get fifty cents a week, you can't give much to the heathen. But I'll do the best I can. My Aunt Jane was fond of missions. Are there any Methodist heathen? I s'pose I ought to give my box to them, rather than to Presbyterian heathen."

"No, it's only after they're converted that they're anything in particular," said Felicity. "Before that, they're just plain heathen. But if you want your money to go to a Methodist missionary you can give it to the Methodist minister at Markdale. I guess the Presbyterians can get along without it, and look after their own heathen."

"Just smell Mrs. Sampson's flowers," said Cecily, as we passed a trim white paling close to the road, over which blew odours sweeter than the perfume of Araby's shore. "Her roses are all out and that bed of Sweet William is a sight by daylight."

"Sweet William is a dreadful name for a flower," said the Story Girl. "William is a man's name, and men are NEVER sweet. They are a great many nice things, but they are NOT sweet and shouldn't be. That is for women. Oh, look at the moonshine on the road in that gap between the spruces! I'd like a dress of moonshine, with stars for buttons."

"It wouldn't do," said Felicity decidedly. "You could see through it."

Which seemed to settle the question of moonshine dresses effectually.

CHAPTER XII.
THE BLUE CHEST OF RACHEL WARD

"It's utterly out of the question," said Aunt Janet seriously. When Aunt Janet said seriously that anything was out of the question it meant that she was thinking about it, and would probably end up by doing it. If a thing really was out of the question she merely laughed and refused to discuss it at all.

The particular matter in or out of the question that opening day of August was a project which Uncle Edward had recently mooted. Uncle Edward's youngest daughter was to be married; and Uncle Edward had written over, urging Uncle Alec, Aunt Janet and Aunt Olivia to go down to Halifax for the wedding and spend a week there.

Uncle Alec and Aunt Olivia were eager to go; but Aunt Janet at first declared it was impossible.

"How could we go away and leave the place to the mercy of all those young ones?" she demanded. "We'd come home and find them all sick, and the house burned down."

"Not a bit of fear of it," scoffed Uncle Roger. "Felicity is as good a housekeeper as you are; and I shall be here to look after them all, and keep them from burning the house down. You've been promising Edward for years to visit him, and you'll never have a better chance. The haying is over and harvest isn't on, and Alec needs a change. He isn't looking well at all."

I think it was Uncle Roger's last argument which convinced Aunt Janet. In the end she decided to go. Uncle Roger's house was to be closed, and he and Peter and the Story Girl were to take up their abode with us.

We were all delighted. Felicity, in especial, seemed to be in seventh heaven. To be left in sole charge of a big house, with three meals a day to plan and prepare, with poultry and cows and dairy and garden to superintend, apparently furnished forth Felicity's conception of Paradise. Of course, we were all to help; but Felicity was to "run things," and she gloried in it.

The Story Girl was pleased, too.

"Felicity is going to give me cooking lessons," she confided to me, as we walked in the orchard. "Isn't that fine? It will be easier when there are no grown-ups around to make me nervous, and laugh if I make mistakes."

Uncle Alec and aunts left on Monday morning. Poor Aunt Janet was full of dismal forebodings, and gave us so many charges and warnings that we did not try to remember any of them; Uncle Alec merely told us to be good and mind what Uncle Roger said. Aunt Olivia laughed at us out of her pansy-blue eyes, and told us she knew exactly what we felt like and hoped we'd have a gorgeous time.

"Mind they go to bed at a decent hour," Aunt Janet called back to Uncle Roger as she drove out of the gate. "And if anything dreadful happens telegraph us."

Then they were really gone and we were all left "to keep house."

Uncle Roger and Peter went away to their work. Felicity at once set the preparations for dinner a-going, and allotted to each of us his portion of service. The Story Girl was to prepare the potatoes; Felix and Dan were to pick and shell the peas; Cecily was to attend the fire; I was to peel the turnips. Felicity made our mouths water by announcing that she was going to make a roly-poly jam pudding for dinner.

I peeled my turnips on the back porch, put them in their pot, and set them on the stove. Then I was at liberty to watch the others, who had longer jobs. The kitchen was a scene of happy activity. The Story Girl peeled her potatoes, somewhat slowly and awkwardly—for she was not deft at household tasks; Dan and Felix shelled peas and tormented Pat by attaching pods to his ears and tail; Felicity, flushed and serious, measured and stirred skilfully.

"I am sitting on a tragedy," said the Story Girl suddenly.

Felix and I stared. We were not quite sure what a "tragedy" was, but we did not think it was an old blue wooden chest, such as the Story Girl was undoubtedly sitting on, if eyesight counted for anything.

The old chest filled up the corner between the table and the wall. Neither Felix nor I had ever thought about it particularly. It was very large and heavy, and Felicity generally said hard things of it when she swept the kitchen.

"This old blue chest holds a tragedy," explained the Story Girl. "I know a story about it."

"Cousin Rachel Ward's wedding things are all in that old chest," said Felicity.

Who was Cousin Rachel Ward? And why were her wedding things shut up in an old blue chest in Uncle Alec's kitchen? We demanded the tale instantly. The Story Girl told it to us as she peeled her potatoes. Perhaps the potatoes suffered—Felicity declared the eyes were not properly done at all—but the story did not.

"It is a sad story," said the Story Girl, "and it happened fifty years ago, when Grandfather and Grandmother King were quite young. Grandmother's cousin Rachel Ward came to spend a winter with them. She belonged to Montreal and she was an orphan too, just like the Family Ghost. I have never heard what she looked like, but she MUST have been beautiful, of course."

"Mother says she was awful sentimental and romantic," interjected Felicity.

"Well, anyway, she met Will Montague that winter. He was handsome— everybody says so"—

"And an awful flirt," said Felicity.

"Felicity, I WISH you wouldn't interrupt. It spoils the effect. What would you feel like if I went and kept stirring things that didn't belong to it into that pudding? I feel just the same way. Well, Will Montague fell in love with Rachel Ward, and she with him, and it was all arranged that they were to be married from here in the spring. Poor Rachel was so happy that winter; she made all her wedding things with her own hands. Girls did, then, you know, for there was no such thing as a sewing-machine. Well, at last in April the wedding day came, and all the guests were here, and Rachel was dressed in her wedding robes, waiting for her bridegroom. And"—the Story Girl laid down her knife and potato and clasped her wet hands—"WILL MONTAGUE NEVER CAME!"

We felt as much of a shock as if we had been one of the expectant guests ourselves.

"What happened to him? Was HE killed too?" asked Felix.

The Story Girl sighed and resumed her work.

"No, indeed. I wish he had been. THAT would have been suitable and romantic. No, it was just something horrid. He had to run away for debt! Fancy! He acted mean right through, Aunt Janet says. He never sent even a word to Rachel, and she never heard from him again."

"Pig!" said Felix forcibly.

"She was broken-hearted of course. When she found out what had happened, she took all her wedding things, and her supply of linen, and some presents that had been given her, and packed them all away in this old blue chest. Then she went away back to Montreal, and took the key with her. She never came back to the Island again—I suppose she couldn't bear to. And she has lived in Montreal ever since and never married. She is an old woman now—nearly seventy-five. And this chest has never been opened since."

"Mother wrote to Cousin Rachel ten years ago," said Cecily, "and asked her if she might open the chest to see if the moths had got into it. There's a crack in the back as big as your finger. Cousin Rachel wrote back that if it wasn't for one thing that was in the trunk she would ask mother to open the chest and dispose of the things as she liked. But she could not bear that any one but herself should see or touch that one thing. So she wanted it left as it was. Ma said she washed her hands of it, moths or no moths. She said if Cousin Rachel had to move that chest every time the floor had to be scrubbed it would cure her of her sentimental nonsense. But I think," concluded Cecily, "that I would feel just like Cousin Rachel in her place."

"What was the thing she couldn't bear any one to see?" I asked.

"Ma thinks it was her wedding dress. But father says he believes it was Will Montague's picture," said Felicity. "He saw her put it in. Father knows some of the things that are in the chest. He was ten years old, and he saw her pack it. There's a white muslin wedding dress and a veil—and—and—a—a"—Felicity dropped her eyes and blushed painfully.

"A petticoat, embroidered by hand from hem to belt," said the Story Girl calmly.

"And a china fruit basket with an apple on the handle," went on Felicity, much relieved. "And a tea set, and a blue candle-stick."

"I'd dearly love to see all the things that are in it," said the Story Girl.

"Pa says it must never be opened without Cousin Rachel's permission," said Cecily.

Felix and I looked at the chest reverently. It had taken on a new significance in our eyes, and seemed like a tomb wherein lay buried some dead romance of the vanished years.

"What happened to Will Montague?" I asked.

"Nothing!" said the Story Girl viciously. "He just went on living and flourishing. He patched up matters with his creditors after awhile, and came back to the Island; and in the end he married a real nice girl, with money, and was very happy. Did you ever HEAR of anything so unjust?"

"Beverley King," suddenly cried Felicity, who had been peering into a pot, "YOU'VE GONE AND PUT THE TURNIPS ON TO BOIL WHOLE JUST LIKE POTATOES!"

"Wasn't that right?" I cried, in an agony of shame.

"Right!" but Felicity had already whisked the turnips out, and was slicing them, while all the others were laughing at me. I had added a tradition on my own account to the family archives.

Uncle Roger roared when he heard it; and he roared again at night over Peter's account of Felix attempting to milk a cow. Felix had previously acquired the knack of extracting milk from the udder. But he had never before tried to "milk a whole cow." He did not get on well; the cow tramped on his foot, and finally upset the bucket.

"What are you to do when a cow won't stand straight?" spluttered Felix angrily.

"That's the question," said Uncle Roger, shaking his head gravely.

Uncle Roger's laughter was hard to bear, but his gravity was harder.

Meanwhile, in the pantry the Story Girl, apron-enshrouded, was being initiated into the mysteries of bread-making. Under Felicity's eyes she set the bread, and on the morrow she was to bake it.

"The first thing you must do in the morning is knead it well," said Felicity, "and the earlier it's done the better—because it's such a warm night."

With that we went to bed, and slept as soundly as if tragedies of blue chests and turnips and crooked cows had no place in the scheme of things at all.

CHAPTER XIII.
AN OLD PROVERB WITH A NEW MEANING

It was half-past five when we boys got up the next morning. We were joined on the stairs by Felicity, yawning and rosy.

"Oh, dear me, I overslept myself. Uncle Roger wanted breakfast at six. Well, I suppose the fire is on anyhow, for the Story Girl is up. I guess she got up early to knead the bread. She couldn't sleep all night for worrying over it."

The fire was on, and a flushed and triumphant Story Girl was taking a loaf of bread from the oven.

"Just look," she said proudly. "I have every bit of the bread baked. I got up at three, and it was lovely and light, so I just gave it a right good kneading and popped it into the oven. And it's all done and out of the way. But the loaves don't seem quite as big as they should be," she added doubtfully.

"Sara Stanley!" Felicity flew across the kitchen. "Do you mean that you put the bread right into the oven after you kneaded it without leaving it to rise a second time?"

The Story Girl turned quite pale.

"Yes, I did," she faltered. "Oh, Felicity, wasn't it right?"

"You've ruined the bread," said Felicity flatly. "It's as heavy as a stone. I declare, Sara Stanley, I'd rather have a little common sense than be a great story teller."

Bitter indeed was the poor Story Girl's mortification.

"Don't tell Uncle Roger," she implored humbly.

"Oh, I won't tell him," promised Felicity amiably. "It's lucky there's enough old bread to do to-day. This will go to the hens. But it's an awful waste of good flour."

The Story Girl crept out with Felix and me to the morning orchard, while Dan and Peter went to do the barn work.

"It isn't ANY use for me to try to learn to cook," she said.

"Never mind," I said consolingly. "You can tell splendid stories."

"But what good would that do a hungry boy?" wailed the Story Girl.

"Boys ain't ALWAYS hungry," said Felix gravely. "There's times when they ain't."

"I don't believe it," said the Story Girl drearily.

"Besides," added Felix in the tone of one who says while there is life there is yet hope, "you may learn to cook yet if you keep on trying."

"But Aunt Olivia won't let me waste the stuff. My only hope was to learn this week. But I suppose Felicity is so disgusted with me now that she won't give me any more lessons."

"I don't care," said Felix. "I like you better than Felicity, even if you can't cook. There's lots of folks can make bread. But there isn't many who can tell a story like you."

"But it's better to be useful than just interesting," sighed the Story Girl bitterly.

And Felicity, who was useful, would, in her secret soul, have given anything to be interesting. Which is the way of human nature.

Company descended on us that afternoon. First came Aunt Janet's sister, Mrs. Patterson, with a daughter of sixteen years and a son of two. They were followed by a buggy-load of Markdale people; and finally, Mrs. Elder Frewen and her sister from Vancouver, with two small daughters of the latter, arrived.

"It never rains but it pours," said Uncle Roger, as he went out to take their horse. But Felicity's foot was on her native heath. She had been baking all the afternoon, and, with a pantry well stocked with biscuits, cookies, cakes, and pies, she cared not if all Carlisle came to tea. Cecily set the table, and the Story Girl waited on it and washed all the dishes afterwards. But all the blushing honours fell to Felicity, who received so many compliments that her airs were quite unbearable for the rest of the week. She presided at the head of the table with as much grace and dignity as if she had been five times twelve years old, and seemed to know by instinct just who took sugar and who took it not. She was flushed with excitement and pleasure, and was so pretty that I could hardly eat for looking at her—which is the highest compliment in a boy's power to pay.

The Story Girl, on the contrary, was under eclipse. She was pale and lustreless from her disturbed night and early rising; and no opportunity offered to tell a melting tale. Nobody took any notice of her. It was Felicity's day.

After tea Mrs. Frewen and her sister wished to visit their father's grave in the Carlisle churchyard. It appeared that everybody wanted to go with them; but it was evident that somebody must stay home with Jimmy Patterson, who had just fallen sound asleep on the kitchen sofa. Dan finally volunteered to look after him. He had a new Henty book which he wanted to finish, and that, he said, was better fun than a walk to the graveyard.

"I think we'll be back before he wakes," said Mrs. Patterson, "and anyhow he is very good and won't be any trouble. Don't let him go outside, though. He has a cold now."

We went away, leaving Dan sitting on the door-sill reading his book, and Jimmy P. snoozing blissfully on the sofa. When we returned—Felix and the girls and I were ahead of the others—Dan was still sitting in precisely the same place and attitude; but there was no Jimmy in sight.

"Dan, where's the baby?" cried Felicity.

Dan looked around. His jaw fell in blank amazement. I never saw any one look as foolish as Dan at that moment.

"Good gracious, I don't know," he said helplessly.

"You've been so deep in that wretched book that he's got out, and dear knows where he is," cried Felicity distractedly.

"I wasn't," cried Dan. "He MUST be in the house. I've been sitting right across the door ever since you left, and he couldn't have got out unless he crawled right over me. He must be in the house."

"He isn't in the kitchen," said Felicity rushing about wildly, "and he couldn't get into the other part of the house, for I shut the hall door tight, and no baby could open it—and it's shut tight yet. So are all the windows. He MUST have gone out of that door, Dan King, and it's your fault."

"He DIDN'T go out of this door," reiterated Dan stubbornly. "I know that."

"Well, where is he, then? He isn't here. Did he melt into air?" demanded Felicity. "Oh, come and look for him, all of you. Don't stand round like ninnies. We MUST find him before his mother gets here. Dan King, you're an idiot!"

Dan was too frightened to resent this, at the time. However and wherever Jimmy had gone, he WAS gone, so much was certain. We tore about the house and yard like maniacs; we looked into every likely and unlikely place. But Jimmy we could not find, anymore than if he had indeed melted into air. Mrs. Patterson came, and we had not found him. Things were getting serious. Uncle Roger and Peter were summoned from the field. Mrs. Patterson became hysterical, and was taken into the spare room with such remedies as could be suggested. Everybody blamed poor Dan. Cecily asked him what he would feel like if Jimmy was never, never found. The Story Girl had a gruesome recollection of some baby at Markdale who had wandered away like that—

"And they never found him till the next spring, and all they found was— HIS SKELETON, with the grass growing through it," she whispered.

"This beats me," said Uncle Roger, when a fruitless hour had elapsed. "I do hope that baby hasn't wandered down to the swamp. It seems impossible he could walk so far; but I must go and see. Felicity, hand me my high boots out from under the sofa, there's a girl."

Felicity, pale and tearful, dropped on her knees and lifted the cretonne frill of the sofa. There, his head pillowed hardly on Uncle Roger's boots, lay Jimmy Patterson, still sound asleep!

"Well, I'll be—jiggered!" said Uncle Roger.

"I KNEW he never went out of the door," cried Dan triumphantly.

When the last buggy had driven away, Felicity set a batch of bread, and the rest of us sat around the back porch steps in the cat's light and ate cherries, shooting the stones at each other. Cecily was in quest of information.

"What does 'it never rains but it pours' mean?"

"Oh, it means if anything happens something else is sure to happen," said the Story Girl. "I'll illustrate. There's Mrs. Murphy. She never had a proposal in her life till she was forty, and then she had three in the one week, and she was so flustered she took the wrong one and has been sorry ever since. Do you see what it means now?"

"Yes, I guess so," said Cecily somewhat doubtfully. Later on we heard her imparting her newly acquired knowledge to Felicity in the pantry.

"'It never rains but it pours' means that nobody wants to marry you for ever so long, and then lots of people do."

CHAPTER XIV.
FORBIDDEN FRUIT

We were all, with the exception of Uncle Roger, more or less grumpy in the household of King next day. Perhaps our nerves had been upset by the excitement attendant on Jimmy Patterson's disappearance. But it is more likely that our crankiness was the result of the supper we had eaten the previous night. Even children cannot devour mince pie, and cold fried pork ham, and fruit cake before going to bed with entire impunity. Aunt Janet had forgotten to warn Uncle Roger to keep an eye on our bedtime snacks, and we ate what seemed good unto us.

Some of us had frightful dreams, and all of us carried chips on our shoulders at breakfast. Felicity and Dan began a bickering which they kept up the entire day. Felicity had a natural aptitude for what we called "bossing," and in her mother's absence she deemed that she had a right to rule supreme. She knew better than to make any attempt to assert authority over the Story Girl, and Felix and I were allowed some length of tether; but Cecily, Dan, and Peter were expected to submit dutifully to her decrees. In the main they did; but on this particular morning Dan was plainly inclined to rebel. He had had time to grow sore over the things that Felicity had said to him when Jimmy Patterson was thought lost, and he began the day with a flatly expressed determination that he was not going to let Felicity rule the roost.

It was not a pleasant day, and to make matters worse it rained until late in the afternoon. The Story Girl had not recovered from the mortifications of the previous day; she would not talk, and she would not tell a single story; she sat on Rachel Ward's chest and ate her breakfast with the air of a martyr. After breakfast she washed the dishes and did the bed-room work in grim silence; then, with a book under one arm and Pat under the other, she betook herself to the window-seat in the upstairs hall, and would not be lured from that retreat, charmed we never so wisely. She stroked the purring Paddy, and read steadily on, with maddening indifference to all our pleadings.

Even Cecily, the meek and mild, was snappish, and complained of headache. Peter had gone home to see his mother, and Uncle Roger had gone to Markdale on business. Sara Ray came up, but was so snubbed by Felicity that she went home, crying. Felicity got the dinner by herself, disdaining to ask or command assistance. She banged things about and rattled the stove covers until even Cecily protested from her sofa. Dan sat on the floor and whittled, his sole aim and object being to make a mess and annoy Felicity, in which noble ambition he succeeded perfectly.

"I wish Aunt Janet and Uncle Alec were home," said Felix. "It's not half so much fun having the grown-ups away as I thought it would be."

"I wish I was back in Toronto," I said sulkily. The mince pie was to blame for THAT wish.

"I wish you were, I'm sure," said Felicity, riddling the fire noisily.

"Any one who lives with you, Felicity King, will always be wishing he was somewhere else," said Dan.

"I wasn't talking to you, Dan King," retorted Felicity, "'Speak when you're spoken to, come when you're called.'"

"Oh, oh, oh," wailed Cecily on the sofa. "I WISH it would stop raining. I WISH my head would stop aching. I WISH ma had never gone away. I WISH you'd leave Felicity alone, Dan."

"I wish girls had some sense," said Dan—which brought the orgy of wishing to an end for the time. A wishing fairy might have had the time of her life in the King kitchen that morning—particularly if she were a cynically inclined fairy.

But even the effects of unholy snacks wear away at length. By tea-time things had brightened up. The rain had ceased, and the old, low-raftered room was full of sunshine which danced on the shining dishes of the dresser, made mosaics on the floor, and flickered over the table whereon a delicious meal was spread. Felicity had put on her blue muslin, and looked so beautiful in it that her good humour was quite restored. Cecily's headache was better, and the Story Girl, refreshed by an afternoon siesta, came down with smiles and sparkling eyes. Dan alone continued to nurse his grievances, and would not even laugh when the Story Girl told us a tale brought to mind by some of the "Rev. Mr. Scott's plums" which were on the table.

"The Rev. Mr. Scott was the man who thought the pulpit door must be made for speerits, you know," she said. "I heard Uncle Edward telling ever so many stories about him. He was called to this congregation, and he laboured here long and faithfully, and was much beloved, though he was very eccentric."

"What does that mean?" asked Peter.

"Hush! It just means queer," said Cecily, nudging him with her elbow. "A common man would be queer, but when it's a minister, it's eccentric."

"When he gets very old," continued the Story Girl, "the Presbytery thought it was time he was retired. HE didn't think so; but the Presbytery had their way, because there were so many of them to one of him. He was retired, and a young man was called to Carlisle. Mr. Scott went to live in town, but he came out to Carlisle very often, and visited all the people regularly, just the same as when he was their minister. The young minister was a very good young man, and tried to do his duty; but he was dreadfully afraid of meeting old Mr. Scott, because he had been told that the old minister was very angry at being set aside, and would likely give him a sound drubbing, if he ever met him. One day the young minister was visiting the Crawfords in Markdale, when they suddenly heard old Mr. Scott's voice in the kitchen. The young minister turned pale as the dead, and implored Mrs. Crawford to hid him. But she couldn't get him out of the room, and all she could do was to hide him in the china closet. The young minister slipped into the china closet, and old Mr. Scott came into the room. He talked very nicely, and read, and prayed. They made very long prayers in those days, you know; and at the end of his prayer he said, 'Oh Lord, bless the poor young man hiding in the closet. Give him courage not to fear the face of man. Make him a burning and a shining light to this sadly abused congregation.' Just imagine the feelings of the young minister in the china closet! But he came right out like a man, though his face was very red, as soon as Mr. Scott had done praying. And Mr. Scott was lovely to him, and shook hands, and never mentioned the china closet. And they were the best of friends ever afterwards."

"How did old Mr. Scott find out the young minister was in the closet?" asked Felix.

"Nobody ever knew. They supposed he had seen him through the window before he came into the house, and guessed he must be in the closet— because there was no way for him to get out of the room."

"Mr. Scott planted the yellow plum tree in Grandfather's time," said Cecily, peeling one of the plums, "and when he did it he said it was as Christian an act as he ever did. I wonder what he meant. I don't see anything very Christian about planting a tree."

"I do," said the Story Girl sagely.

When next we assembled ourselves together, it was after milking, and the cares of the day were done with. We foregathered in the balsam-fragrant aisles of the fir wood, and ate early August apples to such an extent that the Story Girl said we made her think of the Irishman's pig.

"An Irishman who lived at Markdale had a little pig," she said, "and he gave it a pailful of mush. The pig ate the whole pailful, and then the Irishman put the pig IN the pail, and it didn't fill more than half the pail. Now, how was that, when it held a whole pailful of mush?"

This seemed to be a rather unanswerable kind of conundrum. We discussed the problem as we roamed the wood, and Dan and Peter almost quarrelled over it, Dan maintaining that the thing was impossible, and Peter being of the opinion that the mush was somehow "made thicker" in the process of being eaten, and so took up less room. During the discussion we came out to the fence of the hill pasture where grew the "bad berry" bushes.

Just what these "bad berries" were I cannot tell. We never knew their real name. They were small, red-clustered berries of a glossy, seductive appearance, and we were forbidden to eat them, because it was thought they might be poisonous. Dan picked a cluster and held it up.

"Dan King, don't you DARE eat those berries," said Felicity in her "bossiest" tone. "They're poison. Drop them right away."

Now, Dan had not had the slightest intention of eating the berries. But at Felicity's prohibition the rebellion which had smouldered in him all day broke into sudden flame. He would show her!

"I'll eat them if I please, Felicity King," he said in a fury: "I don't believe they're poison. Look here!"

Dan crammed the whole bunch into his capacious mouth and chewed it up.

"They taste great," he said, smacking; and he ate two more clusters, regardless of our horror-stricken protestations and Felicity's pleadings.

We feared that Dan would drop dead on the spot. But nothing occurred immediately. When an hour had passed we concluded that the bad berries were not poison after all, and we looked upon Dan as quite a hero for daring to eat them.

"I knew they wouldn't hurt me," he said loftily. "Felicity's so fond of making a fuss over everything."

Nevertheless, when it grew dark and we returned to the house, I noticed that Dan was rather pale and quiet. He lay down on the kitchen sofa.

"Don't you feel all right, Dan?" I whispered anxiously.

"Shut up," he said.

I shut up.

Felicity and Cecily were setting out a lunch in the pantry when we were all startled by a loud groan from the sofa.

"Oh, I'm sick—I'm awful sick," said Dan abjectly, all the defiance and bravado gone out of him.

We all went to pieces, except Cecily, who alone retained her presence of mind.

"Have you got a pain in your stomach?" she demanded.

"I've got an awful pain here, if that's where my stomach is," moaned Dan, putting his hand on a portion of his anatomy considerably below his stomach. "Oh—oh—oh!"

"Go for Uncle Roger," commanded Cecily, pale but composed. "Felicity, put on the kettle. Dan, I'm going to give you mustard and warm water."

The mustard and warm water produced its proper effect promptly, but gave Dan no relief. He continued to writhe and groan. Uncle Roger, who had been summoned from his own place, went at once for the doctor, telling Peter to go down the hill for Mrs. Ray. Peter went, but returned accompanied by Sara only. Mrs. Ray and Judy Pineau were both away. Sara might better have stayed home; she was of no use, and could only add to the general confusion, wandering aimlessly about, crying and asking if Dan was going to die.

Cecily took charge of things. Felicity might charm the palate, and the Story Girl bind captive the soul; but when pain and sickness wrung the brow it was Cecily who was the ministering angel. She made the writhing Dan go to bed. She made him swallow every available antidote which was recommended in "the doctor's book;" and she applied hot cloths to him until her faithful little hands were half scalded off.

There was no doubt Dan was suffering intense pain. He moaned and writhed, and cried for his mother.

"Oh, isn't it dreadful!" said Felicity, wringing her hands as she walked the kitchen floor. "Oh, why doesn't the doctor come? I TOLD Dan the bad berries were poison. But surely they can't kill people ALTOGETHER."

"Pa's cousin died of eating something forty years ago," sobbed Sara Ray.

"Hold your tongue," said Peter in a fierce whisper. "You oughter have more sense than to say such things to the girls. They don't want to be any worse scared than they are."

"But Pa's cousin DID die," reiterated Sara.

"My Aunt Jane used to rub whisky on for a pain," suggested Peter.

"We haven't any whisky," said Felicity disapprovingly. "This is a temperance house."

"But rubbing whisky on the OUTSIDE isn't any harm," argued Peter. "It's only when you take it inside it is bad for you."

"Well, we haven't any, anyhow," said Felicity. "I suppose blueberry wine wouldn't do in its place?"

Peter did not think blueberry wine would be any good.

It was ten o'clock before Dan began to get better; but from that time he improved rapidly. When the doctor, who had been away from home when Uncle Roger reached Markdale, came at half past ten, he found his patient very weak and white, but free from pain.

Dr. Grier patted Cecily on the head, told her she was a little brick, and had done just the right thing, examined some of the fatal berries and gave it as his opinion that they were probably poisonous, administered some powders to Dan and advised him not to tamper with forbidden fruit in future, and went away.

Mrs. Ray now appeared, looking for Sara, and said she would stay all night with us.

"I'll be much obliged to you if you will," said Uncle Roger. "I feel a bit shook. I urged Janet and Alec to go to Halifax, and took the responsibility of the children while they were away, but I didn't know what I was letting myself in for. If anything had happened I could never have forgiven myself—though I believe it's beyond the power of mortal man to keep watch over the things children WILL eat. Now, you young fry, get straight off to your beds. Dan is out of danger, and you can't do any more good. Not that any of you have done much, except Cecily. She's got a head of her shoulders."

"It's been a horrid day all through," said Felicity drearily, as we climbed the stairs.

"I suppose we made it horrid ourselves," said the Story Girl candidly. "But it'll be a good story to tell sometime," she added.

"I'm awful tired and thankful," sighed Cecily.

We all felt that way.

CHAPTER XV.
A DISOBEDIENT BROTHER

Dan was his own man again in the morning, though rather pale and weak; he wanted to get up, but Cecily ordered him to stay in bed. Fortunately Felicity forgot to repeat the command, so Dan did stay in bed. Cecily carried his meals to him, and read a Henty book to him all her spare time. The Story Girl went up and told him wondrous tales; and Sara Ray brought him a pudding she had made herself. Sara's intentions were good, but the pudding—well, Dan fed most of it to Paddy, who had curled himself up at the foot of the bed, giving the world assurance of a cat by his mellifluous purring.

"Ain't he just a great old fellow?" said Dan. "He knows I'm kind of sick, just as well as a human. He never pays no attention to me when I'm well."

Felix and Peter and I were required to help Uncle Roger in some carpentering work that day, and Felicity indulged in one of the house-cleaning orgies so dear to her soul; so that it was evening before we were all free to meet in the orchard and loll on the grasses of Uncle Stephen's Walk. In August it was a place of shady sweetness, fragrant with the odour of ripening apples, full of dear, delicate shadows. Through its openings we looked afar to the blue rims of the hills and over green, old, tranquil fields, lying the sunset glow. Overhead the lacing leaves made a green, murmurous roof. There was no such thing as hurry in the world, while we lingered there and talked of "cabbages and kings." A tale of the Story Girl's, wherein princes were thicker than blackberries, and queens as common as buttercups, led to our discussion of kings. We wondered what it would be like to be a king. Peter thought it would be fine, only kind of inconvenient, wearing a crown all the time.

"Oh, but they don't," said the Story Girl. "Maybe they used to once, but now they wear hats. The crowns are just for special occasions. They look very much like other people, if you can go by their photographs."

"I don't believe it would be much fun as a steady thing," said Cecily. "I'd like to SEE a queen though. That is one thing I have against the Island—you never have a chance to see things like that here."

"The Prince of Wales was in Charlottetown once," said Peter. "My Aunt Jane saw him quite close by."

"That was before we were born, and such a thing won't happen again until after we're dead," said Cecily, with very unusual pessimism.

"I think queens and kings were thicker long ago," said the Story Girl. "They do seem dreadfully scarce now. There isn't one in this country anywhere. Perhaps I'll get a glimpse of some when I go to Europe."

Well, the Story Girl was destined to stand before kings herself, and she was to be one whom they delighted to honour. But we did not know that, as we sat in the old orchard. We thought it quite sufficiently marvellous that she should expect to have the chance of just seeing them.

"Can a queen do exactly as she pleases?" Sara Ray wanted to know.

"Not nowadays," explained the Story Girl.

"Then I don't see any use in being one," Sara decided.

"A king can't do as he pleases now, either," said Felix. "If he tries to, and if it isn't what pleases other people, the Parliament or something squelches him."

"Isn't 'squelch' a lovely word?" said the Story Girl irrelevantly. "It's so expressive. Squ-u-e-l-ch!"

Certainly it was a lovely word, as the Story Girl said it. Even a king would not have minded being squelched, if it were done to music like that.

"Uncle Roger says that Martin Forbes' wife has squelched HIM," said Felicity. "He says Martin can't call his soul his own since he was married."

"I'm glad of it," said Cecily vindictively.

We all stared. This was so very unlike Cecily.

"Martin Forbes is the brother of a horrid man in Summerside who called me Johnny, that's why," she explained. "He was visiting here with his wife two years ago, and he called me Johnny every time he spoke to me. Just you fancy! I'll NEVER forgive him."

"That isn't a Christian spirit," said Felicity rebukingly.

"I don't care. Would YOU forgive James Forbes if he had called YOU Johnny?" demanded Cecily.

"I know a story about Martin Forbes' grandfather," said the Story Girl. "Long ago they didn't have any choir in the Carlisle church—just a precentor you know. But at last they got a choir, and Andrew McPherson was to sing bass in it. Old Mr. Forbes hadn't gone to church for years, because he was so rheumatic, but he went the first Sunday the choir sang, because he had never heard any one sing bass, and wanted to hear what it was like. Grandfather King asked him what he thought of the choir. Mr.

Forbes said it was 'verra guid,' but as for Andrew's bass, 'there was nae bass aboot it—it was just a bur-r-r-r the hale time.'"

If you could have heard the Story Girl's "bur-r-r-r!" Not old Mr. Forbes himself could have invested it with more of Doric scorn. We rolled over in the cool grass and screamed with laughter.

"Poor Dan," said Cecily compassionately. "He's up there all alone in his room, missing all the fun. I suppose it's mean of us to be having such a good time here, when he has to stay in bed."

"If Dan hadn't done wrong eating the bad berries when he was told not to, he wouldn't be sick," said Felicity. "You're bound to catch it when you do wrong. It was just a Providence he didn't die."

"That makes me think of another story about old Mr. Scott," said the Story Girl. "You know, I told you he was very angry because the Presbytery made him retire. There were two ministers in particular he blamed for being at the bottom of it. One time a friend of his was trying to console him, and said to him,

"'You should be resigned to the will of Providence.'

"'Providence had nothing to do with it,' said old Mr. Scott. 'Twas the McCloskeys and the devil.'"

"You shouldn't speak of the—the—DEVIL," said Felicity, rather shocked.

"Well, that's just what Mr. Scott said."

"Oh, it's all right for a MINISTER to speak of him. But it isn't nice for little girls. If you HAVE to speak of—of—him—you might say the Old Scratch. That is what mother calls him."

"'Twas the McCloskeys and the Old Scratch,'" said the Story Girl reflectively, as if she were trying to see which version was the more effective. "It wouldn't do," she decided.

"I don't think it's any harm to mention the—the—that person, when you're telling a story," said Cecily. "It's only in plain talking it doesn't do. It sounds too much like swearing then."

"I know another story about Mr. Scott," said the Story Girl. "Not long after he was married his wife wasn't quite ready for church one morning when it was time to go. So, just to teach her a lesson, he drove off alone, and left her to walk all the way—it was nearly two miles—in the heat and dust. She took it very quietly. It's the best way, I guess, when you're married to a man like old Mr. Scott. But just a few Sundays after wasn't he late himself! I suppose Mrs. Scott thought that what was sauce for the goose was sauce for the gander, for she slipped out and drove off to church as he had done. Old Mr. Scott finally arrived at the church, pretty hot and dusty, and in none too good a temper. He went into the pulpit, leaned over it and looked at his wife, sitting calmly in her pew at the side.

"'It was cleverly done,' he said, right out loud, 'BUT DINNA TRY IT AGAIN!'"

In the midst of our laughter Pat came down the Walk, his stately tail waving over the grasses. He proved to be the precursor of Dan, clothed and in his right mind.

"Do you think you should have got up, Dan?" said Cecily anxiously.

"I had to," said Dan. "The window was open, and it was more'n I could stand to hear you fellows laughing down here and me missing it all. 'Sides, I'm all right again. I feel fine."

"I guess this will be a lesson to you, Dan King," said Felicity, in her most maddening tone. "I guess you won't forget it in a hurry. You won't go eating the bad berries another time when you're told not to."

Dan had picked out a soft spot in the grass for himself, and was in the act of sitting down, when Felicity's tactful speech arrested him midway. He straightened up and turned a wrathful face on his provoking sister. Then, red with indignation, but without a word, he stalked up the walk.

"Now he's gone off mad," said Cecily reproachfully. "Oh, Felicity, why couldn't you have held your tongue?"

"Why, what did I say to make him mad?" asked Felicity in honest perplexity.

"I think it's awful for brothers and sisters to be always quarrelling," sighed Cecily. "The Cowans fight all the time; and you and Dan will soon be as bad."

"Oh, talk sense," said Felicity. "Dan's got so touchy it isn't safe to speak to him. I should think he'd be sorry for all the trouble he made last night. But you just back him up in everything, Cecily."

"I don't!"

"You do! And you've no business to, specially when mother's away. She left ME in charge."

"You didn't take much charge last night when Dan got sick," said Felix maliciously. Felicity had told him at tea that night he was getting fatter than ever. This was his tit-for-tat. "You were pretty glad to leave it all to Cecily then."

"Who's talking to you?" said Felicity.

"Now, look here," said the Story Girl, "the first thing we know we'll all be quarrelling, and then some of us will sulk all day to-morrow. It's dreadful to spoil a whole day. Just let's all sit still and count a hundred before we say another word."

We sat still and counted the hundred. When Cecily finished she got up and went in search of Dan, resolved to soothe his wounded feelings. Felicity called after her to tell Dan there was a jam turnover she had put away in the pantry specially for him. Felix held out to Felicity a remarkably fine apple which he had been saving for his own consumption; and the Story Girl began a tale of an enchanted maiden in a castle by the sea; but we never heard the end of it. For, just as the evening star was looking whitely through the rosy window of the west, Cecily came flying through the orchard, wringing her hands.

"Oh, come, come quick," she gasped. "Dan's eating the bad berries again— he's et a whole bunch of them—he says he'll show Felicity. I can't stop him. Come you and try."

We rose in a body and rushed towards the house. In the yard we encountered Dan, emerging from the fir wood and champing the fatal berries with unrepentant relish.

"Dan King, do you want to commit suicide?" demanded the Story Girl.

"Look here, Dan," I expostulated. "You shouldn't do this. Think how sick you were last night and all the trouble you made for everybody. Don't eat any more, there's a good chap."

"All right," said Dan. "I've et all I want. They taste fine. I don't believe it was them made me sick."

But now that his anger was over he looked a little frightened. Felicity was not there. We found her in the kitchen, lighting up the fire.

"Bev, fill the kettle with water and put it on to heat," she said in a resigned tone. "If Dan's going to be sick again we've got to be ready for it. I wish mother was home, that's all. I hope she'll never go away again. Dan King, you just wait till I tell her of the way you've acted."

"Fudge! I ain't going to be sick," said Dan. "And if YOU begin telling tales, Felicity King, I'LL tell some too. I know how many eggs mother said you could use while she was away—and I know how many you HAVE used. I counted. So you'd better mind your own business, Miss."

"A nice way to talk to your sister when you may be dead in an hour's time!" retorted Felicity, in tears between her anger and her real alarm about Dan.

But in an hour's time Dan was still in good health, and announced his intention of going to bed. He went, and was soon sleeping as peacefully as if he had nothing on either conscience or stomach. But Felicity declared she meant to keep the water hot until all danger was past; and we sat up to keep her company. We were sitting there when Uncle Roger walked in at eleven o'clock.

"What on earth are you young fry doing up at this time of night?" he asked angrily. "You should have been in your beds two hours ago. And with a roaring fire on a night that's hot enough to melt a brass monkey! Have you taken leave of your senses?"

"It's because of Dan," explained Felicity wearily. "He went and et more of the bad berries—a whole lot of them—and we were sure he'd be sick again. But he hasn't been yet, and now he's asleep."

"Is that boy stark, staring mad?" said Uncle Roger.

"It was Felicity's fault," cried Cecily, who always took Dan's part through evil report and good report. "She told him she guessed he'd learned a lesson and wouldn't do what she'd told him not to again. So he went and et them because she vexed him so."

"Felicity King, if you don't watch out you'll grow up into the sort of woman who drives her husband to drink," said Uncle Roger gravely.

"How could I tell Dan would act so like a mule!" cried Felicity.

"Get off to bed, every one of you. It's a thankful man I'll be when your father and mother come home. The wretched bachelor who undertakes to look after a houseful of children like you is to be pitied. Nobody will ever catch me doing it again. Felicity, is there anything fit to eat in the pantry?"

That last question was the most unkindest cut of all. Felicity could have forgiven Uncle Roger anything but that. It really was unpardonable. She confided to me as we climbed the stairs that she hated Uncle Roger. Her red lips quivered and the tears of wounded pride brimmed over in her beautiful blue eyes. In the dim candle-light she looked unbelievably pretty and appealing. I put my arm about her and gave her a cousinly salute.

"Never you mind him, Felicity," I said. "He's only a grown-up."

CHAPTER XVI.
THE GHOSTLY BELL

Friday was a comfortable day in the household of King. Everybody was in good humour. The Story Girl sparkled through several tales that ranged from the afrites and jinns of Eastern myth, through the piping days of chivalry, down to the homely anecdotes of Carlisle workaday folks. She was in turn an Oriental princess behind a silken veil, the bride who followed her bridegroom to the wars of Palestine disguised as a page, the gallant lady who ransomed her diamond necklace by dancing a coranto with a highwayman on a moonlit heath, and "Buskirk's girl" who joined the Sons and Daughters of Temperance "just to see what was into it;" and in each impersonation she was so thoroughly the thing impersonated that it was a matter of surprise to us when she emerged from each our own familiar Story Girl again.

Cecily and Sara Ray found a "sweet" new knitted lace pattern in an old magazine and spent a happy afternoon learning it and "talking secrets." Chancing—accidentally, I vow—to overhear certain of these secrets, I learned that Sara Ray had named an apple for Johnny Price—"and, Cecily, true's you live, there was eight seeds in it, and you know eight means 'they both love' "—while Cecily admitted that Willy Fraser had written on his slate and showed it to her,

"If you love me as I love you,

No knife can cut our love in two"—

"but, Sara Ray, NEVER you breathe this to a living soul."

Felix also averred that he heard Sara ask Cecily very seriously,

"Cecily, how old must we be before we can have a REAL beau?"

But Sara always denied it; so I am inclined to believe Felix simply made it up himself.

Paddy distinguished himself by catching a rat, and being intolerably conceited about it—until Sara Ray cured him by calling him a "dear, sweet cat," and kissing him between the ears. Then Pat sneaked abjectly off, his tail drooping. He resented being called a sweet cat. He had a sense of humour, had Pat. Very few cats have; and most of them have such an inordinate appetite for flattery that they will swallow any amount of it and thrive thereon. Paddy had a finer taste. The Story Girl and I were the only ones who could pay him compliments to his liking. The Story Girl would box his ears with her fist and say, "Bless your gray heart, Paddy, you're a good sort of old rascal," and Pat would purr his satisfaction; I used to take a handful of the skin on his back, shake him gently and say, "Pat, you've forgotten more than any human being ever knew," and I vow Paddy would lick his chops with delight. But to be called "a sweet cat!" Oh, Sara, Sara!

Felicity tried—and had the most gratifying luck with—a new and complicated cake recipe—a gorgeous compound of a plumminess to make your mouth water. The number of eggs she used in it would have shocked Aunt Janet's thrifty soul, but that cake, like beauty, was its own excuse. Uncle Roger ate three slices of it at tea-time and told Felicity she was an artist. The poor man meant it as a compliment; but Felicity, who knew Uncle Blair was an artist and had a poor opinion of such fry, looked indignant and retorted, indeed she wasn't!

"Peter says there's any amount of raspberries back in the maple clearing," said Dan. "S'posen we all go after tea and pick some?"

"I'd like to," sighed Felicity, "but we'd come home tired and with all the milking to do. You boys better go alone."

"Peter and I will attend to the milking for one evening," said Uncle Roger. "You can all go. I have an idea that a raspberry pie for to-morrow night, when the folks come home, would hit the right spot."

Accordingly, after tea we all set off, armed with jugs and cups. Felicity, thoughtful creature, also took a small basketful of jelly cookies along with her. We had to go back through the maple woods to the extreme end of Uncle Roger's farm—a pretty walk, through a world of green, whispering boughs and spice-sweet ferns, and shifting patches of sunlight. The raspberries were plentiful, and we were not long in filling our receptacles. Then we foregathered around a tiny wood spring, cold and pellucid under its young maples, and ate the jelly cookies; and the Story Girl told us a tale of a haunted spring in a mountain glen where a fair white lady dwelt, who pledged all comers in a golden cup with jewels bright.

"And if you drank of the cup with her," said the Story Girl, her eyes glowing through the emerald dusk about us, "you were never seen in the world again; you were whisked straightway to fairyland, and lived there with a fairy bride. And you never WANTED to come back to earth, because when you drank of the magic cup you forgot all your past life, except for one day in every year when you were allowed to remember it."

"I wish there was such a place as fairyland—and a way to get to it," said Cecily.

"I think there IS such a place—in spite of Uncle Edward," said the Story Girl dreamily, "and I think there is a way of getting there too, if we could only find it."

Well, the Story Girl was right. There is such a place as fairyland—but only children can find the way to it. And they do not know that it is fairyland until they have grown so old that they forget the way. One bitter day, when they seek it and cannot find it, they realize what they have lost; and that is the tragedy of life. On that day the gates of Eden are shut behind them and the age of gold is over. Henceforth they must dwell in the common light of common day. Only a few, who remain children at heart, can ever find that fair, lost path again; and blessed are they above mortals. They, and only they, can bring us tidings from that dear country where we once sojourned and from which we must evermore be exiles. The world calls them its singers and poets and artists and story-tellers; but they are just people who have never forgotten the way to fairyland.

As we sat there the Awkward Man passed by, with his gun over his shoulder and his dog at his side. He did not look like an awkward man, there in the heart of the maple woods. He strode along right masterfully and lifted his head with the air of one who was monarch of all he surveyed.

The Story Girl kissed her fingertips to him with the delightful audacity which was a part of her; and the Awkward Man plucked off his hat and swept her a stately and graceful bow.

"I don't understand why they call him the awkward man," said Cecily, when he was out of earshot.

"You'd understand why if you ever saw him at a party or a picnic," said Felicity, "trying to pass plates and dropping them whenever a woman looked at him. They say it's pitiful to see him."

"I must get well acquainted with that man next summer," said the Story Girl. "If I put it off any longer it will be too late. I'm growing so fast, Aunt Olivia says I'll have to wear ankle skirts next summer. If I begin to look grown-up he'll get frightened of me, and then I'll never find out the Golden Milestone mystery."

"Do you think he'll ever tell you who Alice is?" I asked.

"I have a notion who Alice is already," said the mysterious creature. But she would tell us nothing more.

When the jelly cookies were all eaten it was high time to be moving homeward, for when the dark comes down there are more comfortable places than a rustling maple wood and the precincts of a possibly enchanted spring. When we reached the foot of the orchard and entered it through a gap in the hedge it was the magical, mystical time of "between lights." Off to the west was a daffodil glow hanging over the valley of lost sunsets, and Grandfather King's huge willow rose up against it like a rounded mountain of foliage. In the east, above the maple woods, was a silvery sheen that hinted the moonrise. But the orchard was a place of shadows and mysterious sounds. Midway up the open space in its heart we met Peter; and if ever a boy was given over to sheer terror that boy was Peter. His face was as white as a sunburned face could be, and his eyes were brimmed with panic.

"Peter, what is the matter?" cried Cecily.

"There's—SOMETHING—in the house, RINGING A BELL," said Peter, in a shaking voice. Not the Story Girl herself could have invested that "something" with more of creepy horror. We all drew close together. I felt a crinkly feeling along my back which I had never known before. If Peter had not been so manifestly frightened we might have thought he was trying to "pass a joke" on us. But such abject terror as his could not be counterfeited.

"Nonsense!" said Felicity, but her voice shook. "There isn't a bell in the house to ring. You must have imagined it, Peter. Or else Uncle Roger is trying to fool us."

"Your Uncle Roger went to Markdale right after milking," said Peter. "He locked up the house and gave me the key. There wasn't a soul in it then, that I'm sure of. I druv the cows to the pasture, and I got back about fifteen minutes ago. I set down on the front door steps for a moment, and all at once I heard a bell ring in the house eight times. I tell you I was skeered. I made a bolt for the orchard—and you won't catch me going near that house till your Uncle Roger comes home."

You wouldn't catch any of us doing it. We were almost as badly scared as Peter. There we stood in a huddled demoralized group. Oh, what an eerie place that orchard was! What shadows! What noises! What spooky swooping of bats! You COULDN'T look every way at once, and goodness only knew what might be behind you!

"There CAN'T be anybody in the house," said Felicity.

"Well, here's the key—go and see for yourself," said Peter.

Felicity had no intention of going and seeing.

"I think you boys ought to go," she said, retreating behind the defence of sex. "You ought to be braver than girls."

"But we ain't," said Felix candidly. "I wouldn't be much scared of anything REAL. But a haunted house is a different thing."

"I always thought something had to be done in a place before it could be haunted," said Cecily. "Somebody killed or something like that, you know. Nothing like that ever happened in our family. The Kings have always been respectable."

"Perhaps it is Emily King's ghost," whispered Felix.

"She never appeared anywhere but in the orchard," said the Story Girl. "Oh, oh, children, isn't there something under Uncle Alec's tree?"

We peered fearfully through the gloom. There WAS something— something that wavered and fluttered—advanced—retreated—

"That's only my old apron," said Felicity. "I hung it there to-day when I was looking for the white hen's nest. Oh, what shall we do? Uncle Roger may not be back for hours. I CAN'T believe there's anything in the house."

"Maybe it's only Peg Bowen," suggested Dan.

There was not a great deal of comfort in this. We were almost as much afraid of Peg Bowen as we would be of any spectral visitant.

Peter scoffed at the idea.

"Peg Bowen wasn't in the house before your Uncle Roger locked it up, and how could she get in afterwards?" he said. "No, it isn't Peg Bowen. It's SOMETHING that WALKS."

"I know a story about a ghost," said the Story Girl, the ruling passion strong even in extremity. "It is about a ghost with eyeholes but no eyes—"

"Don't," cried Cecily hysterically. "Don't you go on! Don't you say another word! I can't bear it! Don't you!"

The Story Girl didn't. But she had said enough. There was something in the quality of a ghost with eyeholes but no eyes that froze our young blood.

There never were in all the world six more badly scared children than those who huddled in the old King orchard that August night.

All at once—something—leaped from the bough of a tree and alighted before us. We split the air with a simultaneous shriek. We would have run, one and all, if there had been anywhere to run to. But there wasn't—all around us were only those shadowy arcades. Then we saw with shame that it was only our Paddy.

"Pat, Pat," I said, picking him up, feeling a certain comfort in his soft, solid body. "Stay with us, old fellow."

But Pat would none of us. He struggled out of my clasp and disappeared over the long grasses with soundless leaps. He was no longer our tame, domestic, well acquainted Paddy. He was a strange, furtive animal—a "questing beast."

Presently the moon rose; but this only made matters worse. The shadows had been still before; now they moved and danced, as the night wind tossed the boughs. The old house, with its dreadful secret, was white and clear against the dark background of spruces. We were woefully tired, but we could not sit down because the grass was reeking with dew.

"The Family Ghost only appears in daylight," said the Story Girl. "I wouldn't mind seeing a ghost in daylight. But after dark is another thing."

"There's no such thing as a ghost," I said contemptuously. Oh, how I wished I could believe it!

"Then what rung that bell?" said Peter. "Bells don't ring of themselves, I s'pose, specially when there ain't any in the house to ring."

"Oh, will Uncle Roger never come home!" sobbed Felicity. "I know he'll laugh at us awful, but it's better to be laughed at than scared like this."

Uncle Roger did not come until nearly ten. Never was there a more welcome sound than the rumble of his wheels in the lane. We ran to the orchard gate and swarmed across the yard, just as Uncle Roger alighted at the front door. He stared at us in the moonlight.

"Have you tormented any one into eating more bad berries, Felicity?" he demanded.

"Oh, Uncle Roger, don't go in," implored Felicity seriously. "There's something dreadful in there—something that rings a bell. Peter heard it. Don't go in."

"There's no use asking the meaning of this, I suppose," said Uncle Roger with the calm of despair. "I've gave up trying to fathom you young ones. Peter, where's the key? What yarn have you been telling?"

"I DID hear a bell ring," said Peter stubbornly.

Uncle Roger unlocked and flung open the front door. As he did so, clear and sweet, rang out ten bell-like chimes.

"That's what I heard," cried Peter. "There's the bell!"

We had to wait until Uncle Roger stopped laughing before we heard the explanation. We thought he never WOULD stop.

"That's Grandfather King's old clock striking," he said, as soon as he was able to speak. "Sammy Prott came along after tea, when you were away to the forge, Peter, and I gave him permission to clean the old clock. He had it going merrily in no time. And now it has almost frightened you poor little monkeys to death."

We heard Uncle Roger chuckling all the way to the barn.

"Uncle Roger can laugh," said Cecily, with a quiver in her voice, "but it's no laughing matter to be so scared. I just feel sick, I was so frightened."

"I wouldn't mind if he'd laugh once and have it done with it," said Felicity bitterly. "But he'll laugh at us for a year, and tell the story to every soul that comes to the place."

"You can't blame him for that," said the Story Girl. "I shall tell it, too. I don't care if the joke is as much on myself as any one. A story is a story, no matter who it's on. But it IS hateful to be laughed at—and grown-ups always do it. I never will when I'm grown up. I'll remember better."

"It's all Peter's fault," said Felicity. "I do think he might have had more sense than to take a clock striking for a bell ringing."

"I never heard that kind of a strike before," protested Peter. "It don't sound a bit like other clocks. And the door was shut and the sound kind o' muffled. It's all very fine to say you would have known what it was, but I don't believe you would."

"I wouldn't have," said the Story Girl honestly. "I thought it WAS a bell when I heard it, and the door open, too. Let us be fair, Felicity."

"I'm dreadful tired," sighed Cecily.

We were all "dreadful tired," for this was the third night of late hours and nerve racking strain. But it was over two hours since we had eaten the cookies, and Felicity suggested that a saucerful apiece of raspberries and cream would not be hard to take. It was not, for any one but Cecily, who couldn't swallow a mouthful.

"I'm glad father and mother will be back to-morrow night," she said. "It's too exciting when they're away. That's my opinion."

CHAPTER XVII.
THE PROOF OF THE PUDDING

Felicity was cumbered with many cares the next morning. For one thing, the whole house must be put in apple pie order; and for another, an elaborate supper must be prepared for the expected return of the travellers that night. Felicity devoted her whole attention to this, and left the secondary preparation of the regular meals to Cecily and the Story Girl. It was agreed that the latter was to make a cornmeal pudding for dinner.

In spite of her disaster with the bread, the Story Girl had been taking cooking lessons from Felicity all the week, and getting on tolerably well, although, mindful of her former mistake, she never ventured on anything without Felicity's approval. But Felicity had no time to oversee her this morning.

"You must attend to the pudding yourself," she said. "The recipe's so plain and simple even you can't go astray, and if there's anything you don't understand you can ask me. But don't bother me if you can help it."

The Story Girl did not bother her once. The pudding was concocted and baked, as the Story Girl proudly informed us when we came to the dinner-table, all on her own hook. She was very proud of it; and certainly as far as appearance went it justified her triumph. The slices were smooth and golden; and, smothered in the luscious maple sugar sauce which Cecily had compounded, were very fair to view. Nevertheless, although none of us, not even Uncle Roger or Felicity, said a word at the time, for fear of hurting the Story Girl's feelings, the pudding did not taste exactly as it should. It was tough—decidedly tough—and lacked the richness of flavour which was customary in Aunt Janet's cornmeal puddings. If it had not been for the abundant supply of sauce it would have been very dry eating indeed. Eaten it was, however, to the last crumb. If it were not just what a cornmeal pudding might be, the rest of the bill of fare had been extra good and our appetites matched it.

"I wish I was twins so's I could eat more," said Dan, when he simply had to stop.

"What good would being twins do you?" asked Peter. "People who squint can't eat any more than people who don't squint, can they?"

We could not see any connection between Peter's two questions.

"What has squinting got to do with twins?" asked Dan.

"Why, twins are just people that squint, aren't they?" said Peter.

We thought he was trying to be funny, until we found out that he was quite in earnest. Then we laughed until Peter got sulky.

"I don't care," he said. "How's a fellow to know? Tommy and Adam Cowan, over at Markdale, are twins; and they're both cross-eyed. So I s'posed that was what being twins meant. It's all very fine for you fellows to laugh. I never went to school half as much as you did; and you was brought up in Toronto, too. If you'd worked out ever since you was seven, and just got to school in the winter, there'd be lots of things you wouldn't know, either."

"Never mind, Peter," said Cecily. "You know lots of things they don't."

But Peter was not to be conciliated, and took himself off in high dudgeon. To be laughed at before Felicity—to be laughed at BY Felicity—was something he could not endure. Let Cecily and the Story Girl cackle all they wanted to, and let those stuck-up Toronto boys grin like chessy-cats; but when Felicity laughed at him the iron entered into Peter's soul.

If the Story Girl laughed at Peter the mills of the gods ground out his revenge for him in mid-afternoon. Felicity, having used up all the available cooking materials in the house, had to stop perforce; and she now determined to stuff two new pincushions she had been making for her room. We heard her rummaging in the pantry as we sat on the cool, spruce-shadowed cellar door outside, where Uncle Roger was showing us how to make elderberry pop-guns. Presently she came out, frowning.

"Cecily, do you know where mother put the sawdust she emptied out of that old beaded pincushion of Grandmother King's, after she had sifted the needles out of it? I thought it was in the tin box."

"So it is," said Cecily.

"It isn't. There isn't a speck of sawdust in that box."

The Story Girl's face wore a quite indescribable expression, compound of horror and shame. She need not have confessed. If she had but held her tongue the mystery of the sawdust's disappearance might have forever remained a mystery. She WOULD have held her tongue, as she afterwards confided to me, if it had not been for a horrible fear which flashed into her mind that possibly sawdust puddings were not healthy for people to eat—especially if there might be needles in them—and that if any mischief had been done in that direction it was her duty to undo it if possible at any cost of ridicule to herself.

"Oh, Felicity," she said, her voice expressing a very anguish of humiliation, "I—I—thought that stuff in the box was cornmeal and used it to make the pudding."

Felicity and Cecily stared blankly at the Story Girl. We boys began to laugh, but were checked midway by Uncle Roger. He was rocking himself back and forth, with his hand pressed against his stomach.

"Oh," he groaned, "I've been wondering what these sharp pains I've been feeling ever since dinner meant. I know now. I must have swallowed a needle—several needles, perhaps. I'm done for!"

The poor Story Girl went very white.

"Oh, Uncle Roger, could it be possible? You COULDN'T have swallowed a needle without knowing it. It would have stuck in your tongue or teeth."

"I didn't chew the pudding," groaned Uncle Roger. "It was too tough—I just swallowed the chunks whole."

He groaned and twisted and doubled himself up. But he overdid it. He was not as good an actor as the Story Girl. Felicity looked scornfully at him.

"Uncle Roger, you are not one bit sick," she said deliberately. "You are just putting on."

"Felicity, if I die from the effects of eating sawdust pudding, flavoured with needles, you'll be sorry you ever said such a thing to your poor old uncle," said Uncle Roger reproachfully. "Even if there were no needles in it, sixty-year-old sawdust can't be good for my tummy. I daresay it wasn't even clean."

"Well, you know every one has to eat a peck of dirt in his life," giggled Felicity.

"But nobody has to eat it all at once," retorted Uncle Roger, with another groan. "Oh, Sara Stanley, it's a thankful man I am that your Aunt Olivia is to be home to-night. You'd have me kilt entirely by another day. I believe you did it on purpose to have a story to tell."

Uncle Roger hobbled off to the barn, still holding on to his stomach.

"Do you think he really feels sick?" asked the Story Girl anxiously.

"No, I don't," said Felicity. "You needn't worry over him. There's nothing the matter with him. I don't believe there were any needles in that sawdust. Mother sifted it very carefully."

"I know a story about a man whose son swallowed a mouse," said the Story Girl, who would probably have known a story and tried to tell it if she were being led to the stake. "And he ran and wakened up a very tired doctor just as he had got to sleep.

"'Oh, doctor, my son has swallowed a mouse,' he cried. 'What shall I do?'

"'Tell him to swallow a cat,' roared the poor doctor, and slammed his door.

"Now, if Uncle Roger has swallowed any needles, maybe it would make it all right if he swallowed a pincushion."

We all laughed. But Felicity soon grew sober.

"It seems awful to think of eating a sawdust pudding. How on earth did you make such a mistake?"

"It looked just like cornmeal," said the Story Girl, going from white to red in her shame. "Well, I'm going to give up trying to cook, and stick to things I can do. And if ever one of you mentions sawdust pudding to me I'll never tell you another story as long as I live."

The threat was effectual. Never did we mention that unholy pudding. But the Story Girl could not so impose silence on the grown-ups, especially Uncle Roger. He tormented her for the rest of the summer. Never a breakfast did he sit down to, without gravely inquiring if they were sure there was no sawdust in the porridge. Not a tweak of rheumatism did he feel but he vowed it was due to a needle, travelling about his body. And Aunt Olivia was warned to label all the pincushions in the house. "Contents, sawdust; not intended for puddings."

CHAPTER XVIII.
HOW KISSING WAS DISCOVERED

An August evening, calm, golden, dewless, can be very lovely. At sunset, Felicity, Cecily, and Sara Ray, Dan, Felix, and I were in the orchard, sitting on the cool grasses at the base of the Pulpit Stone. In the west was a field of crocus sky over which pale cloud blossoms were scattered.

Uncle Roger had gone to the station to meet the travellers, and the dining-room table was spread with a feast of fat things.

"It's been a jolly week, take it all round," said Felix, "but I'm glad the grown-ups are coming back to-night, especially Uncle Alec."

"I wonder if they'll bring us anything," said Dan.

"I'm thinking long to hear all about the wedding," said Felicity, who was braiding timothy stalks into a collar for Pat.

"You girls are always thinking about weddings and getting married," said Dan contemptuously.

"We ain't," said Felicity indignantly. "I am NEVER going to get married. I think it is just horrid, so there!"

"I guess you think it would be a good deal horrider not to be," said Dan.

"It depends on who you're married to," said Cecily gravely, seeing that Felicity disdained reply. "If you got a man like father it would be all right. But S'POSEN you got one like Andrew Ward? He's so mean and cross to his wife that she tells him every day she wishes she'd never set eyes on him."

"Perhaps that's WHY he's mean and cross," said Felix.

"I tell you it isn't always the man's fault," said Dan darkly. "When I get married I'll be good to my wife, but I mean to be boss. When I open my mouth my word will be law."

"If your word is as big as your mouth I guess it will be," said Felicity cruelly.

"I pity the man who gets you, Felicity King, that's all," retorted Dan.

"Now, don't fight," implored Cecily.

"Who's fighting?" demanded Dan. "Felicity thinks she can say anything she likes to me, but I'll show her different."

Probably, in spite of Cecily's efforts, a bitter spat would have resulted between Dan and Felicity, had not a diversion been effected at that moment by the Story Girl, who came slowly down Uncle Stephen's Walk.

"Just look how the Story Girl has got herself up!" said Felicity. "Why, she's no more than decent!"

The Story Girl was barefooted and barearmed, having rolled the sleeves of her pink gingham up to her shoulders. Around her waist was twisted a girdle of the blood-red roses that bloomed in Aunt Olivia's garden; on her sleek curls she wore a chaplet of them; and her hands were full of them.

She paused under the outmost tree, in a golden-green gloom, and laughed at us over a big branch. Her wild, subtle, nameless charm clothed her as with a garment. We always remembered the picture she made there; and in later days when we read Tennyson's poems at a college desk, we knew exactly how an oread, peering through the green leaves on some haunted knoll of many fountained Ida, must look.

"Felicity," said the Story Girl reproachfully, "what have you been doing to Peter? He's up there sulking in the granary, and he won't come down, and he says it's your fault. You must have hurt his feelings dreadfully."

"I don't know about his feelings," said Felicity, with an angry toss of her shining head, "but I guess I made his ears tingle all right. I boxed them both good and hard."

"Oh, Felicity! What for?"

"Well, he tried to kiss me, that's what for!" said Felicity, turning very red. "As if I would let a hired boy kiss me! I guess Master Peter won't try anything like that again in a hurry."

The Story Girl came out of her shadows and sat down beside us on the grass.

"Well, in that case," she said gravely, "I think you did right to slap his ears—not because he is a hired boy, but because it would be impertinent in ANY boy. But talking of kissing makes me think of a story I found in Aunt Olivia's scrapbook the other day. Wouldn't you like to hear it? It is called, 'How Kissing Was Discovered.'"

"Wasn't kissing always discovered?" asked Dan.

"Not according to this story. It was just discovered accidentally."

"Well, let's hear about it," said Felix, "although I think kissing's awful silly, and it wouldn't have mattered much if it hadn't ever been discovered."

The Story Girl scattered her roses around her on the grass, and clasped her slim hands over her knees. Gazing dreamily afar at the tinted sky between the apple trees, as if she were looking back to the merry days of the world's gay youth, she began, her voice giving to the words and fancies of the old tale the delicacy of hoar frost and the crystal sparkle of dew.

"It happened long, long ago in Greece—where so many other beautiful things happened. Before that, nobody had ever heard of kissing. And then it was just discovered in the twinkling of an eye. And a man wrote it down and the account has been preserved ever since.

"There was a young shepherd named Glaucon—a very handsome young shepherd—who lived in a little village called Thebes. It became a very great and famous city afterwards, but at this time it was only a little village, very quiet and simple. Too quiet for Glaucon's liking. He grew tired of it, and he thought he would like to go away from home and see something of the world. So he took his knapsack and his shepherd's crook, and wandered away until he came to Thessaly. That is the land of the gods' hill, you know. The name of the hill was Olympus. But it has nothing to do with this story. This happened on another mountain—Mount Pelion.

"Glaucon hired himself to a wealthy man who had a great many sheep. And every day Glaucon had to lead the sheep up to pasture on Mount Pelion, and watch them while they ate. There was nothing else to do, and he would have found the time very long, if he had not been able to play on a flute. So he played very often and very beautifully, as he sat under the trees and watched the wonderful blue sea afar off, and thought about Aglaia.

"Aglaia was his master's daughter. She was so sweet and beautiful that Glaucon fell in love with her the very moment he first saw her; and when he was not playing his flute on the mountain he was thinking about Aglaia, and dreaming that some day he might have flocks of his own, and a dear little cottage down in the valley where he and Aglaia might live.

"Aglaia had fallen in love with Glaucon just as he had with her. But she never let him suspect it for ever so long. He did not know how often she would steal up the mountain and hide behind the rocks near where the sheep pastured, to listen to Glaucon's beautiful music. It was very lovely music, because he was always thinking of Aglaia while he played, though he little dreamed how near him she often was.

"But after awhile Glaucon found out that Aglaia loved him, and everything was well. Nowadays I suppose a wealthy man like Aglaia's father wouldn't be willing to let his daughter marry a hired man; but this was in the Golden Age, you know, when nothing like that mattered at all.

"After that, almost every day Aglaia would go up the mountain and sit beside Glaucon, as he watched the flocks and played on his flute. But he did not play as much as he used to, because he liked better to talk with Aglaia. And in the evening they would lead the sheep home together.

"One day Aglaia went up the mountain by a new way, and she came to a little brook. Something was sparkling very brightly among its pebbles. Aglaia picked it up, and it was the most beautiful little stone that she had ever seen. It was only as large as a pea, but it glittered and flashed in the sunlight with every colour of the rainbow. Aglaia was so delighted with it that she resolved to take it as a present to Glaucon.

"But all at once she heard a stamping of hoofs behind her, and when she turned she almost died from fright. For there was the great god, Pan, and he was a very terrible object, looking quite as much like a goat as a man. The gods were not all beautiful, you know. And, beautiful or not, nobody ever wanted to meet them face to face.

"'Give that stone to me,' said Pan, holding out his hand.

"But Aglaia, though she was frightened, would not give him the stone.

"'I want it for Glaucon,' she said.

"'I want it for one of my wood nymphs,' said Pan, 'and I must have it.'

"He advanced threateningly, but Aglaia ran as hard as she could up the mountain. If she could only reach Glaucon he would protect her. Pan followed her, clattering and bellowing terribly, but in a few minutes she rushed into Glaucon's arms.

"The dreadful sight of Pan and the still more dreadful noise he made, so frightened the sheep that they fled in all directions. But Glaucon was not afraid at all, because Pan was the god of shepherds, and was bound to grant any prayer a good shepherd, who always did his duty, might make. If Glaucon had NOT been a good shepherd dear knows what would have happened to him and Aglaia. But he was; and when he begged Pan to go away and not frighten Aglaia any more, Pan had to go, grumbling a good deal—and Pan's grumblings had a very ugly sound. But still he WENT, and that was the main thing.

"'Now, dearest, what is all this trouble about?' asked Glaucon; and Aglaia told him the story.

"'But where is the beautiful stone?' he asked, when she had finished. 'Didst thou drop it in thy alarm?'

"No, indeed! Aglaia had done nothing of the sort. When she began to run, she had popped it into her mouth, and there it was still, quite safe. Now she poked it out between her red lips, where it glittered in the sunlight.

"'Take it,' she whispered.

"The question was—how was he to take it? Both of Aglaia's arms were held fast to her sides by Glaucon's arms; and if he loosened his clasp ever so little he was afraid she would fall, so weak and trembling was she from her dreadful fright. Then Glaucon had a brilliant idea. He would take the beautiful stone from Aglaia's lips with his own lips.

"He bent over until his lips touched hers—and THEN, he forgot all about the beautiful pebble and so did Aglaia. Kissing was discovered!

"What a yarn!" said Dan, drawing a long breath, when we had come to ourselves and discovered that we were really sitting in a dewy Prince Edward Island orchard instead of watching two lovers on a mountain in Thessaly in the Golden Age. "I don't believe a word of it."

"Of course, we know it wasn't really true," said Felicity.

"Well, I don't know," said the Story Girl thoughtfully. "I think there are two kinds of true things—true things that ARE, and true things that are NOT, but MIGHT be."

"I don't believe there's any but the one kind of trueness," said Felicity. "And anyway, this story couldn't be true. You know there was no such thing as a god Pan."

"How do you know what there might have been in the Golden Age?" asked the Story Girl.

Which was, indeed, an unanswerable question for Felicity.

"I wonder what became of the beautiful stone?" said Cecily.

"Likely Aglaia swallowed it," said Felix practically.

"Did Glaucon and Aglaia ever get married?" asked Sara Ray.

"The story doesn't say. It stops just there," said the Story Girl. "But of course they did. I will tell you what I think. I don't think Aglaia swallowed the stone. I think it just fell to the ground; and after awhile they found it, and it turned out to be of such value that Glaucon could buy all the flocks and herds in the valley, and the sweetest cottage; and he and Aglaia were married right away."

"But you only THINK that," said Sara Ray. "I'd like to be really sure that was what happened."

"Oh, bother, none of it happened," said Dan. "I believed it while the Story Girl was telling it, but I don't now. Isn't that wheels?"

Wheels it was. Two wagons were driving up the lane. We rushed to the house—and there were Uncle Alec and Aunt Janet and Aunt Olivia! The excitement was quite tremendous. Every body talked and laughed at once, and it was not until we were all seated around the supper table that conversation grew coherent. What laughter and questioning and telling of tales followed, what smiles and bright eyes and glad voices. And through it all, the blissful purrs of Paddy, who sat on the window sill behind the Story Girl, resounded through the din like Andrew McPherson's bass—"just a bur-r-r-r the hale time."

"Well, I'm thankful to be home again," said Aunt Janet, beaming on us. "We had a real nice time, and Edward's folks were as kind as could be. But give me home for a steady thing. How has everything gone? How did the children behave, Roger?"

"Like models," said Uncle Roger. "They were as good as gold most of the days."

There were times when one couldn't help liking Uncle Roger.

CHAPTER XIX.
A DREAD PROPHECY

"I've got to go and begin stumping out the elderberry pasture this afternoon," said Peter dolefully. "I tell you it's a tough job. Mr. Roger might wait for cool weather before he sets people to stumping out elderberries, and that's a fact."

"Why don't you tell him so?" asked Dan.

"It ain't my business to tell him things," retorted Peter. "I'm hired to do what I'm told, and I do it. But I can have my own opinion all the same. It's going to be a broiling hot day."

We were all in the orchard, except Felix, who had gone to the post-office. It was the forenoon of an August Saturday. Cecily and Sara Ray, who had come up to spend the day with us—her mother having gone to town— were eating timothy roots. Bertha Lawrence, a Charlottetown girl, who had visited Kitty Marr in June, and had gone to school one day with her, had eaten timothy roots, affecting to consider them great delicacies. The fad was at once taken up by the Carlisle schoolgirls. Timothy roots quite ousted "sours" and young raspberry sprouts, both of which had the real merit of being quite toothsome, while timothy roots were tough and tasteless. But timothy roots were fashionable, therefore timothy roots must be eaten. Pecks of them must have been devoured in Carlisle that summer.

Pat was there also, padding about from one to the other on his black paws, giving us friendly pokes and rubs. We all made much of him except Felicity, who would not take any notice of him because he was the Story Girl's cat.

We boys were sprawling on the grass. Our morning chores were done and the day was before us. We should have been feeling very comfortable and happy, but, as a matter of fact, we were not particularly so.

The Story Girl was sitting on the mint beside the well-house, weaving herself a wreath of buttercups. Felicity was sipping from the cup of clouded blue with an overdone air of unconcern. Each was acutely and miserably conscious of the other's presence, and each was desirous of convincing the rest of us that the other was less than nothing to her. Felicity could not succeed. The Story Girl managed it better. If it had not been for the fact that in all our foregatherings she was careful to sit as far from Felicity as possible, we might have been deceived.

We had not passed a very pleasant week. Felicity and the Story Girl had not been "speaking" to each other, and consequently there had been something rotten in the state of Denmark. An air of restraint was over all our games and conversations.

On the preceding Monday Felicity and the Story Girl had quarrelled over something. What the cause of the quarrel was I cannot tell because I never knew. It remained a "dead secret" between the parties of the first and second part forever. But it was more bitter than the general run of their tiffs, and the consequences were apparent to all. They had not spoken to each other since.

This was not because the rancour of either lasted so long. On the contrary it passed speedily away, not even one low descending sun going down on their wrath. But dignity remained to be considered. Neither would "speak first," and each obstinately declared that she would not speak first, no, not in a hundred years. Neither argument, entreaty, nor expostulation had any effect on those two stubborn girls, nor yet the tears of sweet Cecily, who cried every night about it, and mingled in her pure little prayers fervent petitions that Felicity and the Story Girl might make up.

"I don't know where you expect to go when you die, Felicity," she said tearfully, "if you don't forgive people."

"I have forgiven her," was Felicity's answer, "but I am not going to speak first for all that."

"It's very wrong, and, more than that, it's so uncomfortable," complained Cecily. "It spoils everything."

"Were they ever like this before?" I asked Cecily, as we talked the matter over privately in Uncle Stephen's Walk.

"Never for so long," said Cecily. "They had a spell like this last summer, and one the summer before, but they only lasted a couple of days."

"And who spoke first?"

"Oh, the Story Girl. She got excited about something and spoke to Felicity before she thought, and then it was all right. But I'm afraid it isn't going to be like that this time. Don't you notice how careful the Story Girl is not to get excited? That is such a bad sign."

"We've just got to think up something that will excite her, that's all," I said.

"I'm—I'm praying about it," said Cecily in a low voice, her tear-wet lashes trembling against her pale, round cheeks. "Do you suppose it will do any good, Bev?"

"Very likely," I assured her. "Remember Sara Ray and the money. That came from praying."

"I'm glad you think so," said Cecily tremulously. "Dan said it was no use for me to bother praying about it. He said if they COULDN'T speak God might do something, but when they just WOULDN'T it wasn't likely He would interfere. Dan does say such queer things. I'm so afraid he's going to grow up just like Uncle Robert Ward, who never goes to church, and doesn't believe more than half the Bible is true."

"Which half does he believe is true?" I inquired with unholy curiosity.

"Oh, just the nice parts. He says there's a heaven all right, but no—no— HELL. I don't want Dan to grow up like that. It isn't respectable. And you wouldn't want all kinds of people crowding heaven, now, would you?"

"Well, no, I suppose not," I agreed, thinking of Billy Robinson.

"Of course, I can't help feeling sorry for those who have to go to THE OTHER PLACE," said Cecily compassionately. "But I suppose they wouldn't be very comfortable in heaven either. They wouldn't feel at home. Andrew Marr said a simply dreadful thing about THE OTHER PLACE one night last fall, when Felicity and I were down to see Kitty, and they were burning the potato stalks. He said he believed THE OTHER PLACE must be lots more interesting than heaven because fires were such jolly things. Now, did you ever hear the like?"

"I guess it depends a good deal on whether you're inside or outside the fires," I said.

"Oh, Andrew didn't really mean it, of course. He just said it to sound smart and make us stare. The Marrs are all like that. But anyhow, I'm going to keep on praying that something will happen to excite the Story Girl. I don't believe there is any use in praying that Felicity will speak first, because I am sure she won't."

"But don't you suppose God could make her?" I said, feeling that it wasn't quite fair that the Story Girl should always have to speak first. If she had spoken first the other times it was surely Felicity's turn this time.

"Well, I believe it would puzzle Him," said Cecily, out of the depths of her experience with Felicity.

Peter, as was to be expected, took Felicity's part, and said the Story Girl ought to speak first because she was the oldest. That, he said, had always been his Aunt Jane's rule.

Sara Ray thought Felicity should speak first, because the Story Girl was half an orphan.

Felix tried to make peace between them, and met the usual fate of all peacemakers. The Story Girl loftily told him that he was too young to understand, and Felicity said that fat boys should mind their own business. After that, Felix declared it would serve Felicity right if the Story Girl never spoke to her again.

Dan had no patience with either of the girls, especially Felicity.

"What they both want is a right good spanking," he said.

If only a spanking would mend the matter it was not likely it would ever be mended. Both Felicity and the Story Girl were rather too old to be spanked, and, if they had not been, none of the grown-ups would have thought it worth while to administer so desperate a remedy for what they considered so insignificant a trouble. With the usual levity of grown-ups, they regarded the coldness between the girls as a subject of mirth and jest, and recked not that it was freezing the genial current of our youthful souls, and blighting hours that should have been fair pages in our book of days.

The Story Girl finished her wreath and put it on. The buttercups drooped over her high, white brow and played peep with her glowing eyes. A dreamy smile hovered around her poppy-red mouth—a significant smile which, to those of us skilled in its interpretation, betokened the sentence which soon came.

"I know a story about a man who always had his own opinion—"

The Story Girl got no further. We never heard the story of the man who always had his own opinion. Felix came tearing up the lane, with a newspaper in his hand. When a boy as fat as Felix runs at full speed on a broiling August forenoon, he has something to run for—as Felicity remarked.

"He must have got some bad news at the office," said Sara Ray.

"Oh, I hope nothing has happened to father," I exclaimed, springing anxiously to my feet, a sick, horrible feeling of fear running over me like a cool, rippling wave.

"It's just as likely to be good news he is running for as bad," said the Story Girl, who was no believer in meeting trouble half way.

"He wouldn't be running so fast for good news," said Dan cynically.

We were not left long in doubt. The orchard gate flew open and Felix was among us. One glimpse of his face told us that he was no bearer of glad tidings. He had been running hard and should have been rubicund. Instead, he was "as pale as are the dead." I could not have asked him what was the matter had my life depended on it. It was Felicity who demanded impatiently of my shaking, voiceless brother:

"Felix King, what has scared you?"

Felix held out the newspaper—it was the Charlottetown Daily Enterprise.

"It's there," he gasped. "Look—read—oh, do you—think it's—true? The—end of—the world—is coming to-morrow—at two—o'clock—in the afternoon!"

Crash! Felicity had dropped the cup of clouded blue, which had passed unscathed through so many changing years, and now at last lay shattered on the stone of the well curb. At any other time we should all have been aghast over such a catastrophe, but it passed unnoticed now. What mattered it that all the cups in the world be broken to-day if the crack o' doom must sound to-morrow?

"Oh, Sara Stanley, do you believe it? DO you?" gasped Felicity, clutching the Story Girl's hand. Cecily's prayer had been answered. Excitement had come with a vengeance, and under its stress Felicity had spoken first. But this, like the breaking of the cup, had no significance for us at the moment.

The Story Girl snatched the paper and read the announcement to a group on which sudden, tense silence had fallen. Under a sensational headline, "The Last Trump will sound at Two O'clock To-morrow," was a paragraph to the effect that the leader of a certain noted sect in the United States had predicted that August twelfth would be the Judgment Day, and that all his numerous followers were preparing for the dread event by prayer, fasting, and the making of appropriate white garments for ascension robes.

I laugh at the remembrance now—until I recall the real horror of fear that enwrapped us in that sunny orchard that August morning of long ago; and then I laugh no more. We were only children, be it remembered, with a very firm and simple faith that grown people knew much more than we did, and a rooted conviction that whatever you read in a newspaper must be true. If the Daily Enterprise said that August twelfth was to be the Judgment Day how were you going to get around it?

"Do you believe it, Sara Stanley?" persisted Felicity. "DO you?"

"No—no, I don't believe a word of it," said the Story Girl.

But for once her voice failed to carry conviction—or, rather, it carried conviction of the very opposite kind. It was borne in upon our miserable minds that if the Story Girl did not altogether believe it was true she believed it might be true; and the possibility was almost as dreadful as the certainty.

"It CAN'T be true," said Sara Ray, seeking refuge, as usual, in tears. "Why, everything looks just the same. Things COULDN'T look the same if the Judgment Day was going to be to-morrow."

"But that's just the way it's to come," I said uncomfortably. "It tells you in the Bible. It's to come just like a thief in the night."

"But it tells you another thing in the Bible, too," said Cecily eagerly. "It says nobody knows when the Judgment Day is to come—not even the angels in heaven. Now, if the angels in heaven don't know it, do you suppose the editor of the Enterprise can know it—and him a Grit, too?"

"I guess he knows as much about it as a Tory would," retorted the Story Girl. Uncle Roger was a Liberal and Uncle Alec a Conservative, and the girls held fast to the political traditions of their respective households. "But it isn't really the Enterprise editor at all who is saying it—it's a man in the States who claims to be a prophet. If he IS a prophet perhaps he has found out somehow."

"And it's in the paper, too, and that's printed as well as the Bible," said Dan.

"Well, I'm going to depend on the Bible," said Cecily. "I don't believe it's the Judgment Day to-morrow—but I'm scared, for all that," she added piteously.

That was exactly the position of us all. As in the case of the bell-ringing ghost, we did not believe but we trembled.

"Nobody might have known when the Bible was written," said Dan, "but maybe somebody knows now. Why, the Bible was written thousands of years ago, and that paper was printed this very morning. There's been time to find out ever so much more."

"I want to do so many things," said the Story Girl, plucking off her crown of buttercup gold with a tragic gesture, "but if it's the Judgment Day to-morrow I won't have time to do any of them."

"It can't be much worse than dying, I s'pose," said Felix, grasping at any straw of comfort.

"I'm awful glad I've got into the habit of going to church and Sunday School this summer," said Peter very soberly. "I wish I'd made up my mind before this whether to be a Presbyterian or a Methodist. Do you s'pose it's too late now?"

"Oh, that doesn't matter," said Cecily earnestly. "If—if you're a Christian, Peter, that is all that's necessary."

"But it's too late for that," said Peter miserably. "I can't turn into a Christian between this and two o'clock to-morrow. I'll just have to be satisfied with making up my mind to be a Presbyterian or a Methodist. I wanted to wait till I got old enough to make out what was the difference between them, but I'll have to chance it now. I guess I'll be a Presbyterian, 'cause I want to be like the rest of you. Yes, I'll be a Presbyterian."

"I know a story about Judy Pineau and the word Presbyterian," said the Story Girl, "but I can't tell it now. If to-morrow isn't the Judgment Day I'll tell it Monday."

"If I had known that to-morrow might be the Judgment Day I wouldn't have quarrelled with you last Monday, Sara Stanley, or been so horrid and sulky all the week. Indeed I wouldn't," said Felicity, with very unusual humility.

Ah, Felicity! We were all, in the depths of our pitiful little souls, reviewing the innumerable things we would or would not have done "if we had known." What a black and endless list they made—those sins of omission and commission that rushed accusingly across our young memories! For us the leaves of the Book of Judgment were already opened; and we stood at the bar of our own consciences, than which for youth or eld, there can be no more dread tribunal. I thought of all the evil deeds of my short life—of pinching Felix to make him cry out at family prayers, of playing truant from Sunday School and going fishing one day, of a certain fib—no, no away from this awful hour with all such euphonious evasions—of a LIE I had once told, of many a selfish and unkind word and thought and action. And to-morrow might be the great and terrible day of the last accounting! Oh, if I had only been a better boy!

"The quarrel was as much my fault as yours, Felicity," said the Story Girl, putting her arm around Felicity. "We can't undo it now. But if to-morrow isn't the Judgment Day we must be careful never to quarrel again. Oh, I wish father was here."

"He will be," said Cecily. "If it's the Judgment Day for Prince Edward Island it will be for Europe, too."

"I wish we could just KNOW whether what the paper says is true or not," said Felix desperately. "It seems to me I could brace up if I just KNEW."

But to whom could we appeal? Uncle Alec was away and would not be back until late that night. Neither Aunt Janet nor Uncle Roger were people to whom we cared to apply in such a crisis. We were afraid of the Judgment Day; but we were almost equally afraid of being laughed at. How about Aunt Olivia?

"No, Aunt Olivia has gone to bed with a sick headache and mustn't be disturbed," said the Story Girl. "She said I must get dinner ready, because there was plenty of cold meat, and nothing to do but boil the potatoes and peas, and set the table. I don't know how I can put my thoughts into it when the Judgment Day may be to-morrow. Besides, what is the good of asking the grown-ups? They don't know anything more about this than we do."

"But if they'd just SAY they didn't believe it, it would be a sort of comfort," said Cecily.

"I suppose the minister would know, but he's away on his vacation" said Felicity. "Anyhow, I'll go and ask mother what she thinks of it."

Felicity picked up the Enterprise and betook herself to the house. We awaited her return in dire suspense.

"Well, what does she say?" asked Cecily tremulously.

"She said, 'Run away and don't bother me. I haven't any time for your nonsense.'" responded Felicity in an injured tone. "And I said, 'But, ma, the paper SAYS to-morrow is the Judgment Day,' and ma just said 'Judgment Fiddlesticks!'"

"Well, that's kind of comforting," said Peter. "She can't put any faith in it, or she'd be more worked up."

"If it only wasn't PRINTED!" said Dan gloomily.

"Let's all go over and ask Uncle Roger," said Felix desperately.

That we should make Uncle Roger a court of last resort indicated all too clearly the state of our minds. But we went. Uncle Roger was in his barn-yard, hitching his black mare into the buggy. His copy of the Enterprise was sticking out of his pocket. He looked, as we saw with sinking hearts, unusually grave and preoccupied. There was not a glimmer of a smile about his face.

"You ask him," said Felicity, nudging the Story Girl.

"Uncle Roger," said the Story Girl, the golden notes of her voice threaded with fear and appeal, "the Enterprise says that to-morrow is the Judgment Day? IS it? Do YOU think it is?"

"I'm afraid so," said Uncle Roger gravely. "The Enterprise is always very careful to print only reliable news."

"But mother doesn't believe it," cried Felicity.

Uncle Roger shook his head.

"That is just the trouble," he said. "People won't believe it till it's too late. I'm going straight to Markdale to pay a man there some money I owe him, and after dinner I'm going to Summerside to buy me a new suit. My old one is too shabby for the Judgment Day."

He got into his buggy and drove away, leaving eight distracted mortals behind him.

"Well, I suppose that settles it," said Peter, in despairing tone.

"Is there anything we can do to PREPARE?" asked Cecily.

"I wish I had a white dress like you girls," sobbed Sara Ray. "But I haven't, and it's too late to get one. Oh, I wish I had minded what ma said better. I wouldn't have disobeyed her so often if I'd thought the Judgment Day was so near. When I go home I'm going to tell her about going to the magic lantern show."

"I'm not sure that Uncle Roger meant what he said," remarked the Story Girl. "I couldn't get a look into his eyes. If he was trying to hoax us there would have been a twinkle in them. He can never help that. You know he would think it a great joke to frighten us like this. It's really dreadful to have no grown-ups you can depend on."

"We could depend on father if he was here," said Dan stoutly. "HE'D tell us the truth."

"He would tell us what he THOUGHT was true, Dan, but he couldn't KNOW. He's not such a well-educated man as the editor of the Enterprise. No, there's nothing to do but wait and see."

"Let us go into the house and read just what the Bible does say about it," suggested Cecily.

We crept in carefully, lest we disturb Aunt Olivia, and Cecily found and read the significant portion of Holy Writ. There was little comfort for us in that vivid and terrible picture.

"Well," said the Story Girl finally. "I must go and get the potatoes ready. I suppose they must be boiled even if it is the Judgment Day to-morrow. But I don't believe it is."

"And I've got to go and stump elderberries," said Peter. "I don't see how I can do it—go away back there alone. I'll feel scared to death the whole time."

"Tell Uncle Roger that, and say if to-morrow is the end of the world that there is no good in stumping any more fields," I suggested.

"Yes, and if he lets you off then we'll know he was in earnest," chimed in Cecily. "But if he still says you must go that'll be a sign he doesn't believe it."

Leaving the Story Girl and Peter to peel their potatoes, the rest of us went home, where Aunt Janet, who had gone to the well and found the fragments of the old blue cup, gave poor Felicity a bitter scolding about it. But Felicity bore it very patiently—nay, more, she seemed to delight in it.

"Ma can't believe to-morrow is the last day, or she wouldn't scold like that," she told us; and this comforted us until after dinner, when the Story Girl and Peter came over and told us that Uncle Roger had really gone to Summerside. Then we plunged down into fear and wretchedness again.

"But he said I must go and stump elderberries just the same" said Peter. "He said it might NOT be the Judgment Day to-morrow, though he believed it was, and it would keep me out of mischief. But I just can't stand it back there alone. Some of you fellows must come with me. I don't want you to work, but just for company."

It was finally decided that Dan and Felix should go. I wanted to go also, but the girls protested.

"YOU must stay and keep us cheered up," implored Felicity. "I just don't know how I'm ever going to put in the afternoon. I promised Kitty Marr that I'd go down and spend it with her, but I can't now. And I can't knit any at my lace. I'd just keep thinking, 'What is the use? Perhaps it'll all be burned up to-morrow.'"

So I stayed with the girls, and a miserable afternoon we had of it. The Story Girl again and again declared that she "didn't believe it," but when we asked her to tell a story, she evaded it with a flimsy excuse. Cecily pestered Aunt Janet's life out, asking repeatedly, "Ma, will you be washing Monday?" "Ma, will you be going to prayer meeting Tuesday night?" "Ma, will you be preserving raspberries next week?" and various similar questions. It was a huge comfort to her that Aunt Janet always said, "Yes," or "Of course," as if there could be no question about it.

Sara Ray cried until I wondered how one small head could contain all the tears she shed. But I do not believe she was half as much frightened as disappointed that she had no white dress. In mid-afternoon Cecily came downstairs with her forget-me-not jug in her hand—a dainty bit of china, wreathed with dark blue forget-me-nots, which Cecily prized highly, and in which she always kept her toothbrush.

"Sara, I am going to give you this jug," she said solemnly.

Now, Sara had always coveted this particular jug. She stopped crying long enough to clutch it delightedly.

"Oh, Cecily, thank you. But are you sure you won't want it back if to-morrow isn't the Judgment Day?"

"No, it's yours for good," said Cecily, with the high, remote air of one to whom forget-me-not jugs and all such pomps and vanities of the world were as a tale that is told.

"Are you going to give any one your cherry vase?" asked Felicity, trying to speak indifferently. Felicity had never admired the forget-me-not jug, but she had always hankered after the cherry vase—an affair of white glass, with a cluster of red glass cherries and golden-green glass leaves on its side, which Aunt Olivia had given Cecily one Christmas.

"No, I'm not," answered Cecily, with a change of tone.

"Oh, well, I don't care," said Felicity quickly. "Only, if to-morrow is the last day, the cherry vase won't be much use to you."

"I guess it will be as much use to me as to any one else," said Cecily indignantly. She had sacrificed her dear forget-me-not jug to satisfy some pang of conscience, or propitiate some threatening fate, but surrender her precious cherry vase she could not and would not. Felicity needn't be giving any hints!

With the gathering shades of night our plight became pitiful. In the daylight, surrounded by homely, familiar sights and sounds, it was not so difficult to fortify our souls with a cheering incredulity. But now, in this time of shadows, dread belief clutched us and wrung us with terror. If there had been one wise older friend to tell us, in serious fashion, that we need not be afraid, that the Enterprise paragraph was naught save the idle report of a deluded fanatic, it would have been well for us. But there was not. Our grown-ups, instead, considered our terror an exquisite jest. At that very moment, Aunt Olivia, who had recovered from her headache, and Aunt Janet were laughing in the kitchen over the state the children were in because they were afraid the end of the world was close at hand. Aunt Janet's throaty gurgle and Aunt Olivia's trilling mirth floated out through the open window.

"Perhaps they'll laugh on the other side of their faces to-morrow," said Dan, with gloomy satisfaction.

We were sitting on the cellar hatch, watching what might be our last sunset o'er the dark hills of time. Peter was with us. It was his last Sunday to go home, but he had elected to remain.

"If to-morrow is the Judgment Day I want to be with you fellows," he said.

Sara Ray had also yearned to stay, but could not because her mother had told her she must be home before dark.

"Never mind, Sara," comforted Cecily. "It's not to be till two o'clock to-morrow, so you'll have plenty of time to get up here before anything happens."

"But there might be a mistake," sobbed Sara. "It might be two o'clock to-night instead of to-morrow."

It might, indeed. This was a new horror, which had not occurred to us.

"I'm sure I won't sleep a wink to-night," said Felix.

"The paper SAYS two o'clock to-morrow," said Dan. "You needn't worry, Sara."

But Sara departed, weeping. She did not, however, forget to carry the forget-me-not jug with her. All things considered, her departure was a relief. Such a constantly tearful damsel was not a pleasant companion. Cecily and Felicity and the Story Girl did not cry. They were made of finer, firmer stuff. Dry-eyed, with such courage as they might, they faced whatever might be in store for them.

"I wonder where we'll all be this time to-morrow night," said Felix mournfully, as we watched the sunset between the dark fir boughs. It was an ominous sunset. The sun dropped down amid dark, livid clouds, that turned sullen shades of purple and fiery red behind him.

"I hope we'll be all together, wherever we are," said Cecily gently. "Nothing can be so very bad then."

"I'm going to read the Bible all to-morrow forenoon," said Peter.

When Aunt Olivia came out to go home the Story Girl asked her permission to stay all night with Felicity and Cecily. Aunt Olivia assented lightly, swinging her hat on her arm and including us all in a friendly smile. She looked very pretty, with her big blue eyes and warm-hued golden hair. We loved Aunt Olivia; but just now we resented her having laughed at us with Aunt Janet, and we refused to smile back.

"What a sulky, sulky lot of little people," said Aunt Olivia, going away across the yard, holding her pretty dress up from the dewy grass.

Peter resolved to stay all night with us, too, not troubling himself about anybody's permission. When we went to bed it was settling down for a stormy night, and the rain was streaming wetly on the roof, as if the world, like Sara Ray, were weeping because its end was so near. Nobody forgot or hurried over his prayers that night. We would dearly have loved to leave the candle burning, but Aunt Janet's decree regarding this was as inexorable as any of Mede and Persia. Out the candle must go; and we lay there, quaking, with the wild rain streaming down on the roof above us, and the voices of the storm wailing through the writhing spruce trees.

CHAPTER XX.
THE JUDGMENT SUNDAY

Sunday morning broke, dull and gray. The rain had ceased, but the clouds hung dark and brooding above a world which, in its windless calm, following the spent storm-throe, seemed to us to be waiting "till judgment spoke the doom of fate." We were all up early. None of us, it appeared, had slept well, and some of us not at all. The Story Girl had been among the latter, and she looked very pale and wan, with black shadows under her deep-set eyes. Peter, however, had slept soundly enough after twelve o'clock.

"When you've been stumping out elderberries all the afternoon it'll take more than the Judgment Day to keep you awake all night," he said. "But when I woke up this morning it was just awful. I'd forgot it for a moment, and then it all came back with a rush, and I was worse scared than before."

Cecily was pale but brave. For the first time in years she had not put her hair up in curlers on Saturday night. It was brushed and braided with Puritan simplicity.

"If it's the Judgment Day I don't care whether my hair is curly or not," she said.

"Well," said Aunt Janet, when we all descended to the kitchen, "this is the first time you young ones have ever all got up without being called, and that's a fact."

At breakfast our appetites were poor. How could the grown-ups eat as they did? After breakfast and the necessary chores there was the forenoon to be lived through. Peter, true to his word, got out his Bible and began to read from the first chapter in Genesis.

"I won't have time to read it all through, I s'pose," he said, "but I'll get along as far as I can."

There was no preaching in Carlisle that day, and Sunday School was not till the evening. Cecily got out her Lesson Slip and studied the lesson conscientiously. The rest of us did not see how she could do it. We could not, that was very certain.

"If it isn't the Judgment Day, I want to have the lesson learned," she said, "and if it is I'll feel I've done what was right. But I never found it so hard to remember the Golden Text before."

The long dragging hours were hard to endure. We roamed restlessly about, and went to and fro—all save Peter, who still steadily read away at his Bible. He was through Genesis by eleven and beginning on Exodus.

"There's a good deal of it I don't understand," he said, "but I read every word, and that's the main thing. That story about Joseph and his brother was so int'resting I almost forgot about the Judgment Day."

But the long drawn out dread was beginning to get on Dan's nerves.

"If it is the Judgment Day," he growled, as we went in to dinner, "I wish it'd hurry up and have it over."

"Oh, Dan!" cried Felicity and Cecily together, in a chorus of horror. But the Story Girl looked as if she rather sympathized with Dan.

If we had eaten little at breakfast we could eat still less at dinner. After dinner the clouds rolled away, and the sun came joyously and gloriously out. This, we thought, was a good omen. Felicity opined that it wouldn't have cleared up if it was the Judgment Day. Nevertheless, we dressed ourselves carefully, and the girls put on their white dresses.

Sara Ray came up, still crying, of course. She increased our uneasiness by saying that her mother believed the Enterprise paragraph, and was afraid that the end of the world was really at hand.

"That's why she let me come up," she sobbed. "If she hadn't been afraid I don't believe she would have let me come up. But I'd have died if I couldn't have come. And she wasn't a bit cross when I told her I had gone to the magic lantern show. That's an awful bad sign. I hadn't a white dress, but I put on my white muslin apron with the frills."

"That seems kind of queer," said Felicity doubtfully. "You wouldn't put on an apron to go to church, and so it doesn't seem as if it was proper to put it on for Judgment Day either."

"Well, it's the best I could do," said Sara disconsolately. "I wanted to have something white on. It's just like a dress only it hasn't sleeves."

"Let's go into the orchard and wait," said the Story Girl. "It's one o'clock now, so in another hour we'll know the worst. We'll leave the front door open, and we'll hear the big clock when it strikes two."

No better plan being suggested, we betook ourselves to the orchard, and sat on the boughs of Uncle Alec's tree because the grass was wet. The world was beautiful and peaceful and green. Overhead was a dazzling blue sky, spotted with heaps of white cloud.

"Pshaw, I don't believe there's any fear of it being the last day," said Dan, beginning a whistle out of sheer bravado.

"Well, don't whistle on Sunday anyhow," said Felicity severely.

"I don't see a thing about Methodists or Presbyterians, as far as I've gone, and I'm most through Exodus," said Peter suddenly. "When does it begin to tell about them?"

"There's nothing about Methodists or Presbyterians in the Bible," said Felicity scornfully.

Peter looked amazed.

"Well, how did they happen then?" he asked. "When did they begin to be?"

"I've often thought it such a strange thing that there isn't a word about either of them in the Bible," said Cecily. "Especially when it mentions Baptists—or at least one Baptist."

"Well, anyhow," said Peter, "even if it isn't the Judgment Day I'm going to keep on reading the Bible until I've got clean through. I never thought it was such an int'resting book."

"It sounds simply dreadful to hear you call the Bible an interesting book," said Felicity, with a shudder at the sacrilege. "Why, you might be talking about ANY common book."

"I didn't mean any harm," said Peter, crestfallen.

"The Bible IS an interesting book," said the Story Girl, coming to Peter's rescue. "And there are magnificent stories in it—yes, Felicity, MAGNIFICENT. If the world doesn't come to an end I'll tell you the story of Ruth next Sunday—or look here! I'll tell it anyhow. That's a promise. Wherever we are next Sunday I'll tell you about Ruth."

"Why, you wouldn't tell stories in heaven," said Cecily, in a very timid voice.

"Why not?" said the Story Girl, with a flash of her eyes. "Indeed I shall. I'll tell stories as long as I've a tongue to talk with, or any one to listen."

Ay, doubtless. That dauntless spirit would soar triumphantly above the wreck of matter and the crash of worlds, taking with it all its own wild sweetness and daring. Even the young-eyed cherubim, choiring on meadows of asphodel, might cease their harping for a time to listen to a tale of the vanished earth, told by that golden tongue. Some vague thought of this was in our minds as we looked at her; and somehow it comforted us. Not even the Judgment was so greatly to be feared if after it we were the SAME, our own precious little identities unchanged.

"It must be getting handy two," said Cecily. "It seems as if we'd been waiting here for ever so much longer than an hour."

Conversation languished. We watched and waited nervously. The moments dragged by, each seeming an hour. Would two o'clock never come and end the suspense? We all became very tense. Even Peter had to stop reading. Any unaccustomed sound or sight in the world about us struck on our taut senses like the trump of doom. A cloud passed over the sun and as the sudden shadow swept across the orchard we turned pale and trembled. A wagon rumbling over a plank bridge in the hollow made Sara Ray start up with a shriek. The slamming of a barn door over at Uncle Roger's caused the cold perspiration to break out on our faces.

"I don't believe it's the Judgment Day," said Felix, "and I never have believed it. But oh, I wish that clock would strike two."

"Can't you tell us a story to pass the time?" I entreated the Story Girl.

She shook her head.

"No, it would be no use to try. But if this isn't the Judgment Day I'll have a great one to tell of us being so scared."

Pat presently came galloping up the orchard, carrying in his mouth a big field mouse, which, sitting down before us, he proceeded to devour, body and bones, afterwards licking his chops with great satisfaction.

"It can't be the Judgment Day," said Sara Ray, brightening up. "Paddy would never be eating mice if it was."

"If that clock doesn't soon strike two I shall go out of my seven senses," declared Cecily with unusual vehemence.

"Time always seems long when you're waiting," said the Story Girl. "But it does seem as if we had been here more than an hour."

"Maybe the clock struck and we didn't hear it," suggested Dan. "Somebody'd better go and see."

"I'll go," said Cecily. "I suppose, even if anything happens, I'll have time to get back to you."

We watched her white-clad figure pass through the gate and enter the front door. A few minutes passed—or a few years—we could not have told which. Then Cecily came running at full speed back to us. But when she reached us she trembled so much that at first she could not speak.

"What is it? Is it past two?" implored the Story Girl.

"It's—it's four," said Cecily with a gasp. "The old clock isn't going. Mother forgot to wind it up last night and it stopped. But it's four by the kitchen clock—so it isn't the Judgment Day—and tea is ready—and mother says to come in."

We looked at each other, realizing what our dread had been, now that it was lifted. It was not the Judgment Day. The world and life were still before us, with all their potent lure of years unknown.

"I'll never believe anything I read in the papers again," said Dan, rushing to the opposite extreme.

"I told you the Bible was more to be depended on than the newspapers," said Cecily triumphantly.

Sara Ray and Peter and the Story Girl went home, and we went in to tea with royal appetites. Afterwards, as we dressed for Sunday School upstairs, our spirits carried us away to such an extent that Aunt Janet had to come twice to the foot of the stairs and inquire severely, "Children, have you forgotten what day this is?"

"Isn't it nice that we're going to live a spell longer in this nice world?" said Felix, as we walked down the hill.

"Yes, and Felicity and the Story Girl are speaking again," said Cecily happily.

"And Felicity DID speak first," I said.

"Yes, but it took the Judgment Day to make her. I wish," added Cecily with a sigh, "that I hadn't been in quite such a hurry giving away my forget-me-not jug."

"And I wish I hadn't been in such a hurry deciding I'd be a Presbyterian," said Peter.

"Well, it's not too late for that," said Dan. "You can change your mind now."

"No, sir," said Peter with a flash of spirit, "I ain't one of the kind that says they'll be something just because they're scared, and when the scare is over go back on it. I said I'd be Presbyterian and I mean to stick to it."

"You said you knew a story that had something to do with Presbyterians," I said to the Story Girl. "Tell us it now."

"Oh, no, it isn't the right kind of story to tell on Sunday," she replied. "But I'll tell it to-morrow morning."

Accordingly, we heard it the next morning in the orchard.

"Long ago, when Judy Pineau was young," said the Story Girl, "she was hired with Mrs. Elder Frewen—the first Mrs. Elder Frewen. Mrs. Frewen had been a school-teacher, and she was very particular as to how people talked, and the grammar they used. And she didn't like anything but refined words. One very hot day she heard Judy Pineau say she was 'all in a sweat.' Mrs. Frewen was greatly shocked, and said, 'Judy, you shouldn't say that. It's horses that sweat. You should say you are in a perspiration.' Well, Judy promised she'd remember, because she liked Mrs. Frewen and was anxious to please her. Not long afterwards Judy was scrubbing the kitchen floor one morning, and when Mrs. Frewen came in Judy looked up and said, quite proud over using the right word, 'Oh, Mees Frewen, ain't it awful hot? I declare I'm all in a Presbyterian.'"

CHAPTER XXI.
DREAMERS OF DREAMS

August went out and September came in. Harvest was ended; and though summer was not yet gone, her face was turned westering. The asters lettered her retreating footsteps in a purple script, and over the hills and valleys hung a faint blue smoke, as if Nature were worshipping at her woodland altar. The apples began to burn red on the bending boughs; crickets sang day and night; squirrels chattered secrets of Polichinelle in the spruces; the sunshine was as thick and yellow as molten gold; school opened, and we small denizens of the hill farms lived happy days of harmless work and necessary play, closing in nights of peaceful, undisturbed slumber under a roof watched over by autumnal stars.

At least, our slumbers were peaceful and undisturbed until our orgy of dreaming began.

"I would really like to know what especial kind of deviltry you young fry are up to this time," said Uncle Roger one evening, as he passed through the orchard with his gun on his shoulder, bound for the swamp.

We were sitting in a circle before the Pulpit Stone, each writing diligently in an exercise book, and eating the Rev. Mr. Scott's plums, which always reached their prime of juicy, golden-green flesh and bloomy blue skin in September. The Rev. Mr. Scott was dead and gone, but those plums certainly kept his memory green, as his forgotten sermons could never have done.

"Oh," said Felicity in a shocked tone, when Uncle Roger had passed by, "Uncle Roger SWORE."

"Oh, no, he didn't," said the Story Girl quickly. "'Deviltry' isn't swearing at all. It only means extra bad mischief."

"Well, it's not a very nice word, anyhow," said Felicity.

"No, it isn't," agreed the Story Girl with a regretful sigh. "It's very expressive, but it isn't nice. That is the way with so many words. They're expressive, but they're not nice, and so a girl can't use them."

The Story Girl sighed again. She loved expressive words, and treasured them as some girls might have treasured jewels. To her, they were as lustrous pearls, threaded on the crimson cord of a vivid fancy. When she met with a new one she uttered it over and over to herself in solitude, weighing it, caressing it, infusing it with the radiance of her voice, making it her own in all its possibilities for ever.

"Well, anyhow, it isn't a suitable word in this case," insisted Felicity. "We are not up to any dev—any extra bad mischief. Writing down one's dreams isn't mischief at all."

Certainly it wasn't. Surely not even the straitest sect of the grown-ups could call it so. If writing down your dreams, with agonizing care as to composition and spelling—for who knew that the eyes of generations unborn might not read the record?—were not a harmless amusement, could anything be called so? I trow not.

We had been at it for a fortnight, and during that time we only lived to have dreams and write them down. The Story Girl had originated the idea one evening in the rustling, rain-wet ways of the spruce wood, where we were picking gum after a day of showers. When we had picked enough, we sat down on the moss-grown stones at the end of a long arcade, where it opened out on the harvest-golden valley below us, our jaws exercising themselves vigorously on the spoil of our climbings. We were never allowed to chew gum in school or in company, but in wood and field, orchard and hayloft, such rules were in abeyance.

"My Aunt Jane used to say it wasn't polite to chew gum anywhere," said Peter rather ruefully.

"I don't suppose your Aunt Jane knew all the rules of etiquette," said Felicity, designing to crush Peter with a big word, borrowed from the Family Guide. But Peter was not to be so crushed. He had in him a certain toughness of fibre, that would have been proof against a whole dictionary.

"She did, too," he retorted. "My Aunt Jane was a real lady, even if she was only a Craig. She knew all those rules and she kept them when there was nobody round to see her, just the same as when any one was. And she was smart. If father had had half her git-up-and-git I wouldn't be a hired boy to-day."

"Have you any idea where your father is?" asked Dan.

"No," said Peter indifferently. "The last we heard of him he was in the Maine lumber woods. But that was three years ago. I don't know where he is now, and," added Peter deliberately, taking his gum from his mouth to make his statement more impressive, "I don't care."

"Oh, Peter, that sounds dreadful," said Cecily. "Your own father!"

"Well," said Peter defiantly, "if your own father had run away when you was a baby, and left your mother to earn her living by washing and working out, I guess you wouldn't care much about him either."

"Perhaps your father may come home some of these days with a huge fortune," suggested the Story Girl.

"Perhaps pigs may whistle, but they've poor mouths for it," was all the answer Peter deigned to this charming suggestion.

"There goes Mr. Campbell down the road," said Dan. "That's his new mare. Isn't she a dandy? She's got a skin like black satin. He calls her Betty Sherman."

"I don't think it's very nice to call a horse after your own grandmother," said Felicity.

"Betty Sherman would have thought it a compliment," said the Story Girl.

"Maybe she would. She couldn't have been very nice herself, or she would never have gone and asked a man to marry her," said Felicity.

"Why not?"

"Goodness me, it was dreadful! Would YOU do such a thing yourself?"

"Well, I don't know," said the Story Girl, her eyes gleaming with impish laughter. "If I wanted him DREADFULLY, and HE wouldn't do the asking, perhaps I would."

"I'd rather die an old maid forty times over," exclaimed Felicity.

"Nobody as pretty as you will ever be an old maid, Felicity," said Peter, who never put too fine an edge on his compliments.

Felicity tossed her golden tressed head and tried to look angry, but made a dismal failure of it.

"It wouldn't be ladylike to ask any one to marry you, you know," argued Cecily.

"I don't suppose the Family Guide would think so," agreed the Story Girl lazily, with some sarcasm in her voice. The Story Girl never held the Family Guide in such reverence as did Felicity and Cecily. They pored over the "etiquette column" every week, and could have told you on demand, just exactly what kind of gloves should be worn at a wedding, what you should say when introducing or being introduced, and how you ought to look when your best young man came to see you.

"They say Mrs. Richard Cook asked HER husband to marry her," said Dan.

"Uncle Roger says she didn't exactly ask him, but she helped the lame dog over the stile so slick that Richard was engaged to her before he knew what had happened to him," said the Story Girl. "I know a story about Mrs. Richard Cook's grandmother. She was one of those women who are always saying 'I told you so—'"

"Take notice, Felicity," said Dan aside.

"—And she was very stubborn. Soon after she was married she and her husband quarrelled about an apple tree they had planted in their orchard. The label was lost. He said it was a Fameuse and she declared it was a Yellow Transparent. They fought over it till the neighbours came out to listen. Finally he got so angry that he told her to shut up. They didn't have any Family Guide in those days, so he didn't know it wasn't polite to say shut up to your wife. I suppose she thought she would teach him manners, for would you believe it? That woman did shut up, and never spoke one single word to her husband for five years. And then, in five years' time, the tree bore apples, and they WERE Yellow Transparents. And then she spoke at last. She said, 'I told you so.'"

"And did she talk to him after that as usual?" asked Sara Ray.

"Oh, yes, she was just the same as she used to be," said the Story Girl wearily. "But that doesn't belong to the story. It stops when she spoke at last. You're never satisfied to leave a story where it should stop, Sara Ray."

"Well, I always like to know what happens afterwards," said Sara Ray.

"Uncle Roger says he wouldn't want a wife he could never quarrel with," remarked Dan. "He says it would be too tame a life for him."

"I wonder if Uncle Roger will always stay a bachelor," said Cecily.

"He seems real happy," observed Peter.

"Ma says that it's all right as long as he is a bachelor because he won't take any one," said Felicity, "but if he wakes up some day and finds he is an old bachelor because he can't get any one it'll have a very different flavour."

"If your Aunt Olivia was to up and get married what would your Uncle Roger do for a housekeeper?" asked Peter.

"Oh, but Aunt Olivia will never be married now," said Felicity. "Why, she'll be twenty-nine next January."

"Well, o' course, that's pretty old," admitted Peter, "but she might find some one who wouldn't mind that, seeing she's so pretty."

"It would be awful splendid and exciting to have a wedding in the family, wouldn't it?" said Cecily. "I've never seen any one married, and I'd just love to. I've been to four funerals, but not to one single wedding."

"I've never even got to a funeral," said Sara Ray gloomily.

"There's the wedding veil of the proud princess," said Cecily, pointing to a long drift of filmy vapour in the southwestern sky.

"And look at that sweet pink cloud below it," added Felicity.

"Maybe that little pink cloud is a dream, getting all ready to float down into somebody's sleep," suggested the Story Girl.

"I had a perfectly awful dream last night," said Cecily, with a shudder of remembrance. "I dreamed I was on a desert island inhabited by tigers and natives with two heads."

"Oh!" the Story Girl looked at Cecily half reproachfully. "Why couldn't you tell it better than that? If I had such a dream I could tell it so that everybody else would feel as if they had dreamed it, too."

"Well, I'm not you," countered Cecily, "and I wouldn't want to frighten any one as I was frightened. It was an awful dream—but it was kind of interesting, too."

"I've had some real int'resting dreams," said Peter, "but I can't remember them long. I wish I could."

"Why don't you write them down?" suggested the Story Girl. "Oh—" she turned upon us a face illuminated with a sudden inspiration. "I've an idea. Let us each get an exercise book and write down all our dreams, just as we dream them. We'll see who'll have the most interesting collection. And we'll have them to read and laugh over when we're old and gray."

Instantly we all saw ourselves and each other by inner vision, old and gray—all but the Story Girl. We could not picture her as old. Always, as long as she lived, so it seemed to us, must she have sleek brown curls, a voice like the sound of a harpstring in the wind, and eyes that were stars of eternal youth.

CHAPTER XXII.
THE DREAM BOOKS

The next day the Story Girl coaxed Uncle Roger to take her to Markdale, and there she bought our dream books. They were ten cents apiece, with ruled pages and mottled green covers. My own lies open beside me as I write, its yellowed pages inscribed with the visions that haunted my childish slumbers on those nights of long ago.

On the cover is pasted a lady's visiting card, on which is written, "The Dream Book of Beverley King." Cecily had a packet of visiting cards which she was hoarding against the day when she would be grown up and could put the calling etiquette of the Family Guide into practice; but she generously gave us all one apiece for the covers of our dream books.

As I turn the pages and glance over the (——) records, each one beginning, "Last night I dreamed," the past comes very vividly back to me. I see that bowery orchard, shining in memory with a soft glow of beauty—"the light that never was on land or sea,"—where we sat on those September evenings and wrote down our dreams, when the cares of the day were over and there was nothing to interfere with the pleasing throes of composition. Peter—Dan—Felix—Cecily—Felicity—Sara Ray—the Story Girl—they are all around me once more, in the sweet-scented, fading grasses, each with open dream books and pencil in hand, now writing busily, now staring fixedly into space in search of some elusive word or phrase which might best describe the indescribable. I hear their laughing voices, I see their bright, unclouded eyes. In this little, old book, filled with cramped, boyish writing, there is a spell of white magic that sets the years at naught. Beverley King is a boy once more, writing down his dreams in the old King orchard on the homestead hill, blown over by musky winds.

Opposite to him sits the Story Girl, with her scarlet rosetted head, her beautiful bare feet crossed before her, one slender hand propping her high, white brow, on either side of which fall her glossy curls.

There, to the right, is sweet Cecily of the dear, brown eyes, with a little bloated dictionary beside her—for you dream of so many things you can't spell, or be expected to spell, when you are only eleven. Next to her sits Felicity, beautiful, and conscious that she is beautiful, with hair of spun sunshine, and sea-blue eyes, and all the roses of that vanished summer abloom in her cheeks.

Peter is beside her, of course, sprawled flat on his stomach among the grasses, one hand clutching his black curls, with his dream book on a small, round stone before him—for only so can Peter compose at all, and even then he finds it hard work. He can handle a hoe more deftly than a pencil, and his spelling, even with all his frequent appeals to Cecily, is a fearful and wonderful thing. As for punctuation, he never attempts it, beyond an occasion period, jotted down whenever he happens to think of it, whether in the right place or not. The Story Girl goes over his dreams after he has written them out, and puts in the commas and semicolons, and straightens out the sentences.

Felix sits on the right of the Story Girl, fat and stodgy, grimly in earnest even over dreams. He writes with his knees stuck up to form a writing-desk, and he always frowns fiercely the whole time.

Dan, like Peter, writes lying down flat, but with his back towards us; and he has a dismal habit of groaning aloud, writhing his whole body, and digging his toes into the grass, when he cannot turn a sentence to suit him.

Sara Ray is at his left. There is seldom anything to be said of Sara except to tell where she is. Like Tennyson's Maud, in one respect at least, Sara is splendidly null.

Well, there we sit and write in our dream books, and Uncle Roger passes by and accuses us of being up to dev—to very bad mischief.

Each of us was very anxious to possess the most exciting record; but we were an honourable little crew, and I do not think anything was ever written down in those dream books which had not really been dreamed. We had expected that the Story Girl would eclipse us all in the matter of dreams; but, at least in the beginning, her dreams were no more remarkable than those of the rest of us. In dreamland we were all equal. Cecily, indeed, seemed to have the most decided talent for dramatic dreams. That meekest and mildest of girls was in the habit of dreaming truly terrible things. Almost every night battle, murder, or sudden death played some part in her visions. On the other hand, Dan, who was a somewhat truculent fellow, addicted to the perusal of lurid dime novels which he borrowed from the other boys in school, dreamed dreams of such a peaceful and pastoral character that he was quite disgusted with the resulting tame pages of his dream book.

But if the Story Girl could not dream anything more wonderful than the rest of us, she scored when it came to the telling. To hear her tell a dream was as good—or as bad—as dreaming it yourself.

As far as writing them down was concerned, I believe that I, Beverley King, carried off the palm. I was considered to possess a pretty knack of composition. But the Story Girl went me one better even there, because, having inherited something of her father's talent for drawing, she illustrated her dreams with sketches that certainly caught the spirit of them, whatever might be said of their technical excellence. She had an especial knack for drawing monstrosities; and I vividly recall the picture of an enormous and hideous lizard, looking like a reptile of the pterodactyl period, which she had dreamed of seeing crawl across the roof of the house. On another occasion she had a frightful dream—at least, it seemed frightful while she told us and described the dreadful feeling it had given her—of being chased around the parlour by the ottoman, which made faces at her. She drew a picture of the grimacing ottoman on the margin of her dream book which so scared Sara Ray when she beheld it that she cried all the way home, and insisted on sleeping that night with Judy Pineau lest the furniture take to pursuing her also.

Sara Ray's own dreams never amounted to much. She was always in trouble of some sort—couldn't get her hair braided, or her shoes on the right feet. Consequently, her dream book was very monotonous. The only thing worth mentioning in the way of dreams that Sara Ray ever achieved was when she dreamed that she went up in a balloon and fell out.

"I expected to come down with an awful thud," she said shuddering, "but I lit as light as a feather and woke right up."

"If you hadn't woke up you'd have died," said Peter with a dark significance. "If you dream of falling and DON'T wake you DO land with a thud and it kills you. That's what happens to people who die in their sleep."

"How do you know?" asked Dan skeptically. "Nobody who died in his sleep could ever tell it."

"My Aunt Jane told me so," said Peter.

"I suppose that settles it," said Felicity disagreeably.

"You always say something nasty when I mention my Aunt Jane," said Peter reproachfully.

"What did I say that was nasty?" cried Felicity. "I didn't say a single thing."

"Well, it sounded nasty," said Peter, who knew that it is the tone that makes the music.

"What did your Aunt Jane look like?" asked Cecily sympathetically. "Was she pretty?"

"No," conceded Peter reluctantly, "she wasn't pretty—but she looked like the woman in that picture the Story Girl's father sent her last week—the one with the shiny ring round her head and the baby in her lap. I've seen

Aunt Jane look at me just like that woman looks at her baby. Ma never looks so. Poor ma is too busy washing. I wish I could dream of my Aunt Jane. I never do."

"'Dream of the dead, you'll hear of the living,'" quoted Felix oracularly.

"I dreamed last night that I threw a lighted match into that keg of gunpowder in Mr. Cook's store at Markdale," said Peter. "It blew up—and everything blew up—and they fished me out of the mess—but I woke up before I'd time to find out if I was killed or not."

"One is so apt to wake up just as things get interesting," remarked the Story Girl discontentedly.

"I dreamed last night that I had really truly curly hair," said Cecily mournfully. "And oh, I was so happy! It was dreadful to wake up and find it as straight as ever."

Felix, that sober, solid fellow, dreamed constantly of flying through the air. His descriptions of his aerial flights over the tree-tops of dreamland always filled us with envy. None of the rest of us could ever compass such a dream, not even the Story Girl, who might have been expected to dream of flying if anybody did. Felix had a knack of dreaming anyhow, and his dream book, while suffering somewhat in comparison of literary style, was about the best of the lot when it came to subject matter. Cecily's might be more dramatic, but Felix's was more amusing. The dream which we all counted his masterpiece was the one in which a menagerie had camped in the orchard and the rhinoceros chased Aunt Janet around and around the Pulpit Stone, but turned into an inoffensive pig when it was on the point of catching her.

Felix had a sick spell soon after we began our dream books, and Aunt Janet essayed to cure him by administering a dose of liver pills which Elder Frewen had assured her were a cure-all for every disease the flesh is heir to. But Felix flatly refused to take liver pills; Mexican Tea he would drink, but liver pills he would not take, in spite of his own suffering and Aunt Janet's commands and entreaties. I could not understand his antipathy to the insignificant little white pellets, which were so easy to swallow; but he explained the matter to us in the orchard when he had recovered his usual health and spirits.

"I was afraid to take the liver pills for fear they'd prevent me from dreaming," he said. "Don't you remember old Miss Baxter in Toronto, Bev? And how she told Mrs. McLaren that she was subject to terrible dreams, and finally she took two liver pills and never had any more dreams after that. I'd rather have died than risk it," concluded Felix solemnly.

"I'd an exciting dream last night for once," said Dan triumphantly. "I dreamt old Peg Bowen chased me. I thought I was up to her house and she took after me. You bet I scooted. And she caught me—yes, sir! I felt her skinny hand reach out and clutch my shoulder. I let out a screech—and woke up."

"I should think you did screech," said Felicity. "We heard you clean over into our room."

"I hate to dream of being chased because I can never run," said Sara Ray with a shiver. "I just stand rooted to the ground—and see it coming—and can't stir. It don't sound much written out, but it's awful to go through. I'm sure I hope I'll never dream Peg Bowen chases me. I'll die if I do."

"I wonder what Peg Bowen would really do to a fellow if she caught him," speculated Dan.

"Peg Bowen doesn't need to catch you to do things to you," said Peter ominously. "She can put ill-luck on you just by looking at you—and she will if you offend her."

"I don't believe that," said the Story Girl airily.

"Don't you? All right, then! Last summer she called at Lem Hill's in Markdale, and he told her to clear out or he'd set the dog on her. Peg cleared out, and she went across his pasture, muttering to herself and throwing her arms round. And next day his very best cow took sick and died. How do you account for that?"

"It might have happened anyhow," said the Story Girl—somewhat less assuredly, though.

"It might. But I'd just as soon Peg Bowen didn't look at MY cows," said Peter.

"As if you had any cows!" giggled Felicity.

"I'm going to have cows some day," said Peter, flushing. "I don't mean to be a hired boy all my life. I'll have a farm of my own and cows and everything. You'll see if I won't."

"I dreamed last night that we opened the blue chest," said the Story Girl, "and all the things were there—the blue china candlestick—only it was brass in the dream—and the fruit basket with the apple on it, and the wedding dress, and the embroidered petticoat. And we were laughing, and trying the things on, and having such fun. And Rachel Ward herself came and looked at us—so sad and reproachful—and we all felt ashamed, and I began to cry, and woke up crying."

"I dreamed last night that Felix was thin," said Peter, laughing. "He did look so queer. His clothes just hung loose, and he was going round trying to hold them on."

Everybody thought this was funny, except Felix. He would not speak to Peter for two days because of it. Felicity also got into trouble because of her dreams. One night she woke up, having just had a very exciting dream; but she went to sleep again, and in the morning she could not remember the dream at all. Felicity determined she would never let another dream get away from her in such a fashion; and the next time she wakened in the night—having dreamed that she was dead and buried—she promptly arose, lighted a candle, and proceeded to write the dream down then and there. While so employed she contrived to upset the candle and set fire to her nightgown—a brand-new one, trimmed with any quantity of crocheted lace. A huge hole was burned in it, and when Aunt Janet discovered it she lifted up her voice with no uncertain sound. Felicity had never received a sharper scolding. But she took it very philosophically. She was used to her mother's bitter tongue, and she was not unduly sensitive.

"Anyhow, I saved my dream," she said placidly.

And that, of course, was all that really mattered. Grown people were so strangely oblivious to the truly important things of life. Material for new garments, of night or day, could be bought in any shop for a trifling sum and made up out of hand. But if a dream escape you, in what market-place the wide world over can you hope to regain it? What coin of earthly minting will ever buy back for you that lost and lovely vision?

CHAPTER XXIII.
SUCH STUFF AS DREAMS ARE MADE ON

Peter took Dan and me aside one evening, as we were on our way to the orchard with our dream books, saying significantly that he wanted our advice. Accordingly, we went round to the spruce wood, where the girls would not see us to the rousing of their curiosity, and then Peter told us of his dilemma.

"Last night I dreamed I was in church," he said. "I thought it was full of people, and I walked up the aisle to your pew and set down, as unconcerned as a pig on ice. And then I found that I hadn't a stitch of clothes on—NOT ONE BLESSED STITCH. Now"—Peter dropped his voice—"what is bothering me is this—would it be proper to tell a dream like that before the girls?"

I was of the opinion that it would be rather questionable; but Dan vowed he didn't see why. HE'D tell it quick as any other dream. There was nothing bad in it.

"But they're your own relations," said Peter. "They're no relation to me, and that makes a difference. Besides, they're all such ladylike girls. I guess I'd better not risk it. I'm pretty sure Aunt Jane wouldn't think it was proper to tell such a dream. And I don't want to offend Fel—any of them."

So Peter never told that dream, nor did he write it down. Instead, I remember seeing in his dream book, under the date of September fifteenth, an entry to this effect:—

"Last nite i dremed a drem. it wasent a polit drem so i won't rite it down."

The girls saw this entry but, to their credit be it told, they never tried to find out what the "drem" was. As Peter said, they were "ladies" in the best and truest sense of that much abused appellation. Full of fun and frolic and mischief they were, with all the defects of their qualities and all the wayward faults of youth. But no indelicate thought or vulgar word could have been shaped or uttered in their presence. Had any of us boys ever been guilty of such, Cecily's pale face would have coloured with the blush of outraged purity, Felicity's golden head would have lifted itself in the haughty indignation of insulted womanhood, and the Story Girl's splendid eyes would have flashed with such anger and scorn as would have shrivelled the very soul of the wretched culprit.

Dan was once guilty of swearing. Uncle Alec whipped him for it—the only time he ever so punished any of his children. But it was because Cecily cried all night that Dan was filled with saving remorse and repentance. He vowed next day to Cecily that he would never swear again, and he kept his word.

All at once the Story Girl and Peter began to forge ahead in the matter of dreaming. Their dreams suddenly became so lurid and dreadful and picturesque that it was hard for the rest of us to believe that they were not painting the lily rather freely in their accounts of them. But the Story Girl was the soul of honour; and Peter, early in life, had had his feet set in the path of truthfulness by his Aunt Jane and had never been known to stray from it. When they assured us solemnly that their dreams all happened exactly as they described them we were compelled to believe them. But there was something up, we felt sure of that. Peter and the Story Girl certainly had a secret between them, which they kept for a whole fortnight. There was no finding it out from the Story Girl. She had a knack of keeping secrets, anyhow; and, moreover, all that fortnight she was strangely cranky and petulant, and we found it was not wise to tease her. She was not well, so Aunt Olivia told Aunt Janet.

"I don't know what is the matter with the child," said the former anxiously. "She hasn't seemed like herself the past two weeks. She complains of headache, and she has no appetite, and she is a dreadful colour. I'll have to see a doctor about her if she doesn't get better soon."

"Give her a good dose of Mexican Tea and try that first," said Aunt Janet. "I've saved many a doctor's bill in my family by using Mexican Tea."

The Mexican Tea was duly administered, but produced no improvement in the condition of the Story Girl, who, however, went on dreaming after a fashion which soon made her dream book a veritable curiosity of literature.

"If we can't soon find out what makes Peter and the Story Girl dream like that, the rest of us might as well give up trying to write dream books," said Felix discontentedly.

Finally, we did find out. Felicity wormed the secret out of Peter by the employment of Delilah wiles, such as have been the undoing of many a miserable male creature since Samson's day. She first threatened that she would never speak to him again if he didn't tell her; and then she promised him that, if he did, she would let him walk beside her to and from Sunday School all the rest of the summer, and carry her books for her. Peter was not proof against this double attack. He yielded and told the secret.

I expected the Story Girl would overwhelm him with scorn and indignation. But she took it very coolly.

"I knew Felicity would get it out of him sometime," she said. "I think he has done well to hold out this long."

Peter and the Story Girl, so it appeared, had wooed wild dreams to their pillows by the simple device of eating rich, indigestible things before they went to bed. Aunt Olivia knew nothing about it, of course. She permitted them only a plain, wholesome lunch at bed-time. But during the day the Story Girl would smuggle upstairs various tidbits from the pantry, putting half in Peter's room and half in her own; and the result was these visions which had been our despair.

"Last night I ate a piece of mince pie," she said, "and a lot of pickles, and two grape jelly tarts. But I guess I overdid it, because I got real sick and couldn't sleep at all, so of course I didn't have any dreams. I should have stopped with the pie and pickles and left the tarts alone. Peter did, and he had an elegant dream that Peg Bowen caught him and put him on to boil alive in that big black pot that hangs outside her door. He woke up before the water got hot, though. Well, Miss Felicity, you're pretty smart. But how will you like to walk to Sunday School with a boy who wears patched trousers?"

"I won't have to," said Felicity triumphantly. "Peter is having a new suit made. It's to be ready by Saturday. I knew that before I promised."

Having discovered how to produce exciting dreams, we all promptly followed the example of Peter and the Story Girl.

"There is no chance for me to have any horrid dreams," lamented Sara Ray, "because ma won't let me having anything at all to eat before I go to bed. I don't think it's fair."

"Can't you hide something away through the day as we do?" asked Felicity.

"No." Sara shook her fawn-coloured head mournfully. "Ma always keeps the pantry locked, for fear Judy Pineau will treat her friends."

For a week we ate unlawful lunches and dreamed dreams after our own hearts—and, I regret to say, bickered and squabbled incessantly throughout the daytime, for our digestions went out of order and our tempers followed suit. Even the Story Girl and I had a fight—something that had never happened before. Peter was the only one who kept his normal poise. Nothing could upset that boy's stomach.

One night Cecily came into the pantry with a large cucumber, and proceeded to devour the greater part of it. The grown-ups were away that evening, attending a lecture at Markdale, so we ate our snacks openly, without any recourse to ways that were dark. I remember I supped that night off a solid hunk of fat pork, topped off with a slab of cold plum pudding.

"I thought you didn't like cucumber, Cecily," Dan remarked.

"Neither I do," said Cecily with a grimace. "But Peter says they're splendid for dreaming. He et one that night he had the dream about being caught by cannibals. I'd eat three cucumbers if I could have a dream like that."

Cecily finished her cucumber, and then drank a glass of milk, just as we heard the wheels of Uncle Alec's buggy rambling over the bridge in the hollow. Felicity quickly restored pork and pudding to their own places, and by the time Aunt Janet came in we were all in our respective beds. Soon the house was dark and silent. I was just dropping into an uneasy slumber when I heard a commotion in the girls' room across the hall.

Their door opened and through our own open door I saw Felicity's white-clad figure flit down the stairs to Aunt Janet's room. From the room she had left came moans and cries.

"Cecily's sick," said Dan, springing out of bed. "That cucumber must have disagreed with her."

In a few minutes the whole house was astir. Cecily was sick—very, very sick, there was no doubt of that. She was even worse than Dan had been when he had eaten the bad berries. Uncle Alec, tired as he was from his hard day's work and evening outing, was despatched for the doctor. Aunt Janet and Felicity administered all the homely remedies they could think of, but to no effect. Felicity told Aunt Janet of the cucumber, but Aunt Janet did not think the cucumber alone could be responsible for Cecily's alarming condition.

"Cucumbers are indigestible, but I never knew of them making any one as sick as this," she said anxiously. "What made the child eat a cucumber before going to bed? I didn't think she liked them."

"It was that wretched Peter," sobbed Felicity indignantly. "He told her it would make her dream something extra."

"What on earth did she want to dream for?" demanded Aunt Janet in bewilderment.

"Oh, to have something worth while to write in her dream book, ma. We all have dream books, you know, and every one wants their own to be the most exciting—and we've been eating rich things to make us dream—and it does—but if Cecily—oh, I'll never forgive myself," said Felicity, incoherently, letting all kinds of cats out of the bag in her excitement and alarm.

"Well, I wonder what on earth you young ones will do next," said Aunt Janet in the helpless tone of a woman who gives it up.

Cecily was no better when the doctor came. Like Aunt Janet, he declared that cucumbers alone would not have made her so ill; but when he found out that she had drunk a glass of milk also the mystery was solved.

"Why, milk and cucumbers together make a rank poison," he said. "No wonder the child is sick. There—there now—" seeing the alarmed faces around him, "don't be frightened. As old Mrs. Fraser says, 'It's no deidly.' It won't kill her, but she'll probably be a pretty miserable girl for two or three days."

She was. And we were all miserable in company. Aunt Janet investigated the whole affair and the matter of our dream books was aired in family conclave. I do not know which hurt our feelings most—the scolding we got from Aunt Janet, or the ridicule which the other grown-ups, especially Uncle Roger, showered on us. Peter received an extra "setting down," which he considered rank injustice.

"I didn't tell Cecily to drink the milk, and the cucumber alone wouldn't have hurt her," he grumbled. Cecily was able to be out with us again that day, so Peter felt that he might venture on a grumble. "'Sides, she coaxed me to tell her what would be good for dreams. I just told her as a favour. And now your Aunt Janet blames me for the whole trouble."

"And Aunt Janet says we are never to have anything to eat before we go to bed after this except plain bread and milk," said Felix sadly.

"They'd like to stop us from dreaming altogether if they could," said the Story Girl wrathfully.

"Well, anyway, they can't prevent us from growing up," consoled Dan.

"We needn't worry about the bread and milk rule," added Felicity. "Ma made a rule like that once before, and kept it for a week, and then we just slipped back to the old way. That will be what will happen this time, too. But of course we won't be able to get any more rich things for supper, and our dreams will be pretty flat after this."

"Well, let's go down to the Pulpit Stone and I'll tell you a story I know," said the Story Girl.

We went—and straightway drank of the waters of forgetfulness. In a brief space we were laughing right merrily, no longer remembering our wrongs at the hands of those cruel grown-ups. Our laughter echoed back from the barns and the spruce grove, as if elfin denizens of upper air were sharing in our mirth.

Presently, also, the laughter of the grown-ups mingled with ours. Aunt Olivia and Uncle Roger, Aunt Janet and Uncle Alec, came strolling through the orchard and joined our circle, as they sometimes did when the toil of the day was over, and the magic time 'twixt light and dark brought truce of care and labour. 'Twas then we liked our grown-ups best, for then they seemed half children again. Uncle Roger and Uncle Alec lolled in the grass like boys; Aunt Olivia, looking more like a pansy than ever in the prettiest dress of pale purple print, with a knot of yellow ribbon at her throat, sat with her arm about Cecily and smiled on us all; and Aunt Janet's motherly face lost its every-day look of anxious care.

The Story Girl was in great fettle that night. Never had her tales sparkled with such wit and archness.

"Sara Stanley," said Aunt Olivia, shaking her finger at her after a side-splitting yarn, "if you don't watch out you'll be famous some day."

"These funny stories are all right," said Uncle Roger, "but for real enjoyment give me something with a creep in it. Sara, tell us that story of the Serpent Woman I heard you tell one day last summer."

The Story Girl began it glibly. But before she had gone far with it, I, who was sitting beside her, felt an unaccountable repulsion creeping over me. For the first time since I had known her I wanted to draw away from the Story Girl. Looking around on the faces of the group, I saw that they all shared my feeling. Cecily had put her hands over her eyes. Peter was staring at the Story Girl with a fascinated, horror-strickened gaze. Aunt Olivia was pale and troubled. All looked as if they were held prisoners in the bonds of a fearsome spell which they would gladly break but could not.

It was not our Story Girl who sat there, telling that weird tale in a sibilant, curdling voice. She had put on a new personality like a garment, and that personality was a venomous, evil, loathly thing. I would rather have died than have touched the slim, brown wrist on which she supported herself. The light in her narrowed orbs was the cold, merciless gleam of the serpent's eye. I felt frightened of this unholy creature who had suddenly come in our dear Story Girl's place.

When the tale ended there was a brief silence. Then Aunt Janet said severely, but with a sigh of relief,

"Little girls shouldn't tell such horrible stories."

This truly Aunt Janetian remark broke the spell. The grown-ups laughed, rather shakily, and the Story Girl—our own dear Story Girl once more, and no Serpent Woman—said protestingly,

"Well, Uncle Roger asked me to tell it. I don't like telling such stories either. They make me feel dreadful. Do you know, for just a little while, I felt exactly like a snake."

"You looked like one," said Uncle Roger. "How on earth do you do it?"

"I can't explain how I do it," said the Story Girl perplexedly. "It just does itself."

Genius can never explain how it does it. It would not be genius if it could. And the Story Girl had genius.

As we left the orchard I walked along behind Uncle Roger and Aunt Olivia.

"That was an uncanny exhibition for a girl of fourteen, you know, Roger," said Aunt Olivia musingly. "What is in store for that child?"

"Fame," said Uncle Roger. "If she ever has a chance, that is, and I suppose her father will see to that. At least, I hope he will. You and I, Olivia, never had our chance. I hope Sara will have hers."

This was my first inkling of what I was to understand more fully in later years. Uncle Roger and Aunt Olivia had both cherished certain dreams and ambitions in youth, but circumstances had denied them their "chance" and those dreams had never been fulfilled.

"Some day, Olivia," went on Uncle Roger, "you and I may find ourselves the aunt and uncle of the foremost actress of her day. If a girl of fourteen can make a couple of practical farmers and a pair of matter-of-fact housewives half believe for ten minutes that she really is a snake, what won't she be able to do when she is thirty? Here, you," added Uncle Roger, perceiving me, "cut along and get off to your bed. And mind you don't eat cucumbers and milk before you go."

CHAPTER XXIV.
THE BEWITCHMENT OF PAT

We were all in the doleful dumps—at least, all we "young fry" were, and even the grown-ups were sorry and condescended to take an interest in our troubles. Pat, our own, dear, frolicsome Paddy, was sick again—very, very sick.

On Friday he moped and refused his saucer of new milk at milking time. The next morning he stretched himself down on the platform by Uncle Roger's back door, laid his head on his black paws, and refused to take any notice of anything or anybody. In vain we stroked and entreated and brought him tidbits. Only when the Story Girl caressed him did he give one plaintive little mew, as if to ask piteously why she could not do something for him. At that Cecily and Felicity and Sara Ray all began crying, and we boys felt choky. Indeed, I caught Peter behind Aunt Olivia's dairy later in the day, and if ever a boy had been crying I vow that boy was Peter. Nor did he deny it when I taxed him with it, but he would not give in that he was crying about Paddy. Nonsense!

"What were you crying for, then?" I said.

"I'm crying because—because my Aunt Jane is dead," said Peter defiantly.

"But your Aunt Jane died two years ago," I said skeptically.

"Well, ain't that all the more reason for crying?" retorted Peter. "I've had to do without her for two years, and that's worse than if it had just been a few days."

"I believe you were crying because Pat is so sick," I said firmly.

"As if I'd cry about a cat!" scoffed Peter. And he marched off whistling.

Of course we had tried the lard and powder treatment again, smearing Pat's paws and sides liberally. But to our dismay, Pat made no effort to lick it off.

"I tell you he's a mighty sick cat," said Peter darkly. "When a cat don't care what he looks like he's pretty far gone."

"If we only knew what was the matter with him we might do something," sobbed the Story Girl, stroking her poor pet's unresponsive head.

"I could tell you what's the matter with him, but you'd only laugh at me," said Peter.

We all looked at him.

"Peter Craig, what do you mean?" asked Felicity.

"'Zackly what I say."

"Then, if you know what is the matter with Paddy, tell us," commanded the Story Girl, standing up. She said it quietly; but Peter obeyed. I think he would have obeyed if she, in that tone and with those eyes, had ordered him to cast himself into the depths of the sea. I know I should.

"He's BEWITCHED—that's what's the matter with him," said Peter, half defiantly, half shamefacedly.

"Bewitched? Nonsense!"

"There now, what did I tell you?" complained Peter.

The Story Girl looked at Peter, at the rest of us, and then at poor Pat.

"How could he be bewitched?" she asked irresolutely, "and who could bewitch him?"

"I don't know HOW he was bewitched," said Peter. "I'd have to be a witch myself to know that. But Peg Bowen bewitched him."

"Nonsense!" said the Story Girl again.

"All right," said Peter. "You don't have to believe me."

"If Peg Bowen could bewitch anything—and I don't believe she could— why should she bewitch Pat?" asked the Story Girl. "Everybody here and at Uncle Alec's is always kind to her."

"I'll tell you why," said Peter. "Thursday afternoon, when you fellows were all in school, Peg Bowen came here. Your Aunt Olivia gave her a lunch—a good one. You may laugh at the notion of Peg being a witch, but I notice your folks are always awful good to her when she comes, and awful careful never to offend her."

"Aunt Olivia would be good to any poor creature, and so would mother," said Felicity. "And of course nobody wants to offend Peg, because she is spiteful, and she once set fire to a man's barn in Markdale when he offended her. But she isn't a witch—that's ridiculous."

"All right. But wait till I tell you. When Peg Bowen was leaving Pat stretched out on the steps. She tramped on his tail. You know Pat doesn't like to have his tail meddled with. He slewed himself round and clawed her bare foot. If you'd just seen the look she gave him you'd know whether she was a witch or not. And she went off down the lane, muttering and throwing her hands round, just like she did in Lem Hill's cow pasture. She put a spell on Pat, that's what she did. He was sick the next morning."

We looked at each other in miserable, perplexed silence. We were only children—and we believed that there had been such things as witches once upon a time—and Peg Bowen WAS an eerie creature.

"If that's so—though I can't believe it—we can't do anything," said the Story Girl drearily. "Pat must die."

Cecily began to weep afresh.

"I'd do anything to save Pat's life," she said. "I'd BELIEVE anything."

"There's nothing we can do," said Felicity impatiently.

"I suppose," sobbed Cecily, "we might go to Peg Bowen and ask her to forgive Pat and take the spell off him. She might, if we apologized real humble."

At first we were appalled by the suggestion. We didn't believe that Peg Bowen was a witch. But to go to her—to seek her out in that mysterious woodland retreat of hers which was invested with all the terrors of the unknown! And that this suggestion should come from timid Cecily, of all people! But then, there was poor Pat!

"Would it do any good?" said the Story Girl desperately. "Even if she did make Pat sick I suppose it would only make her crosser if we went and accused her of bewitching him. Besides, she didn't do anything of the sort."

But there was some uncertainty in the Story Girl's voice.

"It wouldn't do any harm to try," said Cecily. "If she didn't make him sick it won't matter if she is cross."

"It won't matter to Pat, but it might to the one who goes to her," said Felicity. "She isn't a witch, but she's a spiteful old woman, and goodness knows what she'd do to us if she caught us. I'm scared of Peg Bowen, and I don't care who knows it. Ever since I can mind ma's been saying, 'If you're not good Peg Bowen will catch you.'"

"If I thought she really made Pat sick and could make him better, I'd try to pacify her somehow," said the Story Girl decidedly. "I'm frightened of her, too—but just look at poor, darling Paddy."

We looked at Paddy who continued to stare fixedly before him with unwinking eyes. Uncle Roger came out and looked at him also, with what seemed to us positively brutal unconcern.

"I'm afraid it's all up with Pat," he said.

"Uncle Roger," said Cecily imploringly, "Peter says Peg Bowen has bewitched Pat for scratching her. Do you think it can be so?"

"Did Pat scratch Peg?" asked Uncle Roger, with a horror-stricken face. "Dear me! Dear me! That mystery is solved. Poor Pat!"

Uncle Roger nodded his head, as if resigning himself and Pat to the worst.

"Do you really think Peg Bowen is a witch, Uncle Roger?" demanded the Story Girl incredulously.

"Do I think Peg Bowen is a witch? My dear Sara, what do YOU think of a woman who can turn herself into a black cat whenever she likes? Is she a witch? Or is she not? I leave it to you."

"Can Peg Bowen turn herself into a black cat?" asked Felix, staring.

"It's my belief that that is the least of Peg Bowen's accomplishments," answered Uncle Roger. "It's the easiest thing in the world for a witch to turn herself into any animal you choose to mention. Yes, Pat is bewitched—no doubt of that—not the least in the world."

"What are you telling those children such stuff for?" asked Aunt Olivia, passing on her way to the well.

"It's an irresistible temptation," answered Uncle Roger, strolling over to carry her pail.

"You can see your Uncle Roger believes Peg is a witch," said Peter.

"And you can see Aunt Olivia doesn't," I said, "and I don't either."

"See here," said the Story Girl resolutely, "I don't believe it, but there MAY be something in it. Suppose there is. The question is, what can we do?"

"I'll tell you what I'D do," said Peter. "I'd take a present for Peg, and ask her to make Pat well. I wouldn't let on I thought she'd made him sick. Then she couldn't be offended—and maybe she'd take the spell off."

"I think we'd better all give her something," said Felicity. "I'm willing to do that. But who's going to take the presents to her?"

"We must all go together," said the Story Girl.

"I won't," cried Sara Ray in terror. "I wouldn't go near Peg Bowen's house for the world, no matter who was with me."

"I've thought of a plan," said the Story Girl. "Let's all give her something, as Felicity says. And let us all go up to her place this evening, and if we see her outside we'll just go quietly and set the things down before her with the letter, and say nothing but come respectfully away."

"If she'll let us," said Dan significantly.

"Can Peg read a letter?" I asked.

"Oh, yes. Aunt Olivia says she is a good scholar. She went to school and was a smart girl until she became crazy. We'll write it very plain."

"What if we don't see her?" asked Felicity.

"We'll put the things on her doorstep then and leave them."

"She may be miles away over the country by this time," sighed Cecily, "and never find them until it's too late for Pat. But it's the only thing to do. What can we give her?"

"We mustn't offer her any money," said the Story Girl. "She's very indignant when any one does that. She says she isn't a beggar. But she'll take anything else. I shall give her my string of blue beads. She's fond of finery."

"I'll give her that sponge cake I made this morning," said Felicity. "I guess she doesn't get sponge cake very often."

"I've nothing but the rheumatism ring I got as a premium for selling needles last winter," said Peter. "I'll give her that. Even if she hasn't got rheumatism it's a real handsome ring. It looks like solid gold."

"I'll give her a roll of peppermint candy," said Felix.

"I'll give one of those little jars of cherry preserve I made," said Cecily.

"I won't go near her," quavered Sara Ray, "but I want to do something for Pat, and I'll send that piece of apple leaf lace I knit last week."

I decided to give the redoubtable Peg some apples from my birthday tree, and Dan declared he would give her a plug of tobacco.

"Oh, won't she be insulted?" exclaimed Felix, rather horrified.

"Naw," grinned Dan. "Peg chews tobacco like a man. She'd rather have it than your rubbishy peppermints, I can tell you. I'll run down to old Mrs. Sampson's and get a plug."

"Now, we must write the letter and take it and the presents to her right away, before it gets dark," said the Story Girl.

We adjourned to the granary to indite the important document, which the Story Girl was to compose.

"How shall I begin it?" she asked in perplexity. "It would never do to say, 'Dear Peg,' and 'Dear Miss Bowen' sounds too ridiculous."

"Besides, nobody knows whether she is Miss Bowen or not," said Felicity. "She went to Boston when she grew up, and some say she was married there and her husband deserted her, and that's why she went crazy. If she's married, she won't like being called Miss."

"Well, how am I to address her?" asked the Story Girl in despair.

Peter again came to the rescue with a practical suggestion.

"Begin it, 'Respected Madam,'" he said. "Ma has a letter a school trustee once writ to my Aunt Jane and that's how it begins."

"Respected Madam," wrote the Story Girl. "We want to ask a very great favour of you and we hope you will kindly grant it if you can. Our favourite cat, Paddy, is very sick, and we are afraid he is going to die. Do you think you could cure him? And will you please try? We are all so fond of him, and he is such a good cat, and has no bad habits. Of course, if any of us tramps on his tail he will scratch us, but you know a cat can't bear to have his tail tramped on. It's a very tender part of him, and it's his only way of preventing it, and he doesn't mean any harm. If you can cure Paddy for us we will always be very, very grateful to you. The accompanying small offerings are a testimonial of our respect and gratitude, and we entreat you to honour us by accepting them.

"Very respectfully yours,

"SARA STANLEY."

"I tell you that last sentence has a fine sound," said Peter admiringly.

"I didn't make that up," admitted the Story Girl honestly. "I read it somewhere and remembered it."

"I think it's TOO fine," criticized Felicity. "Peg Bowen won't know the meaning of such big words."

But it was decided to leave them in and we all signed the letter.

Then we got our "testimonials," and started on our reluctant journey to the domains of the witch. Sara Ray would not go, of course, but she volunteered to stay with Pat while we were away. We did not think it necessary to inform the grown-ups of our errand, or its nature. Grown-ups had such peculiar views. They might forbid our going at all—and they would certainly laugh at us.

Peg Bowen's house was nearly a mile away, even by the short cut past the swamp and up the wooded hill. We went down through the brook field and over the little plank bridge in the hollow, half lost in its surrounding sea of farewell summers. When we reached the green gloom of the woods beyond we began to feel frightened, but nobody would admit it. We walked very closely together, and we did not talk. When you are near the retreat of witches and folk of that ilk the less you say the better, for their feelings are so notoriously touchy. Of course, Peg wasn't a witch, but it was best to be on the safe side.

Finally we came to the lane which led directly to her abode. We were all very pale now, and our hearts were beating. The red September sun hung low between the tall spruces to the west. It did not look to me just right for a sun. In fact, everything looked uncanny. I wished our errand were well over.

A sudden bend in the lane brought us out to the little clearing where Peg's house was before we were half ready to see it. In spite of my fear I looked at it with some curiosity. It was a small, shaky building with a sagging roof, set amid a perfect jungle of weeds. To our eyes, the odd thing about it was that there was no entrance on the ground floor, as there should be in any respectable house. The only door was in the upper story, and was reached by a flight of rickety steps. There was no sign of life about the place except—sight of ill omen—a large black cat, sitting on the topmost step. We thought of Uncle Roger's gruesome hints. Could that black cat be Peg? Nonsense! But still—it didn't look like an ordinary cat. It was so large—and had such green, malicious eyes! Plainly, there was something out of the common about the beastie!

In a tense, breathless silence the Story Girl placed our parcels on the lowest step, and laid her letter on the top of the pile. Her brown fingers trembled and her face was very pale.

Suddenly the door above us opened, and Peg Bowen herself appeared on the threshold. She was a tall, sinewy old woman, wearing a short, ragged, drugget skirt which reached scantly below her knees, a scarlet print blouse, and a man's hat. Her feet, arms, and neck were bare, and she had a battered old clay pipe in her mouth. Her brown face was seamed with a hundred wrinkles, and her tangled, grizzled hair fell unkemptly over her shoulders. She was scowling, and her flashing black eyes held no friendly light.

We had borne up bravely enough hitherto, in spite of our inward, unconfessed quakings. But now our strained nerves gave way, and sheer panic seized us. Peter gave a little yelp of pure terror. We turned and fled across the clearing and into the woods. Down the long hill we tore, like mad, hunted creatures, firmly convinced that Peg Bowen was after us. Wild was that scamper, as nightmare-like as any recorded in our dream books. The Story Girl was in front of me, and I can recall the tremendous leaps she made over fallen logs and little spruce bushes, with her long brown curls streaming out behind her from their scarlet fillet. Cecily, behind me, kept gasping out the contradictory sentences, "Oh, Bev, wait for me," and "Oh, Bev, hurry, hurry!" More by blind instinct than anything else we kept together and found our way out of the woods. Presently we were in the field beyond the brook. Over us was a dainty sky of shell pink, placid cows were pasturing around us; the farewell summers nodded to us in the friendly breezes. We halted, with a glad realization that we were back in our own haunts and that Peg Bowen had not caught us.

"Oh, wasn't that an awful experience?" gasped Cecily, shuddering. "I wouldn't go through it again—I couldn't, not even for Pat."

"It come on a fellow so suddent," said Peter shamefacedly. "I think I could a-stood my ground if I'd known she was going to come out. But when she popped out like that I thought I was done for."

"We shouldn't have run," said Felicity gloomily. "It showed we were afraid of her, and that always makes her awful cross. She won't do a thing for Pat now."

"I don't believe she could do anything, anyway," said the Story Girl. "I think we've just been a lot of geese."

We were all, except Peter, more or less inclined to agree with her. And the conviction of our folly deepened when we reached the granary and found that Pat, watched over by the faithful Sara Ray, was no better. The Story Girl announced that she would take him into the kitchen and sit up all night with him.

"He sha'n't die alone, anyway," she said miserably, gathering his limp body up in her arms.

We did not think Aunt Olivia would give her permission to stay up; but Aunt Olivia did. Aunt Olivia really was a duck. We wanted to stay with her also, but Aunt Janet wouldn't hear of such a thing. She ordered us off to bed, saying that it was positively sinful in us to be so worked up over a cat. Five heart-broken children, who knew that there are many worse friends than dumb, furry folk, climbed Uncle Alec's stairs to bed that night.

"There's nothing we can do now, except pray God to make Pat better," said Cecily.

I must candidly say that her tone savoured strongly of a last resort; but this was owing more to early training than to any lack of faith on Cecily's part. She knew and we knew, that prayer was a solemn rite, not to be lightly held, nor degraded to common uses. Felicity voiced this conviction when she said,

"I don't believe it would be right to pray about a cat."

"I'd like to know why not," retorted Cecily, "God made Paddy just as much as He made you, Felicity King, though perhaps He didn't go to so much trouble. And I'm sure He's abler to help him than Peg Bowen. Anyhow, I'm going to pray for Pat with all my might and main, and I'd like to see you try to stop me. Of course I won't mix it up with more important things. I'll just tack it on after I've finished asking the blessings, but before I say amen."

More petitions than Cecily's were offered up that night on behalf of Paddy. I distinctly heard Felix—who always said his prayers in a loud whisper, owing to some lasting conviction of early life that God could not hear him if he did not pray audibly—mutter pleadingly, after the "important" part of his devotions was over, "Oh, God, please make Pat better by the morning. PLEASE do."

And I, even in these late years of irreverence for the dreams of youth, am not in the least ashamed to confess that when I knelt down to say my boyish prayer, I thought of our little furry comrade in his extremity, and prayed as reverently as I knew how for his healing. Then I went to sleep, comforted by the simple hope that the Great Father would, after "important things" were all attended to, remember poor Pat.

As soon as we were up the next morning we rushed off to Uncle Roger's. But we met Peter and the Story Girl in the lane, and their faces were as the faces of those who bring glad tidings upon the mountains.

"Pat's better," cried the Story Girl, blithe, triumphant. "Last night, just at twelve, he began to lick his paws. Then he licked himself all over and went to sleep, too, on the sofa. When I woke Pat was washing his face, and he has taken a whole saucerful of milk. Oh, isn't it splendid?"

"You see Peg Bowen did put a spell on him," said Peter, "and then she took it off."

"I guess Cecily's prayer had more to do with Pat's getting better than Peg Bowen," said Felicity. "She prayed for Pat over and over again. That is why he's better."

"Oh, all right," said Peter, "but I'd advise Pat not to scratch Peg Bowen again, that's all."

"I wish I knew whether it was the praying or Peg Bowen that cured Pat," said Felix in perplexity.

"I don't believe it was either of them," said Dan. "Pat just got sick and got better again of his own accord."

"I'm going to believe that it was the praying," said Cecily decidedly. "It's so much nicer to believe that God cured Pat than that Peg Bowen did."

"But you oughtn't to believe a thing just 'cause it would be more comfortable," objected Peter. "Mind you, I ain't saying God couldn't cure Pat. But nothing and nobody can't ever make me believe that Peg Bowen wasn't at the bottom of it all."

Thus faith, superstition, and incredulity strove together amongst us, as in all history.

CHAPTER XXV.
A CUP OF FAILURE

One warm Sunday evening in the moon of golden-rod, we all, grown-ups and children, were sitting in the orchard by the Pulpit Stone singing sweet old gospel hymns. We could all sing more or less, except poor Sara Ray, who had once despairingly confided to me that she didn't know what she'd ever do when she went to heaven, because she couldn't sing a note.

That whole scene comes out clearly for me in memory—the arc of primrose sky over the trees behind the old house, the fruit-laden boughs of the orchard, the bank of golden-rod, like a wave of sunshine, behind the Pulpit Stone, the nameless colour seen on a fir wood in a ruddy sunset. I can see Uncle Alec's tired, brilliant, blue eyes, Aunt Janet's wholesome, matronly face, Uncle Roger's sweeping blond beard and red cheeks, and Aunt Olivia's full-blown beauty. Two voices ring out for me above all others in the music that echoes through the halls of recollection. Cecily's sweet and silvery, and Uncle Alec's fine tenor. "If you're a King, you sing," was a Carlisle proverb in those days. Aunt Julia had been the flower of the flock in that respect and had become a noted concert singer. The world had never heard of the rest. Their music echoed only along the hidden ways of life, and served but to lighten the cares of the trivial round and common task.

That evening, after they tired of singing, our grown-ups began talking of their youthful days and doings.

This was always a keen delight to us small fry. We listened avidly to the tales of our uncles and aunts in the days when they, too—hard fact to realize—had been children. Good and proper as they were now, once, so it seemed, they had gotten into mischief and even had their quarrels and disagreements. On this particular evening Uncle Roger told many stories of Uncle Edward, and one in which the said Edward had preached sermons at the mature age of ten from the Pulpit Stone fired, as the sequel will show, the Story Girl's imagination.

"Can't I just see him at it now," said Uncle Roger, "leaning over that old boulder, his cheeks red and his eyes burning with excitement, banging the top of it as he had seen the ministers do in church. It wasn't cushioned, however, and he always bruised his hands in his self-forgetful earnestness. We thought him a regular wonder. We loved to hear him preach, but we didn't like to hear him pray, because he always insisted on praying for each of us by name, and it made us feel wretchedly uncomfortable, somehow.

Alec, do you remember how furious Julia was because Edward prayed one day that she might be preserved from vanity and conceit over her singing?"

"I should think I do," laughed Uncle Alec. "She was sitting right there where Cecily is now, and she got up at once and marched right out of the orchard, but at the gate she turned to call back indignantly, 'I guess you'd better wait till you've prayed the conceit out of yourself before you begin on me, Ned King. I never heard such stuck-up sermons as you preach.' Ned went on praying and never let on he heard her, but at the end of his prayer he wound up with 'Oh, God, I pray you to keep an eye on us all, but I pray you to pay particular attention to my sister Julia, for I think she needs it even more than the rest of us, world without end, Amen.'"

Our uncles roared with laughter over the recollection. We all laughed, indeed, especially over another tale in which Uncle Edward, leaning too far over the "pulpit" in his earnestness, lost his balance altogether and tumbled ingloriously into the grass below.

"He lit on a big Scotch thistle," said Uncle Roger, chuckling, "and besides that, he skinned his forehead on a stone. But he was determined to finish his sermon, and finish it he did. He climbed back into the pulpit, with the tears rolling over his cheeks, and preached for ten minutes longer, with sobs in his voice and drops of blood on his forehead. He was a plucky little beggar. No wonder he succeeded in life."

"And his sermons and prayers were always just about as outspoken as those Julia objected to," said Uncle Alec. "Well, we're all getting on in life and Edward is gray; but when I think of him I always see him a little, rosy, curly-headed chap, laying down the law to us from the Pulpit Stone. It seems like the other day that we were all here together, just as these children are, and now we are scattered everywhere. Julia in California, Edward in Halifax, Alan in South America, Felix and Felicity and Stephen gone to the land that is very far off."

There was a little space of silence; and then Uncle Alec began, in a low, impressive voice, to repeat the wonderful verses of the ninetieth Psalm— verses which were thenceforth bound up for us with the beauty of that night and the memories of our kindred. Very reverently we all listened to the majestic words.

"Lord, thou hast been our dwelling place in all generations. Before the mountains were brought forth, or ever thou hadst formed the earth and the world, even from everlasting to everlasting thou art God.... For a thousand years in thy sight are but as yesterday when it is past, and as a watch in the night.... For all our days are passed away in thy wrath; we spend our years as a tale that is told. The days of our years are threescore and ten; and if by reason of strength they be fourscore years yet is their strength, labour and sorrow; for it is soon cut off and we fly away.... So teach us to number our days that we may apply our hearts unto wisdom.... Oh, satisfy us early with thy mercy; that we may rejoice and be glad all our days.... And let the beauty of the Lord our God be upon us; and establish thou the work of our hands upon us; yea, the work of our hands establish thou it."

The dusk crept into the orchard like a dim, bewitching personality. You could see her—feel her—hear her. She tiptoed softly from tree to tree, ever drawing nearer. Presently her filmy wings hovered over us and through them gleamed the early stars of the autumn night.

The grown-ups rose reluctantly and strolled away; but we children lingered for a moment to talk over an idea the Story Girl broached—a good idea, we thought enthusiastically, and one that promised to add considerable spice to life.

We were on the lookout for some new amusement. Dream books had begun to pall. We no longer wrote in them very regularly, and our dreams were not what they used to be before the mischance of the cucumber. So the Story Girl's suggestion came pat to the psychological moment.

"I've thought of a splendid plan," she said. "It just flashed into my mind when the uncles were talking about Uncle Edward. And the beauty of it is we can play it on Sundays, and you know there are so few things it is proper to play on Sundays. But this is a Christian game, so it will be all right."

"It isn't like the religious fruit basket game, is it?" asked Cecily anxiously.

We had good reason to hope that it wasn't. One desperate Sunday afternoon, when we had nothing to read and the time seemed endless, Felix had suggested that we have a game of fruit-basket; only instead of taking the names of fruits, we were to take the names of Bible characters. This, he argued, would make it quite lawful and proper to play on Sunday. We, too, desirous of being convinced, also thought so; and for a merry hour Lazarus and Martha and Moses and Aaron and sundry other worthies of Holy Writ had a lively time of it in the King orchard. Peter having a Scriptural name of his own, did not want to take another; but we would not allow this, because it would give him an unfair advantage over the rest of us. It would be so much easier to call out your own name than fit your tongue to an unfamiliar one. So Peter retaliated by choosing Nebuchadnezzar, which no one could ever utter three times before Peter shrieked it out once.

In the midst of our hilarity, however, Uncle Alec and Aunt Janet came down upon us. It is best to draw a veil over what followed. Suffice it to say that the recollection gave point to Cecily's question.

"No, it isn't that sort of game at all," said the Story Girl. "It is this; each of you boys must preach a sermon, as Uncle Edward used to do. One of you next Sunday, and another the next, and so on. And whoever preaches the best sermon is to get a prize."

Dan promptly declared he wouldn't try to preach a sermon; but Peter, Felix and I thought the suggestion a very good one. Secretly, I believed I could cut quite a fine figure preaching a sermon.

"Who'll give the prize?" asked Felix.

"I will," said the Story Girl. "I'll give that picture father sent me last week."

As the said picture was an excellent copy of one of Landseer's stags, Felix and I were well pleased; but Peter averred that he would rather have the Madonna that looked like his Aunt Jane, and the Story Girl agreed that if his sermon was the best she would give him that.

"But who's to be the judge?" I said, "and what kind of a sermon would you call the best?"

"The one that makes the most impression," answered the Story Girl promptly. "And we girls must be the judges, because there's nobody else. Now, who is to preach next Sunday?"

It was decided that I should lead off, and I lay awake for an extra hour that night thinking what text I should take for the following Sunday. The next day I bought two sheets of foolscap from the schoolmaster, and after tea I betook myself to the granary, barred the door, and fell to writing my sermon. I did not find it as easy a task as I had anticipated; but I pegged grimly away at it, and by dint of severe labour for two evenings I eventually got my four pages of foolscap filled, although I had to pad the subject-matter not a little with verses of quotable hymns. I had decided to preach on missions, as being a topic more within my grasp than abstruse theological doctrines or evangelical discourses; and, mindful of the need of making an impression, I drew a harrowing picture of the miserable plight of the heathen who in their darkness bowed down to wood and stone. Then I urged our responsibility concerning them, and meant to wind up by reciting, in a very solemn and earnest voice, the verse beginning, "Can we whose souls are lighted." When I had completed my sermon I went over it very carefully again and wrote with red ink—Cecily made it for me out of an aniline dye—the word "thump" wherever I deemed it advisable to chastise the pulpit.

I have that sermon still, all its red thumps unfaded, lying beside my dream book; but I am not going to inflict it on my readers. I am not so proud of it as I once was. I was really puffed up with earthly vanity over it at that time.

Felix, I thought, would be hard put to it to beat it. As for Peter, I did not consider him a rival to be feared. It was unsupposable that a hired boy, with little education and less experience of church-going, should be able to preach better than could I, in whose family there was a real minister.

The sermon written, the next thing was to learn it off by heart and then practise it, thumps included, until I was letter and gesture perfect. I preached it over several times in the granary with only Paddy, sitting immovably on a puncheon, for audience. Paddy stood the test fairly well. At least, he made an adorable listener, save at such times as imaginary rats distracted his attention.

Mr. Marwood had at least three absorbed listeners the next Sunday morning. Felix, Peter and I were all among the chiels who were taking mental notes on the art of preaching a sermon. Not a motion, or glance, or intonation escaped us. To be sure, none of us could remember the text when we got home; but we knew just how you should throw back your head and clutch the edge of the pulpit with both hands when you announced it.

In the afternoon we all repaired to the orchard, Bibles and hymn books in hand. We did not think it necessary to inform the grown-ups of what was in the wind. You could never tell what kink a grown-up would take. They might not think it proper to play any sort of a game on Sunday, not even a Christian game. Least said was soonest mended where grown-ups were concerned.

I mounted the pulpit steps, feeling rather nervous, and my audience sat gravely down on the grass before me. Our opening exercises consisted solely of singing and reading. We had agreed to omit prayer. Neither Felix, Peter nor I felt equal to praying in public. But we took up a collection. The proceeds were to go to missions. Dan passed the plate—Felicity's rosebud plate—looking as preternaturally solemn as Elder Frewen himself. Every one put a cent on it.

Well, I preached my sermon. And it fell horribly flat. I realized that, before I was half way through it. I think I preached it very well; and never a thump did I forget or misplace. But my audience was plainly bored. When I stepped down from the pulpit, after demanding passionately if we whose souls were lighted and so forth, I felt with secret humiliation that my sermon was a failure. It had made no impression at all. Felix would be sure to get the prize.

"That was a very good sermon for a first attempt," said the Story Girl graciously. "It sounded just like real sermons I have heard."

For a moment the charm of her voice made me feel that I had not done so badly after all; but the other girls, thinking it their duty to pay me some sort of a compliment also, quickly dispelled that pleasing delusion.

"Every word of it was true," said Cecily, her tone unconsciously implying that this was its sole merit.

"I often feel," said Felicity primly, "that we don't think enough about the heathens. We ought to think a great deal more."

Sara Ray put the finishing touch to my mortification.

"It was so nice and short," she said.

"What was the matter with my sermon?" I asked Dan that night. Since he was neither judge nor competitor I could discuss the matter with him.

"It was too much like a reg'lar sermon to be interesting," said Dan frankly.

"I should think the more like a regular sermon it was, the better," I said.

"Not if you want to make an impression," said Dan seriously. "You must have something sort of different for that. Peter, now, HE'LL have something different."

"Oh, Peter! I don't believe he can preach a sermon," I said.

"Maybe not, but you'll see he'll make an impression," said Dan.

Dan was neither the prophet nor the son of a prophet, but he had the second sight for once; Peter DID make an impression.

CHAPTER XXVI.
PETER MAKES AN IMPRESSION

Peter's turn came next. He did not write his sermon out. That, he averred, was too hard work. Nor did he mean to take a text.

"Why, who ever heard of a sermon without a text?" asked Felix blankly.

"I am going to take a SUBJECT instead of a text," said Peter loftily. "I ain't going to tie myself down to a text. And I'm going to have heads in it—three heads. You hadn't a single head in yours," he added to me.

"Uncle Alec says that Uncle Edward says that heads are beginning to go out of fashion," I said defiantly—all the more defiantly that I felt I should have had heads in my sermon. It would doubtless have made a much deeper impression. But the truth was I had forgotten all about such things.

"Well, I'm going to have them, and I don't care if they are unfashionable," said Peter. "They're good things. Aunt Jane used to say if a man didn't have heads and stick to them he'd go wandering all over the Bible and never get anywhere in particular."

"What are you going to preach on?" asked Felix.

"You'll find out next Sunday," said Peter significantly.

The next Sunday was in October, and a lovely day it was, warm and bland as June. There was something in the fine, elusive air, that recalled beautiful, forgotten things and suggested delicate future hopes. The woods had wrapped fine-woven gossamers about them and the westering hill was crimson and gold.

We sat around the Pulpit Stone and waited for Peter and Sara Ray. It was the former's Sunday off and he had gone home the night before, but he assured us he would be back in time to preach his sermon. Presently he arrived and mounted the granite boulder as if to the manor born. He was dressed in his new suit and I, perceiving this, felt that he had the advantage of me. When I preached I had to wear my second best suit, for it was one of Aunt Janet's laws that we should take our good suits off when we came home from church. There were, I saw, compensations for being a hired boy.

Peter made quite a handsome little minister, in his navy blue coat, white collar, and neatly bowed tie. His black eyes shone, and his black curls were brushed up in quite a ministerial pompadour, but threatened to tumble over at the top in graceless ringlets.

It was decided that there was no use in waiting for Sara Ray, who might or might not come, according to the humour in which her mother was. Therefore Peter proceeded with the service.

He read the chapter and gave out the hymn with as much SANG FROID as if he had been doing it all his life. Mr. Marwood himself could not have bettered the way in which Peter said,

"We will sing the whole hymn, omitting the fourth stanza."

That was a fine touch which I had not thought of. I began to think that, after all, Peter might be a foeman worthy of my steel.

When Peter was ready to begin he thrust his hands into his pockets—a totally unorthodox thing. Then he plunged in without further ado, speaking in his ordinary conversational tone—another unorthodox thing. There was no shorthand reporter present to take that sermon down; but, if necessary, I could preach it over verbatim, and so, I doubt not, could everyone that heard it. It was not a forgettable kind of sermon.

"Dearly beloved," said Peter, "my sermon is about the bad place—in short, about hell."

An electric shock seemed to run through the audience. Everybody looked suddenly alert. Peter had, in one sentence, done what my whole sermon had failed to do. He had made an impression.

"I shall divide my sermon into three heads," pursued Peter. "The first head is, what you must not do if you don't want to go to the bad place. The second head is, what the bad place is like"—sensation in the audience—"and the third head is, how to escape going there.

"Now, there's a great many things you must not do, and it's very important to know what they are. You ought not to lose no time in finding out. In the first place you mustn't ever forget to mind what grown-up people tell you—that is, GOOD grown-up people."

"But how are you going to tell who are the good grown-up people?" asked Felix suddenly, forgetting that he was in church.

"Oh, that is easy," said Peter. "You can always just FEEL who is good and who isn't. And you mustn't tell lies and you mustn't murder any one. You must be specially careful not to murder any one. You might be forgiven for telling lies, if you was real sorry for them, but if you murdered any one it would be pretty hard to get forgiven, so you'd better be on the safe side. And you mustn't commit suicide, because if you did that you wouldn't have any chance of repenting it; and you mustn't forget to say your prayers and you mustn't quarrel with your sister."

At this point Felicity gave Dan a significant poke with her elbow, and Dan was up in arms at once.

"Don't you be preaching at me, Peter Craig," he cried out. "I won't stand it. I don't quarrel with my sister any oftener than she quarrels with me. You can just leave me alone."

"Who's touching you?" demanded Peter. "I didn't mention no names. A minister can say anything he likes in the pulpit, as long as he doesn't mention any names, and nobody can answer back."

"All right, but just you wait till to-morrow," growled Dan, subsiding reluctantly into silence under the reproachful looks of the girls.

"You must not play any games on Sunday," went on Peter, "that is, any week-day games—or whisper in church, or laugh in church—I did that once but I was awful sorry—and you mustn't take any notice of Paddy—I mean of the family cat at family prayers, not even if he climbs up on your back. And you mustn't call names or make faces."

"Amen," cried Felix, who had suffered many things because Felicity so often made faces at him.

Peter stopped and glared at him over the edge of the Pulpit Stone.

"You haven't any business to call out a thing like that right in the middle of a sermon," he said.

"They do it in the Methodist church at Markdale," protested Felix, somewhat abashed. "I heard them."

"I know they do. That's the Methodist way and it is all right for them. I haven't a word to say against Methodists. My Aunt Jane was one, and I might have been one myself if I hadn't been so scared of the Judgment Day. But you ain't a Methodist. You're a Presbyterian, ain't you?"

"Yes, of course. I was born that way."

"Very well then, you've got to do things the Presbyterian way. Don't let me hear any more of your amens or I'll amen you."

"Oh, don't anybody interrupt again," implored the Story Girl. "It isn't fair. How can any one preach a good sermon if he is always being interrupted? Nobody interrupted Beverley."

"Bev didn't get up there and pitch into us like that," muttered Dan.

"You mustn't fight," resumed Peter undauntedly. "That is, you mustn't fight for the fun of fighting, nor out of bad temper. You must not say bad words or swear. You mustn't get drunk—although of course you wouldn't be likely to do that before you grow up, and the girls never. There's prob'ly a good many other things you mustn't do, but these I've named are the most important. Of course, I'm not saying you'll go to the bad place for sure if you do them. I only say you're running a risk. The devil is looking out for the people who do these things and he'll be more likely to get after them than to waste time over the people who don't do them. And that's all about the first head of my sermon."

At this point Sara Ray arrived, somewhat out of breath. Peter looked at her reproachfully.

"You've missed my whole first head, Sara," he said, "that isn't fair, when you're to be one of the judges. I think I ought to preach it over again for you."

"That was really done once. I know a story about it," said the Story Girl.

"Who's interrupting now?" aid Dan slyly.

"Never mind, tell us the story," said the preacher himself, eagerly leaning over the pulpit.

"It was Mr. Scott who did it," said the Story Girl. "He was preaching somewhere in Nova Scotia, and when he was more than half way through his sermon—and you know sermons were VERY long in those days—a man walked in. Mr. Scott stopped until he had taken his seat. Then he said, 'My friend, you are very late for this service. I hope you won't be late for heaven. The congregation will excuse me if I recapitulate the sermon for our friend's benefit.' And then he just preached the sermon over again from the beginning. It is said that that particular man was never known to be late for church again."

"It served him right," said Dan, "but it was pretty hard lines on the rest of the congregation."

"Now, let's be quiet so Peter can go on with his sermon," said Cecily.

Peter squared his shoulders and took hold of the edge of the pulpit. Never a thump had he thumped, but I realized that his way of leaning forward and fixing this one or that one of his hearers with his eye was much more effective.

"I've come now to the second head of my sermon—what the bad place is like."

He proceeded to describe the bad place. Later on we discovered that he had found his material in an illustrated translation of Dante's Inferno which had once been given to his Aunt Jane as a school prize. But at the time we supposed he must be drawing from Biblical sources. Peter had been reading the Bible steadily ever since what we always referred to as "the Judgment Sunday," and he was by now almost through it. None of the rest of us had ever read the Bible completely through, and we thought Peter must have found his description of the world of the lost in some portion with which we were not acquainted. Therefore, his utterances carried all the weight of inspiration, and we sat appalled before his lurid phrases. He used his own words to clothe the ideas he had found, and the result was a force and simplicity that struck home to our imaginations.

Suddenly Sara Ray sprang to her feet with a scream—a scream that changed into strange laughter. We all, preacher included, looked at her aghast. Cecily and Felicity sprang up and caught hold of her. Sara Ray was really in a bad fit of hysterics, but we knew nothing of such a thing in our experience, and we thought she had gone mad. She shrieked, cried, laughed, and flung herself about.

"She's gone clean crazy," said Peter, coming down out of his pulpit with a very pale face.

"You've frightened her crazy with your dreadful sermon," said Felicity indignantly.

She and Cecily each took Sara by an arm and, half leading, half carrying, got her out of the orchard and up to the house. The rest of us looked at each other in terrified questioning.

"You've made rather too much of an impression, Peter," said the Story Girl miserably.

"She needn't have got so scared. If she'd only waited for the third head I'd have showed her how easy it was to get clear of going to the bad place and go to heaven instead. But you girls are always in such a hurry," said Peter bitterly.

"Do you s'pose they'll have to take her to the asylum?" said Dan in a whisper.

"Hush, here's your father," said Felix.

Uncle Alec came striding down the orchard. We had never before seen Uncle Alec angry. But there was no doubt that he was very angry. His blue eyes fairly blazed at us as he said,

"What have you been doing to frighten Sara Ray into such a condition?"

"We—we were just having a sermon contest," explained the Story Girl tremulously. "And Peter preached about the bad place, and it frightened Sara. That is all, Uncle Alec."

"All! I don't know what the result will be to that nervous delicate child. She is shrieking in there and nothing will quiet her. What do you mean by playing such a game on Sunday, and making a jest of sacred things? No, not a word—" for the Story Girl had attempted to speak. "You and Peter march off home. And the next time I find you up to such doings on Sunday or any other day I'll give you cause to remember it to your latest hour."

The Story Girl and Peter went humbly home and we went with them.

"I CAN'T understand grown-up people," said Felix despairingly. "When Uncle Edward preached sermons it was all right, but when we do it is 'making a jest of sacred things.' And I heard Uncle Alec tell a story once about being nearly frightened to death when he was a little boy, by a minister preaching on the end of the world; and he said, 'That was something like a sermon. You don't hear such sermons nowadays.' But when Peter preaches just such a sermon, it's a very different story."

"It's no wonder we can't understand the grown-ups," said the Story Girl indignantly, "because we've never been grown-up ourselves. But THEY have been children, and I don't see why they can't understand us. Of course, perhaps we shouldn't have had the contest on Sundays. But all the same I think it's mean of Uncle Alec to be so cross. Oh, I do hope poor Sara won't have to be taken to the asylum."

Poor Sara did not have to be. She was eventually quieted down, and was as well as usual the next day; and she humbly begged Peter's pardon for spoiling his sermon. Peter granted it rather grumpily, and I fear that he never really quite forgave Sara for her untimely outburst. Felix, too, felt resentment against her, because he had lost the chance of preaching his sermon.

"Of course I know I wouldn't have got the prize, for I couldn't have made such an impression as Peter," he said to us mournfully, "but I'd like to have had a chance to show what I could do. That's what comes of having those cry-baby girls mixed up in things. Cecily was just as scared as Sara Ray, but she'd more sense than to show it like that."

"Well, Sara couldn't help it," said the Story Girl charitably, "but it does seem as if we'd had dreadful luck in everything we've tried lately. I thought of a new game this morning, but I'm almost afraid to mention it, for I suppose something dreadful will come of it, too."

"Oh, tell us, what is it?" everybody entreated.

"Well, it's a trial by ordeal, and we're to see which of us can pass it. The ordeal is to eat one of the bitter apples in big mouthfuls without making a single face."

Dan made a face to begin with.

"I don't believe any of us can do that," he said.

"YOU can't, if you take bites big enough to fill your mouth," giggled Felicity, with cruelty and without provocation.

"Well, maybe you could," retorted Dan sarcastically. "You'd be so afraid of spoiling your looks that you'd rather die than make a face, I s'pose, no matter what you et."

"Felicity makes enough faces when there's nothing to make faces at," said Felix, who had been grimaced at over the breakfast table that morning and hadn't liked it.

"I think the bitter apples would be real good for Felix," said Felicity. "They say sour things make people thin."

"Let's go and get the bitter apples," said Cecily hastily, seeing that Felix, Felicity and Dan were on the verge of a quarrel more bitter than the apples.

We went to the seedling tree and got an apple apiece. The game was that every one must take a bite in turn, chew it up, and swallow it, without making a face. Peter again distinguished himself. He, and he alone, passed the ordeal, munching those dreadful mouthfuls without so much as a change of expression on his countenance, while the facial contortions the rest of us went through baffled description. In every subsequent trial it was the same. Peter never made a face, and no one else could help making them. It sent him up fifty per cent in Felicity's estimation.

"Peter is a real smart boy," she said to me. "It's such a pity he is a hired boy."

But, if we could not pass the ordeal, we got any amount of fun out of it, at least. Evening after evening the orchard re-echoed to our peals of laughter.

"Bless the children," said Uncle Alec, as he carried the milk pails across the yard. "Nothing can quench their spirits for long."

CHAPTER XXVII.
THE ORDEAL OF BITTER APPLES

I could never understand why Felix took Peter's success in the Ordeal of Bitter Apples so much to heart. He had not felt very keenly over the matter of the sermons, and certainly the mere fact that Peter could eat sour apples without making faces did not cast any reflection on the honour or ability of the other competitors. But to Felix everything suddenly became flat, stale, and unprofitable, because Peter continued to hold the championship of bitter apples. It haunted his waking hours and obsessed his nights. I heard him talking in his sleep about it. If anything could have made him thin the way he worried over this matter would have done it.

For myself, I cared not a groat. I had wished to be successful in the sermon contest, and felt sore whenever I thought of my failure. But I had no burning desire to eat sour apples without grimacing, and I did not sympathize over and above with my brother. When, however, he took to praying about it, I realized how deeply he felt on the subject, and hoped he would be successful.

Felix prayed earnestly that he might be enabled to eat a bitter apple without making a face. And when he had prayed three nights after this manner, he contrived to eat a bitter apple without a grimace until he came to the last bite, which proved too much for him. But Felix was vastly encouraged.

"Another prayer or two, and I'll be able to eat a whole one," he said jubilantly.

But this devoutly desired consummation did not come to pass. In spite of prayers and heroic attempts, Felix could never get beyond that last bite. Not even faith and works in combination could avail. For a time he could not understand this. But he thought the mystery was solved when Cecily came to him one day and told him that Peter was praying against him.

"He's praying that you'll never be able to eat a bitter apple without making a face," she said. "He told Felicity and Felicity told me. She said she thought it was real cute of him. I think that is a dreadful way to talk about praying and I told her so. She wanted me to promise not to tell you, but I wouldn't promise, because I think it's fair for you to know what is going on."

Felix was very indignant—and aggrieved as well.

"I don't see why God should answer Peter's prayers instead of mine," he said bitterly. "I've gone to church and Sunday School all my life, and Peter never went till this summer. It isn't fair."

"Oh, Felix, don't talk like that," said Cecily, shocked. "God MUST be fair. I'll tell you what I believe is the reason. Peter prays three times a day regular—in the morning and at dinner time and at night—and besides that, any time through the day when he happens to think of it, he just prays, standing up. Did you ever hear of such goings-on?"

"Well, he's got to stop praying against me, anyhow," said Felix resolutely. "I won't put up with it, and I'll go and tell him so right off."

Felix marched over to Uncle Roger's, and we trailed after, scenting a scene. We found Peter shelling beans in the granary, and whistling cheerily, as with a conscience void of offence towards all men.

"Look here, Peter," said Felix ominously, "they tell me that you've been praying right along that I couldn't eat a bitter apple. Now, I tell you—"

"I never did!" exclaimed Peter indignantly. "I never mentioned your name. I never prayed that you couldn't eat a bitter apple. I just prayed that I'd be the only one that could."

"Well, that's the same thing," cried Felix. "You've just been praying for the opposite to me out of spite. And you've got to stop it, Peter Craig."

"Well, I just guess I won't," said Peter angrily. "I've just as good a right to pray for what I want as you, Felix King, even if you was brought up in Toronto. I s'pose you think a hired boy hasn't any business to pray for particular things, but I'll show you. I'll just pray for what I please, and I'd like to see you try and stop me."

"You'll have to fight me, if you keep on praying against me," said Felix.

The girls gasped; but Dan and I were jubilant, snuffing battle afar off.

"All right. I can fight as well as pray."

"Oh, don't fight," implored Cecily. "I think it would be dreadful. Surely you can arrange it some other way. Let's all give up the Ordeal, anyway. There isn't much fun in it. And then neither of you need pray about it."

"I don't want to give up the Ordeal," said Felix, "and I won't."

"Oh, well, surely you can settle it some way without fighting," persisted Cecily.

"I'm not wanting to fight," said Peter. "It's Felix. If he don't interfere with my prayers there's no need of fighting. But if he does there's no other way to settle it."

"But how will that settle it?" asked Cecily.

"Oh, whoever's licked will have to give in about the praying," said Peter. "That's fair enough. If I'm licked I won't pray for that particular thing any more."

"It's dreadful to fight about anything so religious as praying," sighed poor Cecily.

"Why, they were always fighting about religion in old times," said Felix. "The more religious anything was the more fighting there was about it."

"A fellow's got a right to pray as he pleases," said Peter, "and if anybody tries to stop him he's bound to fight. That's my way of looking at it."

"What would Miss Marwood say if she knew you were going to fight?" asked Felicity.

Miss Marwood was Felix' Sunday School teacher and he was very fond of her. But by this time Felix was quite reckless.

"I don't care what she would say," he retorted.

Felicity tried another tack.

"You'll be sure to get whipped if you fight with Peter," she said. "You're too fat to fight."

After that, no moral force on earth could have prevented Felix from fighting. He would have faced an army with banners.

"You might settle it by drawing lots," said Cecily desperately.

"Drawing lots is wickeder that fighting," said Dan. "It's a kind of gambling."

"What would Aunt Jane say if she knew you were going to fight?" Cecily demanded of Peter.

"Don't you drag my Aunt Jane into this affair," said Peter darkly.

"You said you were going to be a Presbyterian," persisted Cecily. "Good Presbyterians don't fight."

"Oh, don't they! I heard your Uncle Roger say that Presbyterians were the best for fighting in the world—or the worst, I forget which he said, but it means the same thing."

Cecily had but one more shot in her locker.

"I thought you said in your sermon, Master Peter, that people shouldn't fight."

"I said they oughtn't to fight for fun, or for bad temper," retorted Peter. "This is different. I know what I'm fighting for but I can't think of the word."

"I guess you mean principle," I suggested.

"Yes, that's it," agreed Peter. "It's all right to fight for principle. It's kind of praying with your fists."

"Oh, can't you do something to prevent them from fighting, Sara?" pleaded Cecily, turning to the Story Girl, who was sitting on a bin, swinging her shapely bare feet to and fro.

"It doesn't do to meddle in an affair of this kind between boys," said the Story Girl sagely.

I may be mistaken, but I do not believe the Story Girl wanted that fight stopped. And I am far from being sure that Felicity did either.

It was ultimately arranged that the combat should take place in the fir wood behind Uncle Roger's granary. It was a nice, remote, bosky place where no prowling grown-up would be likely to intrude. And thither we all resorted at sunset.

"I hope Felix will beat," said the Story Girl to me, "not only for the family honour, but because that was a mean, mean prayer of Peter's. Do you think he will?"

"I don't know," I confessed dubiously. "Felix is too fat. He'll get out of breath in no time. And Peter is such a cool customer, and he's a year older than Felix. But then Felix has had some practice. He has fought boys in Toronto. And this is Peter's first fight."

"Did you ever fight?" asked the Story Girl.

"Once," I said briefly, dreading the next question, which promptly came.

"Who beat?"

It is sometimes a bitter thing to tell the truth, especially to a young lady for whom you have a great admiration. I had a struggle with temptation in which I frankly confess I might have been worsted had it not been for a saving and timely remembrance of a certain resolution made on the day preceding Judgment Sunday.

"The other fellow," I said with reluctant honesty.

"Well," said the Story Girl, "I think it doesn't matter whether you get whipped or not so long as you fight a good, square fight."

Her potent voice made me feel that I was quite a hero after all, and the sting went out of my recollection of that old fight.

When we arrived behind the granary the others were all there. Cecily was very pale, and Felix and Peter were taking off their coats. There was a pure yellow sunset that evening, and the aisles of the fir wood were flooded with its radiance. A cool, autumnal wind was whistling among the dark boughs and scattering blood red leaves from the maple at the end of the granary.

"Now," said Dan, "I'll count, and when I say three you pitch in, and hammer each other until one of you has had enough. Cecily, keep quiet. Now, one—two—three!"

Peter and Felix "pitched in," with more zeal than discretion on both sides. As a result, Peter got what later developed into a black eye, and Felix's nose began to bleed. Cecily gave a shriek and ran out of the wood. We thought she had fled because she could not endure the sight of blood, and we were not sorry, for her manifest disapproval and anxiety were damping the excitement of the occasion.

Felix and Peter drew apart after that first onset, and circled about one another warily. Then, just as they had come to grips again, Uncle Alec walked around the corner of the granary, with Cecily behind him.

He was not angry. There was a quizzical look in his eyes. But he took the combatants by their shirt collars and dragged them apart.

"This stops right here, boys," he said. "You know I don't allow fighting."

"Oh, but Uncle Alec, it was this way," began Felix eagerly. "Peter—"

"No, I don't want to hear about it," said Uncle Alec sternly. "I don't care what you were fighting about, but you must settle your quarrels in a different fashion. Remember my commands, Felix. Peter, Roger is looking for you to wash his buggy. Be off."

Peter went off rather sullenly, and Felix, also sullenly, sat down and began to nurse his nose. He turned his back on Cecily.

Cecily "caught it" after Uncle Alec had gone. Dan called her a tell-tale and a baby, and sneered at her until Cecily began to cry.

"I couldn't stand by and watch Felix and Peter pound each other all to pieces," she sobbed. "They've been such friends, and it was dreadful to see them fighting."

"Uncle Roger would have let them fight it out," said the Story Girl discontentedly. "Uncle Roger believes in boys fighting. He says it's as harmless a way as any of working off their original sin. Peter and Felix wouldn't have been any worse friends after it. They'd have been better friends because the praying question would have been settled. And now it can't be—unless Felicity can coax Peter to give up praying against Felix."

For once in her life the Story Girl was not as tactful as her wont. Or—is it possible that she said it out of malice prepense? At all events, Felicity resented the imputation that she had more influence with Peter than any one else.

"I don't meddle with hired boys' prayers," she said haughtily.

"It was all nonsense fighting about such prayers, anyhow," said Dan, who probably thought that since all chance of a fight was over, he might as well avow his real sentiments as to its folly. "Just as much nonsense as praying about the bitter apples in the first place."

"Oh, Dan, don't you believe there is some good in praying?" said Cecily reproachfully.

"Yes, I believe there's some good in some kinds of praying, but not in that kind," said Dan sturdily. "I don't believe God cares whether anybody can eat an apple without making a face or not."

"I don't believe it's right to talk of God as if you were well acquainted with Him," said Felicity, who felt that it was a good chance to snub Dan.

"There's something wrong somewhere," said Cecily perplexedly. "We ought to pray for what we want, of that I'm sure—and Peter wanted to be the only one who could pass the Ordeal. It seems as if he must be right—and yet it doesn't seem so. I wish I could understand it."

"Peter's prayer was wrong because it was a selfish prayer, I guess," said the Story Girl thoughtfully. "Felix's prayer was all right, because it wouldn't have hurt any one else; but it was selfish of Peter to want to be the only one. We mustn't pray selfish prayers."

"Oh, I see through it now," said Cecily joyfully.

"Yes, but," said Dan triumphantly, "if you believe God answers prayers about particular things, it was Peter's prayer He answered. What do you make of that?"

"Oh!" the Story Girl shook her head impatiently. "There's no use trying to make such things out. We only get more mixed up all the time. Let's leave it alone and I'll tell you a story. Aunt Olivia had a letter today from a friend in Nova Scotia, who lives in Shubenacadie. When I said I thought it a funny name, she told me to go and look in her scrap book, and I would find a story about the origin of the name. And I did. Don't you want to hear it?"

Of course we did. We all sat down at the roots of the firs. Felix, having finally squared matters with his nose, turned around and listened also. He would not look at Cecily, but every one else had forgiven her.

The Story Girl leaned that brown head of hers against the fir trunk behind her, and looked up at the apple-green sky through the dark boughs above us. She wore, I remember, a dress of warm crimson, and she had wound around her head a string of waxberries, that looked like a fillet of pearls. Her cheeks were still flushed with the excitement of the evening. In the dim light she was beautiful, with a wild, mystic loveliness, a compelling charm that would not be denied.

"Many, many moons ago, an Indian tribe lived on the banks of a river in Nova Scotia. One of the young braves was named Accadee. He was the tallest and bravest and handsomest young man in the tribe—"

"Why is it they're always so handsome in stories?" asked Dan. "Why are there never no stories about ugly people?"

"Perhaps ugly people never have stories happen to them," suggested Felicity.

"I think they're just as interesting as the handsome people," retorted Dan.

"Well, maybe they are in real life," said Cecily, "but in stories it's just as easy to make them handsome as not. I like them best that way. I just love to read a story where the heroine is beautiful as a dream."

"Pretty people are always conceited," said Felix, who was getting tired of holding his tongue.

"The heroes in stories are always nice," said Felicity, with apparent irrelevance. "They're always so tall and slender. Wouldn't it be awful funny if any one wrote a story about a fat hero—or about one with too big a mouth?"

"It doesn't matter what a man LOOKS like," I said, feeling that Felix and Dan were catching it rather too hotly. "He must be a good sort of chap and DO heaps of things. That's all that's necessary."

"Do any of you happen to want to hear the rest of my story?" asked the Story Girl in an ominously polite voice that recalled us to a sense of our bad manners. We apologized and promised to behave better; she went on, appeased:

"Accadee was all these things that I have mentioned, and he was the best hunter in the tribe besides. Never an arrow of his that did not go straight to the mark. Many and many a snow white moose he shot, and gave the beautiful skin to his sweetheart. Her name was Shuben and she was as lovely as the moon when it rises from the sea, and as pleasant as a summer twilight. Her eyes were dark and soft, her foot was as light as a breeze, and her voice sounded like a brook in the woods, or the wind that comes over the hills at night. She and Accadee were very much in love with each other, and often they hunted together, for Shuben was almost as skilful with her bow and arrow as Accadee himself. They had loved each other ever since they were small pappooses, and they had vowed to love each other as long as the river ran.

"One twilight, when Accadee was out hunting in the woods, he shot a snow white moose; and he took off its skin and wrapped it around him. Then he went on through the woods in the starlight; and he felt so happy and light of heart that he sometimes frisked and capered about just as a real moose would do. And he was doing this when Shuben, who was also out hunting, saw him from afar and thought he was a real moose. She stole cautiously through the woods until she came to the brink of a little valley. Below her stood the snow white moose. She drew her arrow to her eye—alas, she knew the art only too well!—and took careful aim. The next moment Accadee fell dead with her arrow in his heart."

The Story Girl paused—a dramatic pause. It was quite dark in the fir wood. We could see her face and eyes but dimly through the gloom. A silvery moon was looking down on us over the granary. The stars twinkled through the softly waving boughs. Beyond the wood we caught a glimpse of a moonlit world lying in the sharp frost of the October evening. The sky above it was chill and ethereal and mystical.

But all about us were shadows; and the weird little tale, told in a voice fraught with mystery and pathos, had peopled them for us with furtive folk in belt and wampum, and dark-tressed Indian maidens.

"What did Shuben do when she found out she had killed Accadee?" asked Felicity.

"She died of a broken heart before the spring, and she and Accadee were buried side by side on the bank of the river which has ever since borne their names—the river Shubenacadie," said the Story Girl.

The sharp wind blew around the granary and Cecily shivered. We heard Aunt Janet's voice calling "Children, children." Shaking off the spell of firs and moonlight and romantic tale, we scrambled to our feet and went homeward.

"I kind of wish I'd been born an Injun," said Dan. "It must have been a jolly life—nothing to do but hunt and fight."

"It wouldn't be so nice if they caught you and tortured you at the stake," said Felicity.

"No," said Dan reluctantly. "I suppose there'd be some drawback to everything, even being an Injun."

"Isn't it cold?" said Cecily, shivering again. "It will soon be winter. I wish summer could last forever. Felicity likes the winter, and so does the Story Girl, but I don't. It always seems so long till spring."

"Never mind, we've had a splendid summer," I said, slipping my arm about her to comfort some childish sorrow that breathed in her plaintive voice.

Truly, we had had a delectable summer; and, having had it, it was ours forever. "The gods themselves cannot recall their gifts." They may rob us of our future and embitter our present, but our past they may not touch. With all its laughter and delight and glamour it is our eternal possession.

Nevertheless, we all felt a little of the sadness of the waning year. There was a distinct weight on our spirits until Felicity took us into the pantry and stayed us with apple tarts and comforted us with cream. Then we brightened up. It was really a very decent world after all.

CHAPTER XXVIII.
THE TALE OF THE RAINBOW BRIDGE

Felix, so far as my remembrance goes, never attained to success in the Ordeal of Bitter Apples. He gave up trying after awhile; and he also gave up praying about it, saying in bitterness of spirit that there was no use in praying when other fellows prayed against you out of spite. He and Peter remained on bad terms for some time, however.

We were all of us too tired those nights to do any special praying. Sometimes I fear our "regular" prayers were slurred over, or mumbled in anything but reverent haste. October was a busy month on the hill farms. The apples had to be picked, and this work fell mainly to us children. We stayed home from school to do it. It was pleasant work and there was a great deal of fun in it; but it was hard, too, and our arms and backs ached roundly at night. In the mornings it was very delightful; in the afternoons tolerable; but in the evenings we lagged, and the laughter and zest of fresher hours were lacking.

Some of the apples had to be picked very carefully. But with others it did not matter; we boys would climb the trees and shake the apples down until the girls shrieked for mercy. The days were crisp and mellow, with warm sunshine and a tang of frost in the air, mingled with the woodsy odours of the withering grasses. The hens and turkeys prowled about, pecking at windfalls, and Pat made mad rushes at them amid the fallen leaves. The world beyond the orchard was in a royal magnificence of colouring, under the vivid blue autumn sky. The big willow by the gate was a splendid golden dome, and the maples that were scattered through the spruce grove waved blood-red banners over the sombre cone-bearers. The Story Girl generally had her head garlanded with their leaves. They became her vastly. Neither Felicity nor Cecily could have worn them. Those two girls were of a domestic type that assorted ill with the wildfire in Nature's veins. But when the Story Girl wreathed her nut brown tresses with crimson leaves it seemed, as Peter said, that they grew on her—as if the gold and flame of her spirit had broken out in a coronal, as much a part of her as the pale halo seems a part of the Madonna it encircles.

What tales she told us on those far-away autumn days, peopling the russet arcades with folk of an elder world. Many a princess rode by us on her palfrey, many a swaggering gallant ruffled it bravely in velvet and plume adown Uncle Stephen's Walk, many a stately lady, silken clad, walked in that opulent orchard!

When we had filled our baskets they had to be carried to the granary loft, and the contents stored in bins or spread on the floor to ripen further. We ate a good many, of course, feeling that the labourer was worthy of his hire. The apples from our own birthday trees were stored in separate barrels inscribed with our names. We might dispose of them as we willed. Felicity sold hers to Uncle Alec's hired man—and was badly cheated to boot, for he levanted shortly afterwards, taking the apples with him, having paid her only half her rightful due. Felicity has not gotten over that to this day.

Cecily, dear heart, sent most of hers to the hospital in town, and no doubt gathered in therefrom dividends of gratitude and satisfaction of soul, such as can never be purchased by any mere process of bargain and sale. The rest of us ate our apples, or carried them to school where we bartered them for such treasures as our schoolmates possessed and we coveted.

There was a dusky, little, pear-shaped apple—from one of Uncle Stephen's trees—which was our favourite; and next to it a delicious, juicy yellow apple from Aunt Louisa's tree. We were also fond of the big sweet apples; we used to throw them up in the air and let them fall on the ground until they were bruised and battered to the bursting point. Then we sucked on the juice; sweeter was it than the nectar drunk by blissful gods on the Thessalian hill.

Sometimes we worked until the cold yellow sunsets faded out over the darkening distances, and the hunter's moon looked down on us through the sparkling air. The constellations of autumn scintillated above us. Peter and the Story Girl knew all about them, and imparted their knowledge to us generously. I recall Peter standing on the Pulpit Stone, one night ere moonrise, and pointing them out to us, occasionally having a difference of opinion with the Story Girl over the name of some particular star. Job's Coffin and the Northern Cross were to the west of us; south of us flamed Fomalhaut. The Great Square of Pegasus was over our heads. Cassiopeia sat enthroned in her beautiful chair in the north-east; and north of us the Dippers swung untiringly around the Pole Star. Cecily and Felix were the only ones who could distinguish the double star in the handle of the Big Dipper, and greatly did they plume themselves thereon. The Story Girl told us the myths and legends woven around these immemorial clusters, her very voice taking on a clear, remote, starry sound as she talked of them. When she ceased, we came back to earth, feeling as if we had been millions of miles away in the blue ether, and that all our old familiar surroundings were momentarily forgotten and strange.

That night when he pointed out the stars to us from the Pulpit Stone was the last time for several weeks that Peter shared our toil and pastime. The next day he complained of headache and sore throat, and seemed to prefer lying on Aunt Olivia's kitchen sofa to doing any work. As it was not in Peter to be a malingerer he was left in peace, while we picked apples. Felix alone, must unjustly and spitefully, declared that Peter was simply shirking.

"He's just lazy, that's what's the matter with him," he said.

"Why don't you talk sense, if you must talk?" said Felicity. "There's no sense in calling Peter lazy. You might as well say I had black hair. Of course, Peter, being a Craig, has his faults, but he's a smart boy. His father was lazy but his mother hasn't a lazy bone in her body, and Peter takes after her."

"Uncle Roger says Peter's father wasn't exactly lazy," said the Story Girl. "The trouble was, there were so many other things he liked better than work."

"I wonder if he'll ever come back to his family," said Cecily. "Just think how dreadful it would be if OUR father had left us like that!"

"Our father is a King," said Felicity loftily, "and Peter's father was only a Craig. A member of our family COULDN'T behave like that."

"They say there must be a black sheep in every family," said the Story Girl.

"There isn't any in ours," said Cecily loyally.

"Why do white sheep eat more than black?" asked Felix.

"Is that a conundrum?" asked Cecily cautiously. "If it is I won't try to guess the reason. I never can guess conundrums."

"It isn't a conundrum," said Felix. "It's a fact. They do—and there's a good reason for it."

We stopped picking apples, sat down on the grass, and tried to reason it out—with the exception of Dan, who declared that he knew there was a catch somewhere and he wasn't going to be caught. The rest of us could not see where any catch could exist, since Felix solemnly vowed, 'cross his heart, white sheep did eat more than black. We argued over it seriously, but finally had to give it up.

"Well, what is the reason?" asked Felicity.

"Because there's more of them," said Felix, grinning.

I forget what we did to Felix.

A shower came up in the evening and we had to stop picking. After the shower there was a magnificent double rainbow. We watched it from the granary window, and the Story Girl told us an old legend, culled from one of Aunt Olivia's many scrapbooks.

"Long, long ago, in the Golden Age, when the gods used to visit the earth so often that it was nothing uncommon to see them, Odin made a pilgrimage over the world. Odin was the great god of the northland, you know. And wherever he went among men he taught them love and brotherhood, and skilful arts; and great cities sprang up where he had trodden, and every land through which he passed was blessed because one of the gods had come down to men. But many men and women followed Odin himself, giving up all their worldly possessions and ambitions; and to these he promised the gift of eternal life. All these people were good and noble and unselfish and kind; but the best and noblest of them all was a youth named Ving; and this youth was beloved by Odin above all others, for his beauty and strength and goodness. Always he walked on Odin's right hand, and always the first light of Odin's smile fell on him. Tall and straight was he as a young pine, and his long hair was the colour of ripe wheat in the sun; and his blue eyes were like the northland heavens on a starry night.

"In Odin's band was a beautiful maiden named Alin. She was as fair and delicate as a young birch tree in spring among the dark old pines and firs, and Ving loved her with all his heart. His soul thrilled with rapture at the thought that he and she together should drink from the fountain of immortality, as Odin had promised, and be one thereafter in eternal youth.

"At last they came to the very place where the rainbow touched the earth. And the rainbow was a great bridge, built of living colours, so dazzling and wonderful that beyond it the eye could see nothing, only far away a great, blinding, sparkling glory, where the fountain of life sprang up in a shower of diamond fire. But under the Rainbow Bridge rolled a terrible flood, deep and wide and violent, full of rocks and rapids and whirlpools.

"There was a Warder of the bridge, a god, dark and stern and sorrowful. And to him Odin gave command that he should open the gate and allow his followers to cross the Rainbow Bridge, that they might drink of the fountain of life beyond. And the Warder set open the gate.

"'Pass on and drink of the fountain,' he said. 'To all who taste of it shall immortality be given. But only to that one who shall drink of it first shall be permitted to walk at Odin's right hand forever.'

"Then the company passed through in great haste, all fired with a desire to be the first to drink of the fountain and win so marvellous a boon. Last of all came Ving. He had lingered behind to pluck a thorn from the foot of a beggar child he had met on the highway, and he had not heard the Warder's words. But when, eager, joyous, radiant, he set his foot on the rainbow, the stern, sorrowful Warder took him by the arm and drew him back.

"'Ving, strong, noble, and valiant,' he said, 'Rainbow Bridge is not for thee.'

"Very dark grew Ving's face. Hot rebellion rose in his heart and rushed over his pale lips.

"'Why dost thou keep back the draught of immortality from me?' he demanded passionately.

"The Warder pointed to the dark flood that rolled under the bridge.

"'The path of the rainbow is not for thee,' he said, 'but yonder way is open. Ford that flood. On the furthest bank is the fountain of life.'

"'Thou mockest me,' muttered Ving sullenly. 'No mortal could cross that flood. Oh, Master,' he prayed, turning beseechingly to Odin, 'thou didst promise to me eternal life as to the others. Wilt thou not keep that promise? Command the Warder to let me pass. He must obey thee.'

"But Odin stood silent, with his face turned from his beloved, and Ving's heart was filled with unspeakable bitterness and despair.

"'Thou mayest return to earth if thou fearest to essay the flood,' said the Warder.

"'Nay,' said Ving wildly, 'earthly life without Alin is more dreadful than the death which awaits me in yon dark river.'

"And he plunged fiercely in. He swam, and struggled, he buffetted the turmoil. The waves went over his head again and again, the whirlpools caught him and flung him on the cruel rocks. The wild, cold spray beat on his eyes and blinded him, so that he could see nothing, and the roar of the river deafened him so that he could hear nothing; but he felt keenly the wounds and bruises of the cruel rocks, and many a time he would have given up the struggle had not the thought of sweet Alin's loving eyes brought him the strength and desire to struggle as long as it was possible. Long, long, long, to him seemed that bitter and perilous passage; but at last he won through to the furthest side. Breathless and reeling, his vesture torn, his great wounds bleeding, he found himself on the shore where the fountain of immortality sprang up. He staggered to its brink and drank of its clear stream. Then all pain and weariness fell away from him, and he rose up, a god, beautiful with immortality. And as he did there came rushing over the Rainbow Bridge a great company—the band of fellow travellers. But all were too late to win the double boon. Ving had won to it through the danger and suffering of the dark river."

The rainbow had faded out, and the darkness of the October dusk was falling.

"I wonder," said Dan meditatively, as we went away from that redolent spot, "what it would be like to live for ever in this world."

"I expect we'd get tired of it after awhile," said the Story Girl. "But," she added, "I think it would be a goodly while before I would."

CHAPTER XXIX.
THE SHADOW FEARED OF MAN

We were all up early the next morning, dressing by candlelight. But early as it was we found the Story Girl in the kitchen when we went down, sitting on Rachel Ward's blue chest and looking important.

"What do you think?" she exclaimed. "Peter has the measles! He was dreadfully sick all night, and Uncle Roger had to go for the doctor. He was quite light-headed, and didn't know any one. Of course he's far too sick to be taken home, so his mother has come up to wait on him, and I'm to live over here until he is better."

This was mingled bitter and sweet. We were sorry to hear that Peter had the measles; but it would be jolly to have the Story Girl living with us all the time. What orgies of story telling we should have!

"I suppose we'll all have the measles now," grumbled Felicity. "And October is such an inconvenient time for measles—there's so much to do."

"I don't believe any time is very convenient to have the measles," Cecily said.

"Oh, perhaps we won't have them," said the Story Girl cheerfully. "Peter caught them at Markdale, the last time he was home, his mother says."

"I don't want to catch the measles from Peter," said Felicity decidedly. "Fancy catching them from a hired boy!"

"Oh, Felicity, don't call Peter a hired boy when he's sick," protested Cecily.

During the next two days we were very busy—too busy to tell tales or listen to them. Only in the frosty dusk did we have time to wander afar in realms of gold with the Story Girl. She had recently been digging into a couple of old volumes of classic myths and northland folklore which she had found in Aunt Olivia's attic; and for us, god and goddess, laughing nymph and mocking satyr, norn and valkyrie, elf and troll, and "green folk" generally, were real creatures once again, inhabiting the orchards and woods and meadows around us, until it seemed as if the Golden Age had returned to earth.

Then, on the third day, the Story Girl came to us with a very white face. She had been over to Uncle Roger's yard to hear the latest bulletin from the sick room. Hitherto they had been of a non-committal nature; but now it was only too evident that she had bad news.

"Peter is very, very sick," she said miserably. "He has caught cold someway—and the measles have struck in—and—and—" the Story Girl wrung her brown hands together—"the doctor is afraid he—he—won't get better."

We all stood around, stricken, incredulous.

"Do you mean," said Felix, finding voice at length, "that Peter is going to die?"

The Story Girl nodded miserably.

"They're afraid so."

Cecily sat down by her half filled basket and began to cry. Felicity said violently that she didn't believe it.

"I can't pick another apple to-day and I ain't going to try," said Dan.

None of us could. We went to the grown-ups and told them so; and the grown-ups, with unaccustomed understanding and sympathy, told us that we need not. Then we roamed about in our wretchedness and tried to comfort one another. We avoided the orchard; it was for us too full of happy memories to accord with our bitterness of soul. Instead, we resorted to the spruce wood, where the hush and the sombre shadows and the soft, melancholy sighing of the wind in the branches over us did not jar harshly on our new sorrow.

We could not really believe that Peter was going to die—to DIE. Old people died. Grown-up people died. Even children of whom we had heard died. But that one of US—of our merry little band—should die was unbelievable. We could not believe it. And yet the possibility struck us in the face like a blow. We sat on the mossy stones under the dark old evergreens and gave ourselves up to wretchedness. We all, even Dan, cried, except the Story Girl.

"I don't see how you can be so unfeeling, Sara Stanley," said Felicity reproachfully. "You've always been such friends with Peter—and made out you thought so much of him—and now you ain't shedding a tear for him."

I looked at the Story Girl's dry, piteous eyes, and suddenly remembered that I had never seen her cry. When she told us sad tales, in a voice laden with all the tears that had ever been shed, she had never shed one of her own.

"I can't cry," she said drearily. "I wish I could. I've a dreadful feeling here—" she touched her slender throat—"and if I could cry I think it would make it better. But I can't."

"Maybe Peter will get better after all," said Dan, swallowing a sob. "I've heard of lots of people who went and got better after the doctor said they were going to die."

"While there's life there's hope, you know," said Felix. "We shouldn't cross bridges till we come to them."

"Those are only proverbs," said the Story Girl bitterly. "Proverbs are all very fine when there's nothing to worry you, but when you're in real trouble they're not a bit of help."

"Oh, I wish I'd never said Peter wasn't fit to associate with," moaned Felicity. "If he ever gets better I'll never say such a thing again—I'll never THINK it. He's just a lovely boy and twice as smart as lots that aren't hired out."

"He was always so polite and good-natured and obliging," sighed Cecily.

"He was just a real gentleman," said the Story Girl.

"There ain't many fellows as fair and square as Peter," said Dan.

"And such a worker," said Felix.

"Uncle Roger says he never had a boy he could depend on like Peter," I said.

"It's too late to be saying all these nice things about him now," said the Story Girl. "He won't ever know how much we thought of him. It's too late."

"If he gets better I'll tell him," said Cecily resolutely.

"I wish I hadn't boxed his ears that day he tried to kiss me," went on Felicity, who was evidently raking her conscience for past offences in regard to Peter. "Of course I couldn't be expected to let a hir—to let a boy kiss me. But I needn't have been so cross about it. I might have been more dignified. And I told him I just hated him. That wasn't true, but I s'pose he'll die thinking it is. Oh, dear me, what makes people say things they've got to be so sorry for afterwards?"

"I suppose if Peter d-d-dies he'll go to heaven anyhow," sobbed Cecily. "He's been real good all this summer, but he isn't a church member."

"He's a Presbyterian, you know," said Felicity reassuringly. Her tone expressed her conviction that that would carry Peter through if anything would. "We're none of us church members. But of course Peter couldn't be sent to the bad place. That would be ridiculous. What would they do with him there, when he's so good and polite and honest and kind?"

"Oh, I think he'll be all right, too," sighed Cecily, "but you know he never did go to church and Sunday School before this summer."

"Well, his father run away, and his mother was too busy earning a living to bring him up right," argued Felicity. "Don't you suppose that anybody, even God, would make allowances for that?"

"Of course Peter will go to heaven," said the Story Girl. "He's not grown up enough to go anywhere else. Children always go to heaven. But I don't want him to go there or anywhere else. I want him to stay right here. I know heaven must be a splendid place, but I'm sure Peter would rather be here, having fun with us."

"Sara Stanley," rebuked Felicity. "I should think you wouldn't say such things at such a solemn time. You're such a queer girl."

"Wouldn't you rather be here yourself than in heaven?" said the Story Girl bluntly. "Wouldn't you now, Felicity King? Tell the truth, 'cross your heart."

But Felicity took refuge from this inconvenient question in tears.

"If we could only DO something to help Peter!" I said desperately. "It seems dreadful not to be able to do a single thing."

"There's one thing we can do," said Cecily gently. "We can pray for him."

"So we can," I agreed.

"I'm going to pray like sixty," said Felix energetically.

"We'll have to be awful good, you know," warned Cecily. "There's no use praying if you're not good."

"That will be easy," sighed Felicity. "I don't feel a bit like being bad. If anything happens to Peter I feel sure I'll never be naughty again. I won't have the heart."

We did, indeed, pray most sincerely for Peter's recovery. We did not, as in the case of Paddy, "tack it on after more important things," but put it in the very forefront of our petitions. Even skeptical Dan prayed, his skepticism falling away from him like a discarded garment in this valley of the shadow, which sifts out hearts and tries souls, until we all, grown-up or children, realize our weakness, and, finding that our own puny strength is as a reed shaken in the wind, creep back humbly to the God we have vainly dreamed we could do without.

Peter was no better the next day. Aunt Olivia reported that his mother was broken-hearted. We did not again ask to be released from work. Instead, we went at it with feverish zeal. If we worked hard there was less time for grief and grievious thoughts. We picked apples and dragged them to the granary doggedly. In the afternoon Aunt Janet brought us a lunch of apple turnovers; but we could not eat them. Peter, as Felicity reminded us with a burst of tears, had been so fond of apple turnovers.

And, oh, how good we were! How angelically and unnaturally good! Never was there such a band of kind, sweet-tempered, unselfish children in any orchard. Even Felicity and Dan, for once in their lives, got through the day without any exchange of left-handed compliments. Cecily confided to me that she never meant to put her hair up in curlers on Saturday nights again, because it was pretending. She was so anxious to repent of something, sweet girl, and this was all she could think of.

During the afternoon Judy Pineau brought up a tear-blotted note from Sara Ray. Sara had not been allowed to visit the hill farm since Peter had developed measles. She was an unhappy little exile, and could only relieve her anguish of soul by daily letters to Cecily, which the faithful and obliging Judy Pineau brought up for her. These epistles were as gushingly underlined as if Sara had been a correspondent of early Victorian days.

Cecily did not write back, because Mrs. Ray had decreed that no letters must be taken down from the hill farm lest they carry infection. Cecily had offered to bake every epistle thoroughly in the oven before sending it; but Mrs. Ray was inexorable, and Cecily had to content herself by sending long verbal messages with Judy Pineau.

"My OWN DEAREST Cecily," ran Sara's letter. "I have just heard the sad news about POOR DEAR PETER. I can't describe MY FEELINGS. They are DREADFUL. I have been crying ALL THE AFTERNOON. I wish I could FLY to you, but ma will not let me. She is afraid I will catch the measles, but I would rather have the measles A DOZEN TIMES OVER than be sepparated from you all like this. But I have felt, ever since the Judgment Sunday that I MUST OBEY MA BETTER than I used to do. If ANYTHING HAPPENS to Peter and you are let see him BEFORE IT HAPPENS give him MY LOVE and tell him HOW SORRY I AM, and that I hope we will ALL meet in A BETTER WORLD Everything in school is about the same. The master is awful cross by spells. Jimmy Frewen walked home with Nellie Bowan last night from prayer-meeting and HER ONLY FOURTEEN. Don't you think it horrid BEGINNING SO YOUNG? YOU AND ME would NEVER do anything like that till we were GROWN UP, would we? Willy Fraser looks SO LONESOME in school these days. I must stop for ma says I waste FAR TOO MUCH TIME writing letters. Tell Judy ALL THE NEWS for me.

"Your OWN TRUE FRIEND,

"P.S. Oh I DO hope Peter will get better. Ma is going to get me a new brown dress for the winter.

"S. R."

When evening came we went to our seats under the whispering, sighing fir trees. It was a beautiful night—clear, windless, frosty. Some one galloped down the road on horseback, lustily singing a comic song. How dared he? We felt that it was an insult to our wretchedness. If Peter were going to—going to—well, if anything happened to Peter, we felt so miserably sure that the music of life would be stilled for us for ever. How could any one in the world be happy when we were so unhappy?

Presently Aunt Olivia came down the long twilight arcade. Her bright hair was uncovered and she looked slim and queen-like in her light dress. We thought Aunt Olivia very pretty then. Looking back from a mature standpoint I realize that she must have been an unusually beautiful woman; and she looked her prettiest as she stood under the swaying boughs in the last faint light of the autumn dusk and smiled down at our woebegone faces.

"Dear, sorrowful little people, I bring you glad tidings of great joy," she said. "The doctor has just been here, and he finds Peter much better, and thinks he will pull through after all."

We gazed up at her in silence for a few moments. When we had heard the news of Paddy's recovery we had been noisy and jubilant; but we were very quiet now. We had been too near something dark and terrible and menacing; and though it was thus suddenly removed the chill and shadow of it were about us still. Presently the Story Girl, who had been standing up, leaning against a tall fir, slipped down to the ground in a huddled fashion and broke into a very passion of weeping. I had never heard any one cry so, with dreadful, rending sobs. I was used to hearing girls cry. It was as much Sara Ray's normal state as any other, and even Felicity and Cecily availed themselves occasionally of the privilege of sex. But I had never heard any girl cry like this. It gave me the same unpleasant sensation which I had felt one time when I had seen my father cry.

"Oh, don't, Sara, don't," I said gently, patting her convulsed shoulder.

"You ARE a queer girl," said Felicity—more tolerantly than usual however—"you never cried a speck when you thought Peter was going to die—and now when he is going to get better you cry like that."

"Sara, child, come with me," said Aunt Olivia, bending over her. The Story Girl got up and went away, with Aunt Olivia's arms around her. The sound of her crying died away under the firs, and with it seemed to go the dread and grief that had been our portion for hours. In the reaction our spirits rose with a bound.

"Oh, ain't it great that Peter's going to be all right?" said Dan, springing up.

"I never was so glad of anything in my whole life," declared Felicity in shameless rapture.

"Can't we send word somehow to Sara Ray to-night?" asked Cecily, the ever-thoughtful. "She's feeling so bad—and she'll have to feel that way till to-morrow if we can't."

"Let's all go down to the Ray gate and holler to Judy Pineau till she comes out," suggested Felix.

Accordingly, we went and "hollered," with a right good will. We were much taken aback to find that Mrs. Ray came to the gate instead of Judy, and rather sourly demanded what we were yelling about. When she heard our news, however, she had the decency to say she was glad, and to promise she would convey the good tidings to Sara—"who is already in bed, where all children of her age should be," added Mrs. Ray severely.

WE had no intention of going to bed for a good two hours yet. Instead, after devoutly thanking goodness that our grown-ups, in spite of some imperfections, were not of the Mrs. Ray type, we betook ourselves to the granary, lighted a huge lantern which Dan had made out of a turnip, and proceeded to devour all the apples we might have eaten through the day but had not. We were a blithe little crew, sitting there in the light of our goblin lantern. We had in very truth been given beauty for ashes and the oil of joy for mourning. Life was as a red rose once more.

"I'm going to make a big batch of patty-pans, first thing in the morning," said Felicity jubilantly. "Isn't it queer? Last night I felt just like praying, and tonight I feel just like cooking."

"We mustn't forget to thank God for making Peter better," said Cecily, as we finally went to the house.

"Do you s'pose Peter wouldn't have got better anyway?" said Dan.

"Oh, Dan, what makes you ask such questions?" exclaimed Cecily in real distress.

"I dunno," said Dan. "They just kind of come into my head, like. But of course I mean to thank God when I say my prayers to-night. That's only decent."

CHAPTER XXX.
A COMPOUND LETTER

Once Peter was out of danger he recovered rapidly, but he found his convalescence rather tedious; and Aunt Olivia suggested to us one day that we write a "compound letter" to amuse him, until he could come to the window and talk to us from a safe distance. The idea appealed to us; and, the day being Saturday and the apples all picked, we betook ourselves to the orchard to compose our epistles, Cecily having first sent word by a convenient caller to Sara Ray, that she, too, might have a letter ready. Later, I, having at that time a mania for preserving all documents relating to our life in Carlisle, copied those letters in the blank pages at the back of my dream book. Hence I can reproduce them verbatim, with the bouquet they have retained through all the long years since they were penned in that autumnal orchard on the hill, with its fading leaves and frosted grasses, and the "mild, delightsome melancholy" of the late October day enfolding.

CECILY'S LETTER

"DEAR PETER:—I am so very glad and thankful that you are going to get better. We were so afraid you would not last Tuesday, and we felt dreadful, even Felicity. We all prayed for you. I think the others have stopped now, but I keep it up every night still, for fear you might have a relaps. (I don't know if that is spelled right. I haven't the dixonary handy, and if I ask the others Felicity will laugh at me, though she cannot spell lots of words herself.) I am saving some of the Honourable Mr. Whalen's pears for you. I've got them hid where nobody can find them. There's only a dozen because Dan et all the rest, but I guess you will like them. We have got all the apples picked, and are all ready to take the measles now, if we have to, but I hope we won't. If we have to, though, I'd rather catch them from you than from any one else, because we are acquainted with you. If I do take the measles and anything happens to me Felicity is to have my cherry vase. I'd rather give it to the Story Girl, but Dan says it ought to be kept in the family, even if Felicity is a crank. I haven't anything else valuable, since I gave Sara Ray my forget-me-not jug, but if you would like anything I've got let me know and I'll leave instructions for you to have it. The Story Girl has told us some splendid stories lately. I wish I was clever like her. Ma says it doesn't matter if you're not clever as long as you are good, but I am not even very good.

"I think this is all my news, except that I want to tell you how much we all think of you, Peter. When we heard you were sick we all said nice things about you, but we were afraid it was too late, and I said if you got better I'd tell you. It is easier to write it than to tell it out to your face. We think you are smart and polite and obliging and a great worker and a gentleman.

"Your true friend,

"CECILY KING.

"P.S. If you answer my letter don't say anything about the pears, because I don't want Dan to find out there's any left. C. K."

FELICITY'S LETTER

"DEAR PETER:—Aunt Olivia says for us all to write a compound letter to cheer you up. We are all awful glad you are getting better. It gave us an awful scare when we heard you were going to die. But you will soon be all right and able to get out again. Be careful you don't catch cold. I am going to bake some nice things for you and send them over, now that the doctor says you can eat them. And I'll send you my rosebud plate to eat off of. I'm only lending it, you know, not giving it. I let very few people use it because it is my greatest treasure. Mind you don't break it. Aunt Olivia must always wash it, not your mother.

"I do hope the rest of us won't catch the measles. It must look horrid to have red spots all over your face. We all feel pretty well yet. The Story Girl says as many queer things as ever. Felix thinks he is getting thin, but he is fatter than ever, and no wonder, with all the apples he eats. He has give up trying to eat the bitter apples at last. Beverley has grown half an inch since July, by the mark on the hall door, and he is awful pleased about it. I told him I guessed the magic seed was taking effect at last, and he got mad. He never gets mad at anything the Story Girl says, and yet she is so sarkastic by times. Dan is pretty hard to get along with as usul, but I try to bear pashently with him. Cecily is well and says she isn't going to curl her hair any more. She is so conscienshus. I am glad my hair curls of itself, ain't you?

"We haven't seen Sara Ray since you got sick. She is awful lonesome, and Judy says she cries nearly all the time but that is nothing new. I'm awful sorry for Sara but I'm glad I'm not her. She is going to write you a letter too. You'll let me see what she puts in it, won't you? You'd better take some Mexican Tea now. It's a great blood purifyer.

"I am going to get a lovely dark blue dress for the winter. It is ever so much prettier than Sara Ray's brown one. Sara Ray's mother has no taste. The Story Girl's father is sending her a new red dress, and a red velvet cap from Paris. She is so fond of red. I can't bear it, it looks so common. Mother says I can get a velvet hood too. Cecily says she doesn't believe it's right to wear velvet when it's so expensive and the heathen are crying for the gospel. She got that idea from a Sunday School paper but I am going to get my hood all the same.

"Well, Peter, I have no more news so I will close for this time.

"hoping you will soon be quite well, I remain

"yours sincerely,

"FELICITY KING.

"P.S. The Story Girl peeked over my shoulder and says I ought to have signed it 'yours affeckshunately,' but I know better, because the Family Guide has told lots of times how you should sign yourself when you are writing to a young man who is only a friend. F. K."

FELIX' LETTER

"DEAR PETER:—I am awful glad you are getting better. We all felt bad when we thought you wouldn't, but I felt worse than the others because we hadn't been on very good terms lately and I had said mean things about you. I'm sorry and, Peter, you can pray for anything you like and I won't ever object again. I'm glad Uncle Alec interfered and stopped the fight. If I had licked you and you had died of the measles it would have been a dreadful thing.

"We have all the apples in and haven't much to do just now and we are having lots of fun but we wish you were here to join in. I'm a lot thinner than I was. I guess working so hard picking apples is a good thing to make you thin. The girls are all well. Felicity puts on as many airs as ever, but she makes great things to eat. I have had some splendid dreams since we gave up writing them down. That is always the way. We ain't going to school till we're sure we are not going to have the measles. This is all I can think of, so I will draw to a close. Remember, you can pray for anything you like. FELIX KING."

SARA RAY'S LETTER

"DEAR PETER:—I never wrote to A BOY before, so PLEASE excuse ALL mistakes. I am SO glad you are getting better. We were SO afraid you were GOING TO DIE. I CRIED ALL NIGHT about it. But now that you are OUT OF DANGER will you tell me WHAT IT REALLY FEELS LIKE to think you are going to die? Does it FEEL QUEER? Were you VERY badly frightened?

"Ma won't let me go up the hill AT ALL now. I would DIE if it was not for Judy Pinno. (The French names are SO HARD TO SPELL.) JUDY IS VERY OBLIGING and I feel that she SIMPATHISES WITH ME. In my

LONELY HOURS I read my dream book and Cecily's old letters and they are SUCH A COMFORT to me. I have been reading one of the school library books too. I is PRETTY GOOD but I wish they had got more LOVE STORIES because they are so exciting. But the master would not let them.

"If you had DIED, Peter, and YOUR FATHER had heard it wouldn't he have FELT DREADFUL? We are having BEAUTIFUL WEATHER and the seenary is fine since the leaves turned. I think there is nothing so pretty as Nature after all.

"I hope ALL DANGER from the measles will soon be over and we can ALL MEET AGAIN AT THE HOME ON THE HILL. Till then FAREWELL.

"Your true friend,

"SARA RAY.

"P. S. Don't let Felicity see this letter. S. R."

DAN'S LETTER

"DEAR OLD PETE:—Awful glad you cheated the doctor. I thought you weren't the kind to turn up your toes so easy. You should of heard the girls crying.

"They're all getting their winter finery now and the talk about it would make you sick. The Story Girl is getting hers from Paris and Felicity is awful jealous though she pretends she isn't. I can see through her.

"Kitt Mar was up here Thursday to see the girls. She's had the measles so she isn't scared. She's a great girl to laugh. I like a girl that laughs, don't you?

"We had a call from Peg Bowen yesterday. You should of seen the Story Girl hustling Pat out of the way, for all she says she don't believe he was bewitched. Peg had your rheumatism ring on and the Story Girl's blue beads and Sara Ray's lace soed across the front of her dress. She wanted some tobacco and some pickles. Ma gave her some pickles but said we didn't have no tobacco and Peg went off mad but I guess she wouldn't bewitch anything on account of the pickles.

"I ain't any hand to write letters so I guess I'll stop. Hope you'll be out soon. DAN."

THE STORY GIRL'S LETTER

"DEAR PETER:—Oh, how glad I am that you are getting better! Those days when we thought you wouldn't were the hardest of my whole life. It seemed too dreadful to be true that perhaps you would die. And then when we heard you were going to get better that seemed too good to be true. Oh, Peter, hurry up and get well, for we are having such good times and we miss you so much. I have coaxed Uncle Alec not to burn his potato stalks till you are well, because I remember how you always liked to see the potato stalks burn. Uncle Alec consented, though Aunt Janet said it was high time they were burned. Uncle Roger burned his last night and it was such fun.

"Pat is splendid. He has never had a sick spell since that bad one. I would send him over to be company for you, but Aunt Janet says no, because he might carry the measles back. I don't see how he could, but we must obey Aunt Janet. She is very good to us all, but I know she does not approve of me. She says I'm my father's own child. I know that doesn't mean anything complimentary because she looked so queer when she saw that I had heard her, but I don't care. I'm glad I'm like father. I had a splendid letter from him this week, with the darlingest pictures in it. He is painting a new picture which is going to make him famous. I wonder what Aunt Janet will say then.

"Do you know, Peter, yesterday I thought I saw the Family Ghost at last. I was coming through the gap in the hedge, and I saw somebody in blue standing under Uncle Alec's tree. How my heart beat! My hair should have stood up on end with terror but it didn't. I felt to see, and it was lying down quite flat. But it was only a visitor after all. I don't know whether I was glad or disappointed. I don't think it would be a pleasant experience to see the ghost. But after I had seen it think what a heroine I would be!

"Oh, Peter, what do you think? I have got acquainted with the Awkward Man at last. I never thought it would be so easy. Yesterday Aunt Olivia wanted some ferns, so I went back to the maple woods to get them for her, and I found some lovely ones by the spring. And while I was sitting there, looking into the spring who should come along but the Awkward Man himself. He sat right down beside me and began to talk. I never was so surprised in my life. We had a very interesting talk, and I told him two of my best stories, and a great many of my secrets into the bargain. They may say what they like, but he was not one bit shy or awkward, and he has beautiful eyes. He did not tell me any of his secrets, but I believe he will some day. Of course I never said a word about his Alice-room. But I gave him a hint about his little brown book. I said I loved poetry and often felt like writing it, and then I said, 'Do you ever feel like that, Mr. Dale?' He said, yes, he sometimes felt that way, but he did not mention the brown book. I thought he might have. But after all I don't like people who tell you everything the first time you meet them, like Sara Ray. When he went away he said, 'I hope I shall have the pleasure of meeting you again,' just as seriously and politely as if I was a grown-up young lady. I am sure he could never have said it if I had been really grown up. I told him it was likely he would and that he wasn't to mind if I had a longer skirt on next time, because I'd be just the same person.

"I told the children a beautiful new fairy story to-day. I made them go to the spruce wood to hear it. A spruce wood is the proper place to tell fairy stories in. Felicity says she can't see that it makes any difference where you tell them, but oh, it does. I wish you had been there to hear it too, but when you are well I will tell it over again for you.

"I am going to call the southernwood 'appleringie' after this. Beverley says that is what they call it in Scotland, and I think it sounds so much more poetical than southernwood. Felicity says the right name is 'Boy's Love,' but I think that sounds silly.

"Oh, Peter, shadows are such pretty things. The orchard is full of them this very minute. Sometimes they are so still you would think them asleep. Then they go laughing and skipping. Outside, in the oat field, they are always chasing each other. They are the wild shadows. The shadows in the orchard are the tame shadows.

"Everything seems to be rather tired growing except the spruces and chrysanthemums in Aunt Olivia's garden. The sunshine is so thick and yellow and lazy, and the crickets sing all day long. The birds are nearly all gone and most of the maple leaves have fallen.

"Just to make you laugh I'll write you a little story I heard Uncle Alec telling last night. It was about Elder Frewen's grandfather taking a pair of rope reins to lead a piano home. Everybody laughed except Aunt Janet. Old Mr. Frewen was HER grandfather too, and she wouldn't laugh. One day when old Mr. Frewen was a young man of eighteen his father came home and said, 'Sandy, I bought a piano at Simon Ward's sale to-day. You're to go to-morrow and bring it home.' So next day Sandy started off on horseback with a pair of rope reins to lead the piano home. He thought it was some kind of livestock.

"And then Uncle Roger told about old Mark Ward who got up to make a speech at a church missionary social when he was drunk. (Of course he didn't get drunk at the social. He went there that way.) And this was his speech.

"'Ladies and gentlemen, Mr. Chairman, I can't express my thoughts on this grand subject of missions. It's in this poor human critter'—patting himself on the breast—'but he can't git it out.'

"I'll tell you these stories when you get well. I can tell them ever so much better than I can write them.

"I know Felicity is wondering why I'm writing such a long letter, so perhaps I'd better stop. If your mother reads it to you there is a good deal of it she may not understand, but I think your Aunt Jane would.

"I remain

"your very affectionate friend,

"SARA STANLEY."

I did not keep a copy of my own letter, and I have forgotten everything that was in it, except the first sentence, in which I told Peter I was awful glad he was getting better.

Peter's delight on receiving our letters knew no bounds. He insisted on answering them and his letter, painstakingly disinfected, was duly delivered to us. Aunt Olivia had written it at his dictation, which was a gain, as far as spelling and punctuation went. But Peter's individuality seemed merged and lost in Aunt Olivia's big, dashing script. Not until the Story Girl read the letter to us in the granary by jack-o-lantern light, in a mimicry of Peter's very voice, did we savour the real bouquet of it.

PETER'S LETTER

"DEAR EVERYBODY, BUT ESPECIALLY FELICITY:—I was awful glad to get your letters. It makes you real important to be sick, but the time seems awful long when you're getting better. Your letters were all great, but I liked Felicity's best, and next to hers the Story Girl's. Felicity, it will be awful good of you to send me things to eat and the rosebud plate. I'll be awful careful of it. I hope you won't catch the measles, for they are not nice, especially when they strike in, but you would look all right, even if you did have red spots on your face. I would like to try the Mexican Tea, because you want me to, but mother says no, she doesn't believe in it, and Burtons Bitters are a great deal healthier. If I was you I would get the velvet hood all right. The heathen live in warm countries so they don't want hoods.

"I'm glad you are still praying for me, Cecily, for you can't trust the measles. And I'm glad you're keeping you know what for me. I don't believe anything will happen to you if you do take the measles; but if anything does I'd like that little red book of yours, The Safe Compass, just to remember you by. It's such a good book to read on Sundays. It is interesting and religious, too. So is the Bible. I hadn't quite finished the Bible before I took the measles, but ma is reading the last chapters to me. There's an awful lot in that book. I can't understand the whole of it, since I'm only a hired boy, but some parts are real easy.

"I'm awful glad you have such a good opinion of me. I don't deserve it, but after this I'll try to. I can't tell you how I feel about all your kindness. I'm like the fellow the Story Girl wrote about who couldn't get it out. I have the picture the Story Girl gave me for my sermon on the wall at the foot of my bed. I like to look at it, it looks so much like Aunt Jane.

"Felix, I've given up praying that I'd be the only one to eat the bitter apples, and I'll never pray for anything like that again. It was a horrid mean prayer. I didn't know it then, but after the measles struck in I found out it was. Aunt Jane wouldn't have liked it. After this I'm going to pray prayers I needn't be ashamed of.

"Sara Ray, I don't know what it feels like to be going to die because I didn't know I was going to die till I got better. Mother says I was luny most of the time after they struck in. It was just because they struck in I was luny. I ain't luny naturally, Felicity. I will do what you asked in your postscript, Sara, although it will be hard.

"I'm glad Peg Bowen didn't catch you, Dan. Maybe she bewitched me that night we were at her place, and that is why the measles struck in. I'm awful glad Mr. King is going to leave the potato stalks until I get well, and I'm obliged to the Story Girl for coaxing him. I guess she will find out about Alice yet. There were some parts of her letter I couldn't see through, but when the measles strike in, they leave you stupid for a spell. Anyhow, it was a fine letter, and they were all fine, and I'm awful glad I have so many nice friends, even if I am only a hired boy. Perhaps I'd never have found it out if the measles hadn't struck in. So I'm glad they did but I hope they never will again.

"Your obedient servant,

"PETER CRAIG."

CHAPTER XXXI.
ON THE EDGE OF LIGHT AND DARK

We celebrated the November day when Peter was permitted to rejoin us by a picnic in the orchard. Sara Ray was also allowed to come, under protest; and her joy over being among us once more was almost pathetic. She and Cecily cried in one another's arms as if they had been parted for years.

We had a beautiful day for our picnic. November dreamed that it was May. The air was soft and mellow, with pale, aerial mists in the valleys and over the leafless beeches on the western hill. The sere stubble fields brooded in glamour, and the sky was pearly blue. The leaves were still thick on the apple trees, though they were russet hued, and the after-growth of grass was richly green, unharmed as yet by the nipping frosts of previous nights. The wind made a sweet, drowsy murmur in the boughs, as of bees among apple blossoms.

"It's just like spring, isn't it?" asked Felicity.

The Story Girl shook her head.

"No, not quite. It looks like spring, but it isn't spring. It's as if everything was resting—getting ready to sleep. In spring they're getting ready to grow. Can't you FEEL the difference?"

"I think it's just like spring," insisted Felicity.

In the sun-sweet place before the Pulpit Stone we boys had put up a board table. Aunt Janet allowed us to cover it with an old tablecloth, the worn places in which the girls artfully concealed with frost-whitened ferns. We had the kitchen dishes, and the table was gaily decorated with Cecily's three scarlet geraniums and maple leaves in the cherry vase. As for the viands, they were fit for the gods on high Olympus. Felicity had spent the whole previous day and the forenoon of the picnic day in concocting them. Her crowning achievement was a rich little plum cake, on the white frosting of which the words "Welcome Back" were lettered in pink candies. This was put before Peter's place, and almost overcame him.

"To think that you'd go to so much trouble for me!" he said, with a glance of adoring gratitude at Felicity. Felicity got all the gratitude, although the Story Girl had originated the idea and seeded the raisins and beaten the eggs, while Cecily had trudged all the way to Mrs. Jameson's little shop below the church to buy the pink candies. But that is the way of the world.

"We ought to have grace," said Felicity, as we sat down at the festal board. "Will any one say it?"

She looked at me, but I blushed to the roots of my hair and shook my head sheepishly. An awkward pause ensued; it looked as if we would have to proceed without grace, when Felix suddenly shut his eyes, bent his head, and said a very good grace without any appearance of embarrassment. We looked at him when it was over with an increase of respect.

"Where on earth did you learn that, Felix?" I asked.

"It's the grace Uncle Alec says at every meal," answered Felix.

We felt rather ashamed of ourselves. Was it possible that we had paid so little attention to Uncle Alec's grace that we did not recognize it when we heard it on other lips?

"Now," said Felicity jubilantly, "let's eat everything up."

In truth, it was a merry little feast. We had gone without our dinners, in order to "save our appetites," and we did ample justice to Felicity's good things. Paddy sat on the Pulpit Stone and watched us with great yellow eyes, knowing that tidbits would come his way later on. Many witty things were said—or at least we thought them witty—and uproarious was the laughter. Never had the old King orchard known a blither merrymaking or lighter hearts.

The picnic over, we played games until the early falling dusk, and then we went with Uncle Alec to the back field to burn the potato stalks—the crowning delight of the day.

The stalks were in heaps all over the field, and we were allowed the privilege of setting fire to them. 'Twas glorious! In a few minutes the field was alight with blazing bonfires, over which rolled great, pungent clouds of smoke. From pile to pile we ran, shrieking with delight, to poke each up with a long stick and watch the gush of rose-red sparks stream off into the night. In what a whirl of smoke and firelight and wild, fantastic, hurtling shadows we were!

When we grew tired of our sport we went to the windward side of the field and perched ourselves on the high pole fence that skirted a dark spruce wood, full of strange, furtive sounds. Over us was a great, dark sky, blossoming with silver stars, and all around lay dusky, mysterious reaches of meadow and wood in the soft, empurpled night. Away to the east a shimmering silveryness beneath a palace of aerial cloud foretokened moonrise. But directly before us the potato field, with its wreathing smoke and sullen flames, the gigantic shadow of Uncle Alec crossing and recrossing it, reminded us of Peter's famous description of the bad place, and probably suggested the Story Girl's remark.

"I know a story," she said, infusing just the right shade of weirdness into her voice, "about a man who saw the devil. Now, what's the matter, Felicity?"

"I can never get used to the way you mention the—the—that name," complained Felicity. "To hear you speak of the Old Scratch any one would think he was just a common person."

"Never mind. Tell us the story," I said curiously.

"It is about Mrs. John Martin's uncle at Markdale," said the Story Girl. "I heard Uncle Roger telling it the other night. He didn't know I was sitting on the cellar hatch outside the window, or I don't suppose he would have told it. Mrs. Martin's uncle's name was William Cowan, and he has been dead for twenty years; but sixty years ago he was a young man, and a very wild, wicked young man. He did everything bad he could think of, and never went to church, and he laughed at everything religious, even the devil. He didn't believe there was a devil at all. One beautiful summer Sunday evening his mother pleaded with him to go to church with her, but he would not. He told her that he was going fishing instead, and when church time came he swaggered past the church, with his fishing rod over his shoulder, singing a godless song. Half way between the church and the harbour there was a thick spruce wood, and the path ran through it. When William Cowan was half way through it SOMETHING came out of the wood and walked beside him."

I have never heard anything more horribly suggestive than that innocent word "something," as enunciated by the Story Girl. I felt Cecily's hand, icy cold, clutching mine.

"What—what—was IT like?" whispered Felix, curiosity getting the better of his terror.

"IT was tall, and black, and hairy," said the Story Girl, her eyes glowing with uncanny intensity in the red glare of the fires, "and IT lifted one great, hairy hand, with claws on the end of it, and clapped William Cowan, first on one shoulder and then on the other, and said, 'Good sport to you, brother.' William Cowan gave a horrible scream and fell on his face right there in the wood. Some of the men around the church door heard the scream, and they rushed down to the wood. They saw nothing but William Cowan, lying like a dead man on the path. They took him up and carried him home; and when they undressed him to put him to bed, there, on each shoulder, was the mark of a big hand, BURNED INTO THE FLESH. It was weeks before the burns healed, and the scars never went away. Always, as long as William Cowan lived, he carried on his shoulders the prints of the devil's hand."

I really do not know how we should ever have got home, had we been left to our own devices. We were cold with fright. How could we turn our backs on the eerie spruce wood, out of which SOMETHING might pop at any moment? How cross those long, shadowy fields between us and our rooftree? How venture through the darkly mysterious bracken hollow?

Fortunately, Uncle Alec came along at this crisis and said he thought we'd better come home now, since the fires were nearly out. We slid down from the fence and started, taking care to keep close together and in front of Uncle Alec.

"I don't believe a word of that yarn," said Dan, trying to speak with his usual incredulity.

"I don't see how you can help believing it," said Cecily. "It isn't as if it was something we'd read of, or that happened far away. It happened just down at Markdale, and I've seen that very spruce wood myself."

"Oh, I suppose William Cowan got a fright of some kind," conceded Dan, "but I don't believe he saw the devil."

"Old Mr. Morrison at Lower Markdale was one of the men who undressed him, and he remembers seeing the marks," said the Story Girl triumphantly.

"How did William Cowan behave afterwards?" I asked.

"He was a changed man," said the Story Girl solemnly. "Too much changed. He never was known to laugh again, or even smile. He became a very religious man, which was a good thing, but he was dreadfully gloomy and thought everything pleasant sinful. He wouldn't even eat any more than was actually necessary to keep him alive. Uncle Roger says that if he had been a Roman Catholic he would have become a monk, but, as he was a Presbyterian, all he could do was to turn into a crank."

"Yes, but your Uncle Roger was never clapped on the shoulder and called brother by the devil," said Peter. "If he had, he mightn't have been so precious jolly afterwards himself."

"I do wish to goodness," said Felicity in exasperation, "that you'd stop talking of the—the—of such subjects in the dark. I'm so scared now that I keep thinking father's steps behind us are SOMETHING'S. Just think, my own father!"

The Story Girl slipped her arm through Felicity's.

"Never mind," she said soothingly. "I'll tell you another story—such a beautiful story that you'll forget all about the devil."

She told us one of Hans Andersen's most exquisite tales; and the magic of her voice charmed away all our fear, so that when we reached the bracken hollow, a lake of shadow surrounded by the silver shore of moonlit fields, we all went through it without a thought of His Satanic Majesty at all. And beyond us, on the hill, the homelight was glowing from the farmhouse window like a beacon of old loves.

CHAPTER XXXII.
THE OPENING OF THE BLUE CHEST

November wakened from her dream of May in a bad temper. The day after the picnic a cold autumn rain set in, and we got up to find our world a drenched, wind-writhen place, with sodden fields and dour skies. The rain was weeping on the roof as if it were shedding the tears of old sorrows; the willow by the gate tossed its gaunt branches wildly, as if it were some passionate, spectral thing, wringing its fleshless hands in agony; the orchard was haggard and uncomely; nothing seemed the same except the staunch, trusty, old spruces.

It was Friday, but we were not to begin going to school again until Monday, so we spent the day in the granary, sorting apples and hearing tales. In the evening the rain ceased, the wind came around to the northwest, freezing suddenly, and a chilly yellow sunset beyond the dark hills seemed to herald a brighter morrow.

Felicity and the Story Girl and I walked down to the post-office for the mail, along a road where fallen leaves went eddying fitfully up and down before us in weird, uncanny dances of their own. The evening was full of eerie sounds—the creaking of fir boughs, the whistle of the wind in the tree-tops, the vibrations of strips of dried bark on the rail fences. But we carried summer and sunshine in our hearts, and the bleak unloveliness of the outer world only intensified our inner radiance.

Felicity wore her new velvet hood, with a coquettish little collar of white fur about her neck. Her golden curls framed her lovely face, and the wind stung the pink of her cheeks to crimson. On my left hand walked the Story Girl, her red cap on her jaunty brown head. She scattered her words along the path like the pearls and diamonds of the old fairy tale. I remember that I strutted along quite insufferably, for we met several of the Carlisle boys and I felt that I was an exceptionally lucky fellow to have such beauty on one side and such charm on the other.

There was one of father's thin letters for Felix, a fat, foreign letter for the Story Girl, addressed in her father's minute handwriting, a drop letter for Cecily from some school friend, with "In Haste" written across the corner, and a letter for Aunt Janet, postmarked Montreal.

"I can't think who that is from," said Felicity. "Nobody in Montreal ever writes to mother. Cecily's letter is from Em Frewen. She always puts 'In Haste' on her letters, no matter what is in them."

When we reached home, Aunt Janet opened and read her Montreal letter. Then she laid it down and looked about her in astonishment.

"Well, did ever any mortal!" she said.

"What in the world is the matter?" said Uncle Alec.

"This letter is from James Ward's wife in Montreal," said Aunt Janet solemnly. "Rachel Ward is dead. And she told James' wife to write to me and tell me to open the old blue chest."

"Hurrah!" shouted Dan.

"Donald King," said his mother severely, "Rachel Ward was your relation and she is dead. What do you mean by such behaviour?"

"I never was acquainted with her," said Dan sulkily. "And I wasn't hurrahing because she is dead. I hurrahed because that blue chest is to be opened at last."

"So poor Rachel is gone," said Uncle Alec. "She must have been an old woman—seventy-five I suppose. I remember her as a fine, blooming young woman. Well, well, and so the old chest is to be opened at last. What is to be done with its contents?"

"Rachel left instructions about them," answered Aunt Janet, referring to the letter. "The wedding dress and veil and letters are to be burned. There are two jugs in it which are to be sent to James' wife. The rest of the things are to be given around among the connection. Each members is to have one, 'to remember her by.'"

"Oh, can't we open it right away this very night?" said Felicity eagerly.

"No, indeed!" Aunt Janet folded up the letter decidedly. "That chest has been locked up for fifty years, and it'll stand being locked up one more night. You children wouldn't sleep a wink to-night if we opened it now. You'd go wild with excitement."

"I'm sure I won't sleep anyhow," said Felicity. "Well, at least you'll open it the first thing in the morning, won't you, ma?"

"No, I'll do nothing of the sort," was Aunt Janet's pitiless decree. "I want to get the work out of the way first—and Roger and Olivia will want to be here, too. We'll say ten o'clock to-morrow forenoon."

"That's sixteen whole hours yet," sighed Felicity.

"I'm going right over to tell the Story Girl," said Cecily. "Won't she be excited!"

We were all excited. We spent the evening speculating on the possible contents of the chest, and Cecily dreamed miserably that night that the moths had eaten everything in it.

The morning dawned on a beautiful world. A very slight fall of snow had come in the night—just enough to look like a filmy veil of lace flung over the dark evergreens, and the hard frozen ground. A new blossom time seemed to have revisited the orchard. The spruce wood behind the house appeared to be woven out of enchantment. There is nothing more beautiful than a thickly growing wood of firs lightly powdered with new-fallen snow. As the sun remained hidden by gray clouds, this fairy-beauty lasted all day.

The Story Girl came over early in the morning, and Sara Ray, to whom faithful Cecily had sent word, was also on hand. Felicity did not approve of this.

"Sara Ray isn't any relation to our family," she scolded to Cecily, "and she has no right to be present."

"She's a particular friend of mine," said Cecily with dignity. "We have her in everything, and it would hurt her feelings dreadfully to be left out of this. Peter is no relation either, but he is going to be here when we open it, so why shouldn't Sara?"

"Peter ain't a member of the family YET, but maybe he will be some day. Hey, Felicity?" said Dan.

"You're awful smart, aren't you, Dan King?" said Felicity, reddening. "Perhaps you'd like to send for Kitty Marr, too—though she DOES laugh at your big mouth."

"It seems as if ten o'clock would never come," sighed the Story Girl. "The work is all done, and Aunt Olivia and Uncle Roger are here, and the chest might just as well be opened right away."

"Mother SAID ten o'clock and she'll stick to it," said Felicity crossly. "It's only nine now."

"Let us put the clock on half an hour," said the Story Girl. "The clock in the hall isn't going, so no one will know the difference."

We all looked at each other.

"I wouldn't dare," said Felicity irresolutely.

"Oh, if that's all, I'll do it," said the Story Girl.

When ten o'clock struck Aunt Janet came into the kitchen, remarking innocently that it hadn't seemed anytime since nine. We must have looked horribly guilty, but none of the grown-ups suspected anything. Uncle Alec brought in the axe, and pried off the cover of the old blue chest, while everybody stood around in silence.

Then came the unpacking. It was certainly an interesting performance. Aunt Janet and Aunt Olivia took everything out and laid it on the kitchen table. We children were forbidden to touch anything, but fortunately we were not forbidden the use of our eyes and tongues.

"There are the pink and gold vases Grandmother King gave her," said Felicity, as Aunt Olivia unwrapped from their tissue paper swathings a pair of slender, old-fashioned, twisted vases of pink glass, over which little gold leaves were scattered. "Aren't they handsome?"

"And oh," exclaimed Cecily in delight, "there's the china fruit basket with the apple on the handle. Doesn't it look real? I've thought so much about it. Oh, mother, please let me hold it for a minute. I'll be as careful as careful."

"There comes the china set Grandfather King gave her," said the Story Girl wistfully. "Oh, it makes me feel sad. Think of all the hopes that Rachel Ward must have put away in this chest with all her pretty things."

Following these, came a quaint little candlestick of blue china, and the two jugs which were to be sent to James' wife.

"They ARE handsome," said Aunt Janet rather enviously. "They must be a hundred years old. Aunt Sara Ward gave them to Rachel, and she had them for at least fifty years. I should have thought one would have been enough for James' wife. But of course we must do just as Rachel wished. I declare, here's a dozen tin patty pans!"

"Tin patty pans aren't very romantic," said the Story Girl discontentedly.

"I notice that you are as fond as any one of what is baked in them," said Aunt Janet. "I've heard of those patty pans. An old servant Grandmother King had gave them to Rachel. Now we are coming to the linen. That was Uncle Edward Ward's present. How yellow it has grown."

We children were not greatly interested in the sheets and tablecloths and pillow-cases which now came out of the capacious depths of the old blue chest. But Aunt Olivia was quite enraptured over them.

"What sewing!" she said. "Look, Janet, you'd almost need a magnifying glass to see the stitches. And the dear, old-fashioned pillow-slips with buttons on them!"

"Here are a dozen handkerchiefs," said Aunt Janet. "Look at the initial in the corner of each. Rachel learned that stitch from a nun in Montreal. It looks as if it was woven into the material."

"Here are her quilts," said Aunt Olivia. "Yes, there is the blue and white counterpane Grandmother Ward gave her—and the Rising Sun quilt her Aunt Nancy made for her—and the braided rug. The colours are not faded one bit. I want that rug, Janet."

Underneath the linen were Rachel Ward's wedding clothes. The excitement of the girls waxed red hot over these. There was a Paisley shawl in the wrappings in which it had come from the store, and a wide scarf of some yellowed lace. There was the embroidered petticoat which had cost Felicity such painful blushes, and a dozen beautifully worked sets of the fine muslin "undersleeves" which had been the fashion in Rachel Ward's youth.

"This was to have been her appearing out dress," said Aunt Olivia, lifting out a shot green silk. "It is all cut to pieces—but what a pretty soft shade it was! Look at the skirt, Janet. How many yards must it measure around?"

"Hoopskirts were in then," said Aunt Janet. "I don't see her wedding hat here. I was always told that she packed it away, too."

"So was I. But she couldn't have. It certainly isn't here. I have heard that the white plume on it cost a small fortune. Here is her black silk mantle. It seems like sacrilege to meddle with these clothes."

"Don't be foolish, Olivia. They must be unpacked at least. And they must all be burned since they have cut so badly. This purple cloth dress is quite good, however. It can be made over nicely, and it would become you very well, Olivia."

"No, thank you," said Aunt Olivia, with a little shudder. "I should feel like a ghost. Make it over for yourself, Janet."

"Well, I will, if you don't want it. I am not troubled with fancies. That seems to be all except this box. I suppose the wedding dress is in it."

"Oh," breathed the girls, crowding about Aunt Olivia, as she lifted out the box and cut the cord around it. Inside was lying a dress of soft silk, that had once been white but was now yellowed with age, and, enfolding it like a mist, a long, white bridal veil, redolent with some strange, old-time perfume that had kept its sweetness through all the years.

"Poor Rachel Ward," said Aunt Olivia softly. "Here is her point lace handkerchief. She made it herself. It is like a spider's web. Here are the letters Will Montague wrote her. And here," she added, taking up a crimson velvet case with a tarnished gilt clasp, "are their photographs—his and hers."

We looked eagerly at the daguerreotypes in the old case.

"Why, Rachel Ward wasn't a bit pretty!" exclaimed the Story Girl in poignant disappointment.

No, Rachel Ward was not pretty, that had to be admitted. The picture showed a fresh young face, with strongly marked, irregular features, large black eyes, and black curls hanging around the shoulders in old-time style.

"Rachel wasn't pretty," said Uncle Alec, "but she had a lovely colour, and a beautiful smile. She looks far too sober in that picture."

"She has a beautiful neck and bust," said Aunt Olivia critically.

"Anyhow, Will Montague was really handsome," said the Story Girl.

"A handsome rogue," growled Uncle Alec. "I never liked him. I was only a little chap of ten but I saw through him. Rachel Ward was far too good for him."

We would dearly have liked to get a peep into the letters, too. But Aunt Olivia would not allow that. They must be burned unread, she declared. She took the wedding dress and veil, the picture case, and the letters away with her. The rest of the things were put back into the chest, pending their ultimate distribution. Aunt Janet gave each of us boys a handkerchief. The Story Girl got the blue candlestick, and Felicity and Cecily each got a pink and gold vase. Even Sara Ray was made happy by the gift of a little china plate, with a loudly coloured picture of Moses and Aaron before Pharaoh in the middle of it. Moses wore a scarlet cloak, while Aaron disported himself in bright blue. Pharaoh was arrayed in yellow. The plate had a scalloped border with a wreath of green leaves around it.

"I shall never use it to eat off," said Sara rapturously. "I'll put it up on the parlour mantelpiece."

"I don't see much use in having a plate just for ornament," said Felicity.

"It's nice to have something interesting to look at," retorted Sara, who felt that the soul must have food as well as the body.

"I'm going to get a candle for my candlestick, and use it every night to go to bed with," said the Story Girl. "And I'll never light it without thinking of poor Rachel Ward. But I DO wish she had been pretty."

"Well," said Felicity, with a glance at the clock, "it's all over, and it has been very interesting. But that clock has got to be put back to the right time some time through the day. I don't want bedtime coming a whole half-hour before it ought to."

In the afternoon, when Aunt Janet was over at Uncle Roger's, seeing him and Aunt Olivia off to town, the clock was righted. The Story Girl and

Peter came over to stay all night with us, and we made taffy in the kitchen, which the grown-ups kindly gave over to us for that purpose.

"Of course it was very interesting to see the old chest unpacked," said the Story Girl as she stirred the contents of a saucepan vigorously. "But now that it is over I believe I am sorry that it is opened. It isn't mysterious any longer. We know all about it now, and we can never imagine what things are in it any more."

"It's better to know than to imagine," said Felicity.

"Oh, no, it isn't," said the Story Girl quickly. "When you know things you have to go by facts. But when you just dream about things there's nothing to hold you down."

"You're letting the taffy scorch, and THAT'S a fact you'd better go by," said Felicity sniffing. "Haven't you got a nose?"

When we went to bed, that wonderful white enchantress, the moon, was making an elf-land of the snow-misted world outside. From where I lay I could see the sharp tops of the spruces against the silvery sky. The frost was abroad, and the winds were still and the land lay in glamour.

Across the hall, the Story Girl was telling Felicity and Cecily the old, old tale of Argive Helen and "evil-hearted Paris."

"But that's a bad story," said Felicity when the tale was ended. "She left her husband and run away with another man."

"I suppose it was bad four thousand years ago," admitted the Story Girl. "But by this time the bad must have all gone out of it. It's only the good that could last so long."

Our summer was over. It had been a beautiful one. We had known the sweetness of common joys, the delight of dawns, the dream and glamour of noontides, the long, purple peace of carefree nights. We had had the pleasure of bird song, of silver rain on greening fields, of storm among the trees, of blossoming meadows, and of the converse of whispering leaves. We had had brotherhood with wind and star, with books and tales, and hearth fires of autumn. Ours had been the little, loving tasks of every day, blithe companionship, shared thoughts, and adventuring. Rich were we in the memory of those opulent months that had gone from us—richer than we then knew or suspected. And before us was the dream of spring. It is always safe to dream of spring. For it is sure to come; and if it be not just as we have pictured it, it will be infinitely sweeter.

THE END.

Milton Keynes UK
Ingram Content Group UK Ltd.
UKHW040838141024
449705UK00006B/348